THE DAILY STUDY BIBLE

THE GOSPEL
of
JOHN

Volume 1

THE GOSPEL

of

JOHN

Volume 1

(Chapters 1 to 7)

Translated
with an Introduction and Interpretation
by

WILLIAM BARCLAY

THE WESTMINSTER PRESS
PHILADELPHIA

First published by The Saint Andrew Press
Edinburgh, Scotland
First Edition, July, 1955
Second Edition, November, 1956

Bible, N. T. John — Commentaries

Library of Congress Catalog Card No.: 58-5035

Typeset in Great Britain
Printed in the United States of America

It may truly be said that this series of Daily Bible Studies began almost accidently. A series which the Church of Scotland was using came to an end, and another series was immediately required. I was asked to write a volume on *Acts*, and, at the moment, had no intention beyond that. But one volume followed another, until the demand for one volume became a plan to write on the whole New Testament.

The translation which is given in each volume claims no special merit. It was included in order that the reader might be able to carry both the text of the New Testament and the comments on it wherever he went, and that he might be able to read it anywhere. While I was making the translation, the translations of Moffatt, Weymouth, and Knox were ever beside me. *The American Revised Standard Version, The Twentieth Century New Testament,* and *The New Testament in Plain English,* by Charles Kingsley Williams, have been in constant use. Since its publication, I have consistently consulted *The Authentic New Testament,* translated by Hugh J. Schonfield.

I cannot see another edition of these books going out to the public without expressing my very deep and sincere gratitude to the Church of Scotland Publications Committee for allowing me the privilege of first beginning, and then continuing, this series. And in particular I wish to express my very great gratitude to the convener, Rev. R. G. Macdonald, O.B.E., M.A., D.D., and to the committee's secretary and manager, Rev. Andrew McCosh, M.A., S.T.M., for constant encouragement and never-failing sympathy and help.

As these volumes went on, the idea of the whole series developed. The aim is to make the results of modern scholarship available to the non-technical reader in a form that it does not require a theological education to understand; and then to seek to make the teaching of the New Testament books relevant to life and work to-day. The whole aim of these books is summed up in Richard of Chichester's famous prayer; they are meant to enable men and women to know Jesus Christ more clearly, to love Him more dearly, and to follow Him more nearly. It is my prayer that they may do something to make that possible.

THE GOSPEL OF JOHN

FOREWORD

With this volume we come to the *Gospel according to St. John*. I would like to point out one new feature in the setting out of these Daily Bible Studies. None of the sections for each day has been allowed to become too long. In former volumes I put everything that I wished to say about any passage into the reading for one day. In this volume, if there was a great deal to be said about any passage, I have asked the reader to spend two or even more days studying the passage with me.

The Gospel according to St. John is to many people the most precious book in the Bible. It is an amazing book. It can be read and loved without any commentary at all. Throughout the generations simple people have fed their hearts and nourished their souls on it with nothing but the text of the Authorised Version in their hands. But the more we study *John*, the more wealth arises out of it. There are times when I was forced to take it, especially in the first chapter, almost verse by verse, for every verse was overflowing with riches. It is my hope and my prayer that many will find the patience necessary for this detailed study of *John*, for only thus will its words reveal their full riches. There is many a phrase in *John* whose greatness a man will not exhaust in a life-time, let alone in a day. It was necessary in writing of *John* to write a fairly long introduction. There is no book which gains so much from being set against the background from which it emerged. Again I hope that those who read these books will have the patience to read their way through the Introduction both before and after they have studied the gospel itself.

The literature on *John* is immense. For the English reader there is no volume so good as that of my chief, Dr. G. H. C. Macgregor, in the Moffatt Commentary. It is the ideal commentary for the English reader. B. F. Westcott wrote two magnificent commentaries on *John*, one on the Greek text, and one on the English text. There is an immense amount of material in the commentary by J. H. Bernard in the International Critical Commentary. The commentary by Marcus Dods in the Expositor's Greek Testament is still full of illumination. Of the older commentaries that by Godet is outstanding. This book of mine has come to this stage before the promised commentary by C. K. Barrett has come into my hands, but it is not too much to say that that is a volume which the whole world of New Testament scholarship awaits with expectation. There are excellent general works on the Fourth Gospel by E. F. Scott, R. H. Strachan, W. F. Howard and C. H. Dodd. There is a small but excellent *Introduction to the Fourth Gospel*, by E. Basil Redlich, which is the best thing of its kind for the English reader, and there are very many who know and love the late William Temple's exposition of the gospel. It would be impossible to set down all my debts to those who have written on this gospel.

I would like to offer my most sincere thanks to all those who have written to me about previous volumes. Their thanks and their appreciation and their encouragement has been very uplifting; and their suggestions and their criticisms have been most helpful. It is my prayer that one of the greatest books in all the world will unfold for us even more of its treasures as we study it together.

WILLIAM BARCLAY.

TRINITY COLLEGE,
GLASGOW.
May, 1955.

CONTENTS

THE GOSPEL OF JOHN

CONTENTS

THE GOSPEL OF JOHN

CONTENTS

CONTENTS

INTRODUCTION TO THE FOURTH GOSPEL

The Gospel of the Eagle's Eye

For many Christian people the Gospel according to
St. John is the most precious book in the New Testament.
It is the book on which above all they feed their minds,
and nourish their hearts, and in which they rest their
souls. Very often on stained glass windows and the like
the gospel writers are represented in symbol by the figures
of the four beasts whom the writer of the *Revelation* saw
around the throne (*Revelation* 4: 7). The emblems are
variously distributed among the gospel writers, but a
common allocation is that the *man* stands for *Mark*,
which is the plainest, the most straightforward and the
most human of the gospels; the *lion* stands for *Matthew*,
for he specially saw Jesus as the Messiah and the Lion
of the Tribe of Judah; the *ox* stands for *Luke*, because
the ox is the animal of service and sacrifice, and Luke saw
Jesus as the great servant of men and the universal sacrifice
for all mankind; the *eagle* stands for *John*, because the
eagle of all living creatures alone can look straight into
the sun and not be dazzled, and John of all the New
Testament writers has the most penetrating gaze into the
eternal mysteries and the eternal truths, and into the very
mind of God. It is true that there are many people who
find themselves closer to God and to Jesus Christ in *John*
than in any other book in the world.

The Gospel that is Different

But we have only to read the Fourth Gospel in the most
cursory way to see that it is quite different from the other
three. It omits so many things that they include. The
Fourth Gospel has no account of the Birth of Jesus, of
His Baptism, of His Temptations; it tells us nothing of the
Last Supper, nothing of Gethsemane, and nothing of the
Ascension. It has no word of the healing of any people
possessed by devils and evil spirits. And, perhaps most

surprising of all, it has no parables, and none of these stories which Jesus told, and which are so priceless a part of the other three gospels. In the other three gospels Jesus speaks, either in these wonderful stories, or in short, memorable, epigrammatic, simple, vivid sentences which stick in the memory. But in the Fourth Gospel the speeches of Jesus are often a whole chapter long; they are often involved, argumentative pronouncements quite unlike the vivid, pithy, unforgettable sayings of the other three gospels.

Even more surprising than that, the account in the Fourth Gospel of the facts of the life and ministry of Jesus is often different from that in the other three gospels. (i) *John* has a different account of the *beginning* of the ministry of Jesus. In the other three gospels it is quite definitely stated that Jesus did not emerge as a preacher until after John the Baptist had been imprisoned. " Now after John was put in prison Jesus came into Galilee, preaching the gospel of the Kingdom of God " (*Mark* 1: 14; *Luke* 3: 18, 20; *Matthew* 4: 12). But in *John* there is a quite considerable period during which the ministry of Jesus overlapped with the activity of John the Baptist (*John* 3: 22-30; 4: 1, 2). (ii) *John* has a different account of the *scene* of Jesus' ministry. In the other three gospels the main scene of Jesus' ministry is in Galilee, and He does not reach Jerusalem until the last week of His life. In *John* the main scene of Jesus' ministry is in Jerusalem and Judaea, with only occasional withdrawals to Galilee (*John* 2: 1-12; 4: 35—5: 1; 6: 1—7: 14). In *John* Jesus is in Jerusalem for a Passover which occurred at the same time as the Cleansing of the Temple, as John tells the story (*John* 2: 13); He is in Jerusalem at the time of an unnamed feast (*John* 5: 1); He is there for the Feast of Tabernacles (*John* 7: 2, 10); He is there at the Feast of Dedication in the winter-time (*John* 10: 22). In fact according to the Fourth Gospel Jesus never left Jerusalem after that feast; after chapter 10 He is in

Jerusalem all the time, which would mean a stay of months, from the winter-time of the Feast of the Dedication to the spring-time of the Passover at which He was crucified. In point of fact in this particular matter *John* is surely right. The other gospels show us Jesus mourning over Jerusalem as the last week came on. " O Jerusalem, Jerusalem, thou that killest the prophets and stonest them that are sent unto thee, how often would I have gathered thy children together, even as a hen gathereth her chicks under her wings—and ye would not! " (*Matthew* 23: 37=*Luke* 13: 34). Now it is clear that Jesus could not have said that unless He had paid repeated visits to Jerusalem, and had made repeated appeals to the city. It was impossible for Him to say that on a first visit to the Holy City. In this *John* is unquestionably right. It was in fact this difference of scene which provided Eusebius with one of the earliest explanations of the difference between the Fourth Gospel and the other three gospels. He said that in his day (about A.D. 300) many people who were scholars held the following view of the four gospels. Matthew at first preached to the Hebrew people. The day came when he had to leave them and to go to other nations. Before he went he set down his story of the life of Jesus in Hebrew, " and thus compensated those whom he was obliged to leave for the loss of his presence." After Mark and Luke had published their gospels, John was still preaching the story of Jesus orally. " Finally he proceeded to write for the following reason. The three gospels already mentioned having come into the hands of all and into his hands too, they say that he fully accepted them and bore witness to their truthfulness; *but there was lacking in them an account of the deeds done by Christ at the beginning of His ministry.* . . . They therefore say that John, being asked to do it for this reason, gave in his gospel an account of the period which had been omitted by the earlier evangelists, and of the deeds done by the Saviour during that period; that is, of the deeds

done before the imprisonment of John the Baptist. . . .
John therefore records the deeds of Christ which were
performed *before* the Baptist was cast into prison, but the
other three evangelists mention the events which happened
after that time. . . . The *Gospel according to John* contains
the *first* acts of Christ, while the others give an account
of *the latter part* of His life." (Eusebius, *The Ecclesiastical
History* 5: 24). So then according to Eusebius there is
no contradiction or difference at all between the Fourth
Gospel and the other three; the difference is due to the
fact that the Fourth Gospel is describing a ministry in
Jerusalem, at least in its earlier chapters, which preceded
the ministry in Galilee, and which took place while John
the Baptist was still at liberty. And it may well be that
this explanation of Eusebius is at least in part correct.
(iii) *John* has a different account of the *duration* of Jesus'
ministry. The other three gospels, on the face of it, imply
that Jesus' ministry lasted only one year. Within the
ministry there is only one Passover Feast. In *John* there
are *three* Passovers, one at the Cleansing of the Temple
(*John* 2: 13); one near the Feeding of the Five Thousand
(*John* 6: 4); and the final Passover at which Jesus went
to the Cross. According to *John* the ministry of Jesus
would take a minimum of two years, and probably a
period nearer three years, to cover its events. Again
John is unquestionably right. If we read the other three
gospels closely and carefully we can see that *John* is right.
When the disciples plucked the ears of corn (*Mark* 2: 23)
it must have been spring-time. When the five thousand
were fed, they sat down on the *green grass* (*Mark* 6: 39),
and therefore it must have been spring-time again, and
there must have been a year between the two events.
There follows the tour through Tyre and Sidon, and the
Transfiguration. At the Transfiguration Peter wished to
build three booths and to stay there. It is most natural
to think that it was the time of the Feast of Tabernacles
or Booths and that that is why Peter made the suggestion

(*Mark* 9: 5). That would make the date early in October. There follows the space between that and the last Passover in April. And therefore, behind the narrative of the other three gospels there lies the fact that Jesus' ministry actually did last for at least three years, and again *John* is right. (iv) It sometimes even happens that *John* differs in matters of fact from the other three gospels. Of that there are two outstanding examples. First, *John* puts the Cleansing of the Temple at the *beginning* of Jesus' ministry (*John* 2: 13-22), the other three gospels put it at the *end* (*Mark* 11: 15-17; *Matthew* 21: 12, 13; *Luke* 19: 45, 46). Second, when we study the narratives carefully, as we shall come to do, we will see that *John* dates the crucifixion of Jesus on the day before the Passover, while the other three gospels date it on the day of the Passover.

We can never shut our eyes to the obvious differences between *John* and the other three gospels.

John's Special Knowledge

One thing is certain—if John differs from the other three gospels, it is not because of ignorance and lack of information. The plain fact is that, if he omits much that they tell us, he also tells us much of which they had nothing to say. It is John alone who tells us of the Marriage Feast at Cana of Galilee (2: 1-11); of the coming of Nicodemus to Jesus (3: 1-15); of the woman of Samaria (4); of the raising of Lazarus (11); of the way in which Jesus washed His disciples' feet (13: 1-17); of Jesus' wonderful teaching about the Holy Spirit, the Comforter, which is scattered through chapters 14 to 17. It is only in *John* that some of the disciples really come alive. It is in *John* alone that Thomas speaks (11: 16; 14: 5; 20: 24-29); that Andrew becomes a real personality (1: 40, 41; 6: 8, 9; 12: 22); that we get a glimpse of the character of Philip (6: 5-7; 14: 8, 9); that we hear the carping protest of Judas at the Anointing at Bethany (12: 4). And the strange thing about *John* is that these little extra touches are intensely revealing. *John's* pictures of Thomas and Andrew and Philip are like little cameos or vignettes in which the features of the character of these men are etched in a way that we cannot forget.

Still further, again and again *John* has little extra details which read like the memories of one who was there. The loaves which the lad brought to Jesus were *barley* loaves (6: 9); when Jesus came to the disciples as they crossed the lake in the storm they had rowed between three and four miles (6: 19); there were six stone waterpots at Cana of Galilee (2: 6); it is only *John* who tells of the crown of thorns (19: 5), and the four soldiers gambling for the seamless robe as Jesus died (19: 23); he knows the exact weight of the myrrh and aloes which were used to anoint the dead body of Jesus (19: 39); he remembers how the perfume of the ointment filled the house at the Anointing at Bethany (11: 32). Many of these things are such apparently unimportant details that they are inexplicable unless they are the memories of a man who was there.

However much *John* may differ from the other three gospels, that difference is not to be explained by ignorance and by lack of knowledge. Rather it is to be explained by the fact that he had *more* knowledge, or better sources, or a more vivid memory than the others had.

A further evidence of the specialised knowledge of the writer of the Fourth Gospel is his *detailed knowledge of Palestine and of Jerusalem*. He knows how long it took to build the Temple (2: 20); that the Jews and the Samaritans have a permanent quarrel (4: 9); he knows the low Jewish view of women (4: 9); he knows the way in which the Jews regard the Sabbath (5: 10; 7: 21-23; 9: 14). His knowledge of the geography of Palestine is intimate. He knows of two Bethanys, one of which is beyond Jordan (1: 28; 12: 1); he knows that Bethsaida was the home of some of the disciples (1: 44; 12: 21); that Cana is in Galilee (2: 1; 4: 6; 21: 2); that Sychar is near Shechem (4: 5).

He has what one might call a street by street knowledge of Jerusalem. He knows the sheepgate and the pool near it (5: 1); the Pool of Siloam (9: 7); Solomon's Porch (10: 23); the brook Kidron (18: 1); the pavement which is called Gabbatha (19: 13); Golgotha, which is like a skull (19: 17). Now it must be remembered that Jerusalem was destroyed in A.D. 70 and that John did not write until A.D. 100 or thereby; and yet from his memory he knows Jerusalem like the back of his hand.

The Circumstances in which John wrote

We have now seen that there are very real differences between the Fourth Gospel and the other three gospels; and we have seen that, whatever the reason of these differences, it was not lack of knowledge. We must now go on to ask, What was the aim with which John wrote his gospel? If we can discover his aim we will discover why he selected and treated his facts as he did.

The Fourth Gospel was written in Ephesus round about the year A.D. 100. By that time two special features had emerged in the situation of the Christian Church. First, *Christianity had gone out into the Gentile world.* By that time the Christian Church was no longer predominantly Jewish; it was in fact overwhelmingly Gentile. The vast majority of its members now came, not from a Jewish, but an Hellenistic background. That being so, *Christianity had to be restated.* It was not that the truth of Christianity had changed; but the terms and the categories in which that truth was to be stated had to be changed. Take but one instance. A Greek might take up the *Gospel according to St. Matthew.* No sooner had he opened it than he was confronted with a long genealogy. Genealogies were familiar enough to the Jew, but quite unintelligible to the Greek. He would read on. He would be confronted with a Jesus who was the Son of David, a king of whom the Greeks had never heard, and the symbol of a racial and nationalist ambition which was nothing to the Greek.

He would be faced with the picture of Jesus as Messiah, a term of which the Greek had never heard. Must the Greek who wished to become a Christian be compelled to reorganise his whole thinking into Jewish categories? Must he learn a good deal about Jewish history and Jewish apocalyptic literature (which told about the coming of the Messiah) before he could become a Christian? As E. J. Goodspeed phrased it: " Was there no way in which he might be introduced directly to the values of Christian salvation without being for ever routed, we might even say, detoured, through Judaism? " The Greek was one of the world's great thinkers. Had he to abandon all his own great intellectual heritage in order to think entirely in Jewish terms and categories of thought?

John faced that problem fairly and squarely. And he found one of the greatest solutions which ever entered into the mind of man. Later on, in the commentary, we shall deal much more fully with John's great solution. At the moment we touch on it only briefly. The Greeks had two great conceptions.

(a) They had the conception of the *Logos*. In Greek *logos* means two things—it means *word* and it means *reason*. The Jew was entirely familiar with the all-powerful word of God. " God said, Let there be light; and there was light " (*Genesis* I: 3). The Greek was entirely familiar with the thought of reason. The Greek looked at this world; he saw a magnificent and a splendid and a dependable order. Night and day came with unfailing regularity; the year kept its seasons in unvarying course; the stars and the planets moved in their unaltering path; nature had her unvarying laws. What produces this order? The Greek answered unhesitatingly, The *Logos* of God, the mind of God is responsible for the majestic order of the world. The Greek went on, What is it that gives man power to think, to reason and to know? What makes him a rational, thinking creature? Again the Greek answered unhesitatingly, The *Logos* of God, the mind of

God dwelling within a man makes the man a thinking, reasonable being. So John seized on this. It was in this category that he thought of Jesus. He said to the Greeks, " All your lives you have been fascinated by this great, guiding, controlling mind of God. The mind of God has come to earth in the man Jesus. Look at Him and you see what the mind and thought of God are like." John had discovered a new category in which the Greek might think of Jesus, a category in which Jesus was presented as nothing less than God acting in the form of a man.

(b) They had the conception of the two worlds. The Greek always conceived of two worlds. The one was the world in which we live. It was a wonderful world in its way but it was a world of shadows and copies and unrealities. The other was the real world, in which the great realities of which our earthly things are only poor, pale copies stand for ever. To the Greek the unseen world was the real world; the seen world was only shadowy unreality. It was Plato who systematised this way of thinking in his doctrine of forms or ideas. He held that in the unseen world there was the perfect pattern of everything, and the things of this world were shadowy copies of these eternal patterns. To put it quite simply, Plato held that somewhere there was a perfect pattern of a table of which all earthly tables are inadequate copies; somewhere there was the perfect pattern of the good and the beautiful of which all earthly goodness and earthly beauty are imperfect and inadequate copies. And the great reality, the supreme idea, the pattern of all patterns, and the form of all forms is God. Now the great problem was how to get into this world of reality, how to get out of our shadows into the eternal truths. It is John's answer that that is what Jesus enables us to do. Jesus *is* reality come to earth. The Greek word for *real* in this sense is *alēthinos*; it is very closely connected with the word *alēthēs*, which means *true*, and *alētheia*, which means *the truth*. When the Authorised Version comes on *alēthinos* it translates it *true*; it would be far better to translate it *real*. Jesus is the *real* light (1: 9); Jesus is the *real* bread (6: 32); Jesus is the *real* vine (15: 1); to Jesus belongs the *real* judgment (8: 16). Jesus alone has reality in our world of shadows and imperfections.

Now something follows from that. Every action that Jesus did was, therefore, not only an act in time, but a window which allows us to see into reality. That is what John means when he talks of Jesus' miracles as *signs* (*sēmeia*). The wonderful works of Jesus were not simply wonderful; they were windows opening on to the reality which is God. This explains the way in which John tells the miracle stories. He tells them in a quite different way from the other three gospel writers. There are two differences.

(*a*) In the Fourth Gospel we miss the note of compassion which is in the miracle stories of the other gospels. In the other gospels Jesus is moved with compassion for the leper (*Mark* 1: 41); His sympathy goes out to Jairus (*Mark* 5: 22); He is sorry for the father of the epileptic boy (*Mark* 9: 14); when He raised to life the son of the widow of Nain, Luke says with an infinite tenderness, " He gave him back to his mother " (*Luke* 7: 15). But in *John* the miracles are not so much deeds of compassion as deeds which demonstrate the glory of Christ. After the miracle at Cana of Galilee, John comments: " This beginning of miracles did Jesus in Cana of Galilee, *and manifested forth His glory* " (*John* 2: 11). The raising of Lazarus happens " *for the glory* of God " (*John* 11: 4). The blind man's blindness existed to allow a demonstration of the glory of the works of God (*John* 9: 3). To John it was not that there was no love and compassion in the miracles; but it was that in every one of them he saw the glory of the reality of God breaking into time and into human affairs.

(*b*) Further, it must have been a fact that everyone can see that often the miracles of Jesus in the Fourth Gospel are followed by a long discourse. The feeding of the five thousand is followed by the long discourse on the Bread of Life (chapter 6); the healing of the blind man springs from the saying that Jesus is the Light of the World (chapter 9); the raising of Lazarus leads up to the saying that Jesus is the resurrection and the life (chapter II). To John the miracles were not simply single events in time; they were illustrations, examples, insights into that which God is always doing and what Jesus always is; they are windows into the reality of God. Jesus did not only once feed five thousand people; that is only an illustration that He is for ever the real Bread of Life. Jesus did not only once open the eyes of a blind man; He is for ever the Light of the World. Jesus did not only once raise Lazarus from the dead; He is for ever and for all men the resurrection and the life. To John a miracle was never an isolated act; it was always a window into the reality of that which Jesus always was and always is and always did and always does. It was with this in his mind that that great scholar Clement of Alexandria (about A.D. 230) arrived at one of the most famous and true of all verdicts about the purpose and origin and aim of the Fourth Gospel. It was his view that the gospels containing the genealogies had been written first—that is, *Luke* and *Matthew*; that then Mark at the request of many who had heard Peter preach composed his gospel, which embodied the preaching material of Peter; and that then " last of all, John, perceiving that what had reference to the bodily things of Jesus' ministry had been sufficiently related, and encouraged by his friends, and inspired by the Holy Spirit, wrote *a spiritual gospel*." (Quoted in Eusebius, *The Ecclesiastical History* 6: 14). What Clement meant was that John was not so much interested in the mere facts, as in the meaning of the facts, that it was not facts that he was after, but truth. John did not see the events of Jesus' life simply as events in time; he saw them as windows looking into eternity, and he pressed towards the spiritual meaning of the events and the words of Jesus' life in a way that the other three gospels did not attempt. That is still one of the truest verdicts on the Fourth Gospel that has ever been arrived at. John did write, not an historical, but a spiritual gospel.

So then, first of all, John presented Jesus as the mind of God in a person come to earth, and as the one person who possesses reality instead of shadows, and who can lead men out of the shadows into the real world which Plato and the great Greeks had dreamed of. The Christianity which had once been clothed in Jewish categories has taken to itself the greatness of the thought of the Greeks.

The Rise of the Heresies.

The second of the great facts which confronted the Church when the Fourth Gospel was written was *the rise of heresy within the Church.* It was now seventy years since Jesus had been crucified. By this time the Church was an organisation and an institution. Theologies and creeds were being thought out and stated; and inevitably the thoughts of at least some people went down mistaken ways, and heresies resulted. A heresy is seldom a complete lie and a complete untruth; a heresy usually results when one side, one part, one facet of the truth is unduly emphasised. We can see at least two of the heresies and mistakes which the writer of the Fourth Gospel was seeking to combat.

(*a*) There were certain Christians, especially Jewish Christians, who gave too high a place to John the Baptist. There was something about John which had an inevitable appeal to the Jews. John walked in the prophetic succession and talked with the prophetic voice. We in fact know that in later times there was an accepted sect of John the Baptist within the orthodox Jewish faith. In *Acts* 19: 1-7 we come upon a little group of twelve men who are on the fringe of the Christian Church but who have never got beyond the baptism of John. Over and over again the Fourth Gospel quietly, but definitely, relegates John to

his proper place. Over and over again John himself denies
that he has ever claimed or possessed the highest place,
and without qualification yields that place to Jesus.
We have already seen that in the other gospels the ministry
of Jesus did not begin until John had been put into prison,
but that in the Fourth Gospel the ministry of Jesus and the
ministry of John overlap. John may well have used that
arrangement to show John and Jesus in actual meeting,
and to show that John used these meetings to admit, and
to urge others to admit, the supremacy of Jesus. It is
carefully pointed out that John is not that Light (I: 8).
John is shown as quite definitely disclaiming all Messianic
claims (I: 20ff; 3: 28; 4: 1; 10: 41). It is not even
allowed to think of John as the highest witness (5: 36).
There is no criticism at all of John in the Fourth Gospel;
but there is a rebuke to those who would give John a place
which ought to belong to Jesus and to Jesus alone.

(b) There was a certain type of heresy which was very
widely spread in the days when the Fourth Gospel was
written. It is called by the general name of *Gnosticism*.
Without some understanding of it much of John's greatness
and much of his aim will be missed. The basic doctrine of
Gnosticism was that matter is essentially evil and spirit
is essentially good. The Gnostics went on to argue that
since that is so God Himself cannot touch matter, therefore
God did not create the world. What God did was to put
out a series of emanations. Each of these emanations was
further from God, until at last there was an emanation
so distant from God that it could touch matter. That
emanation was the creator of the world. By itself that idea
is bad enough, but it was made worse by an addition. The
Gnostics held that each emanation knew less and less
about God, until there was a stage when the emanations
were not only ignorant of God, but actually hostile to God.
So the Gnostics finally came to the conclusion that the
creator god was not only different from the real God, but
was also quite ignorant of and actively hostile to Him.

Cerintnus, one of the leaders of the Gnostics, said that " the world was created, not by God, but by a certain power far separate from Him, and far distant from that Power who is over the universe, and ignorant of the God who is over all." The Gnostics believed that God had nothing to do with the creating of the world. That is why John begins his gospel with the ringing statement: " All things were made by Him; and without Him was not anything made that was made " (*John* I: 3). That is why John insists that " God so loved the *world* " (*John* 3: 16). In face of the Gnostics who so mistakenly spiritualised God into a being who could not possibly have anything to do with the world, in answer to what could only be a godless world, John presented the Christian doctrine of the God who made the world and whose presence fills the world that He has made.

The beliefs of the Gnostics impinged on their ideas of Jesus. Their beliefs had two different effects on their ideas of Jesus. (*a*) Some of the Gnostics held that Jesus was one of the emanations which had proceeded from God. They held that Jesus was not in any real sense divine; that He was only a kind of demi-god who was more or less distant from the real God; that He was simply one of a chain of lesser beings between God and the world. (*b*) Some of the Gnostics held that Jesus had no real body. On their beliefs Jesus could not have had a body. A body is matter and God could not touch matter; they therefore held that Jesus was a kind of phantom without real flesh and blood. They held, for instance, that when He stepped on the ground He left no footprint, for His body had neither weight nor substance. They could never have said: " The Word became *flesh* " (*John* I: 14). Augustine tells how he had read much in the work of the philosophers of his day; he had found much that was very like what was in the New Testament, but, he said: " ' The Word was made flesh and dwelt among us ' I did not read there." That is why John in his *First Letter* insists that Jesus came *in the flesh,* and declares that any one who denies that fact is moved by the spirit of antichrist (I *John* 4: 3). This particular heresy is known as *Docetism.* Docetism comes from the Greek word *dokein* which means *to seem;* and the heresy is so called because it held that Jesus only *seemed* to be a man. (c) There were some Gnostics who held a variation of that heresy. They held that Jesus was a man into whom the Spirit of God came at His Baptism; that Spirit remained with Him throughout His life until the end; but since the Spirit of God could never suffer and die, that Spirit left Him before He was crucified. They gave Jesus' cry on the Cross as: " My power, my power, why hast thou forsaken me? " And in their books they told of people talking on the Mount of Olives to a form which looked exactly like Jesus while the man Jesus died on the Cross.

So then the Gnostic heresies issued in one of two beliefs. The Gnostics believed either that Jesus was not really divine, but that He was simply one of a series of emanations from God, a kind of demi-god, or, that He was not in any sense human but that He was a kind of phantom in the shape of a man. The Gnostic beliefs at one and the same time destroyed the real godhead and the real manhood of Jesus.

The Humanity of Jesus

The fact that John is out to correct both these Gnostic tendencies explains a curious paradoxical double emphasis in his gospel. On the one hand, there is no gospel which so uncompromisingly stresses the real manhood and the real humanity of Jesus. Jesus was angry with those who bought and sold in the Temple courts (2: 15); He was physically tired as He sat by the well which was near Sychar in Samaria (4: 6); His disciples offered Him food in the way in which they would offer it to any hungry man (4: 31); He had sympathy with those who were hungry and with those who were afraid (6: 5, 20); He knew grief and He wept tears as any mourner might do (11: 33, 35, 38); in the agony of the Cross the cry of His parched lips was: " I thirst " (19: 28). The Fourth Gospel shows us a Jesus who was no shadowy, docetic figure; it shows us one who knew the weariness of an exhausted body and the wounds of a distressed mind and heart. It is the truly human Jesus which the Fourth Gospel sets before us.

The Deity of Jesus

But on the other hand, there is no gospel which sets before us such a view of the deity and the godhead of Jesus. (a) John stresses the *pre-existence* of Jesus. " Before Abraham was," said Jesus, " I am " (8: 58). He talks of the glory which He had with the Father before the world was made (17: 5). Again and again He speaks of His coming down from heaven (6: 33-38). John saw in Jesus one who had always been, even before the world began. (b) The Fourth Gospel stresses more than any of the gospels the *omniscience* of Jesus. It is John's view that apparently miraculously Jesus knew the past record of the woman of Samaria (4: 16, 17); apparently without anyone telling Him He knew how long the man beside the healing pool had been ill (5: 6); before He asked it He knew the answer to the question which He asked Philip (6: 6); He knew that Judas would betray Him (6: 61-64); He knew the death of Lazarus before anyone had told Him of it (11: 14). John saw in Jesus one who had a special and miraculous knowledge, independent of anything which any man might tell Him. He needed to ask no questions, as John saw it, because He knew all the answers. (c) The Fourth Gospel stresses the fact, again as John saw it, that Jesus always acted entirely on His own initiative and quite uninfluenced by anyone else. It was not His mother's request which moved Him to the miracle at Cana of Galilee; it was His own personal decision (2: 4); the urging of His brothers had nothing to do with the visit which He paid to Jerusalem at the Feast of Tabernacles (7: 10); no man took His life from Him, no man could; He laid it down purely voluntarily and of His own free-will (10: 18; 19: 11). As John saw it, Jesus had a divine independence from all human influence. He was self-moved and self-determined.

So we see that to meet the Gnostics and their strange beliefs, John presents us with a Jesus who was undeniably human, and who yet was equally undeniably divine.

The Author of the Fourth Gospel

We have seen that the aim of the writer of the Fourth Gospel was to present the Christian faith in such a way that it would commend itself to the Greek world to which Christianity had gone out, and to combat the heresies and mistaken ideas which had arisen within the Church. Now we must go on to ask, Who is the author of the Fourth Gospel? Tradition answers unanimously that the author was John the Apostle. We shall see that beyond doubt the authority of John lies behind the gospel, although it may well be that the actual form and penmanship of the gospel did not come from his hand. Let us, then, collect what we know about this John. He was the younger son of Zebedee, who possessed a fishing boat on the Sea of Galilee and who was well enough off to be able to employ hired servants to help him with his work (*Mark* 1: 19, 20). His mother was Salome, and it seems likely that this Salome was the sister of Mary, the mother of Jesus (*Matthew* 27: 56; *Mark* 16: 1). With his brother James He obeyed the call of Jesus to follow Him (*Mark* 1: 20). It would seem that James and John were in partnership with Peter in the fishing trade (*Luke* 5: 7-10). He was one of the inner circle of the disciples, for the lists of the disciples always begin with the names of Peter, James and John; and there were certain great occasions when Jesus took these three specially with Him (*Mark* 3: 17; 5: 37; 9: 3; 14: 33). In character he was clearly a turbulent and ambitious man. Jesus gave to him and to his brother the name *Boanerges*, which the gospel writers take to mean *Sons of Thunder*. John and his brother James were completely exclusive and intolerant (*Mark* 9: 38; *Luke* 9: 49). So violent was their temper that they were prepared to blast a Samaritan village out of existence because it would not give them hospitality when they were on their journey to Jerusalem (*Luke* 9: 54). Either they or their mother Salome had the ambition that when Jesus came into His Kingdom, they might be His principal ministers of state (*Mark* 10: 35; *Matthew* 20: 20). It was Peter and John who were entrusted with the arrangements for the Last Supper (*Luke* 22: 8). In the other three gospels John appears as a leader of the apostolic band, one of the inner circle, and yet a turbulent, ambitious and intolerant character. In the *Book of Acts* John always appears as the companion of Peter, and he himself never speaks at all. His name is still one of the three names at the head of the apostolic list (*Acts* 1: 13). He is with Peter when the lame man is healed at the Beautiful Gate of the Temple (*Acts* 3: 1ff). With Peter he is brought before the Sanhedrin and faces the Jewish leaders with a courage and a boldness that astonished them (*Acts* 4: 1-13). With Peter he goes from Jerusalem to Samaria to survey the work done by Philip (*Acts* 8: 14). In Paul's letters he appears only once. In *Galatians* 2: 9 he is named as one of the pillars of the Church along with Peter and James, and with them is depicted as giving his approval to the work of Paul.

It is clear that John was a strange mixture. He was one of the leaders of the Twelve; he was one of the inner circle of Jesus' closest friends; and yet at the same time he was a man of temper and ambition and intolerance, and yet of courage.

We may follow John into the stories which were told of him in the early Church. Eusebius tells us that he was banished to Patmos in the reign of Domitian (Eusebius, *The Ecclesiastical History* 3: 23). In the same passage

Eusebius tells a characteristic story about John, a story which he received from Clement of Alexandria. John became a kind of bishop of Asia Minor. He was visiting one of his churches which was near Ephesus. In the congregation he saw a tall and exceptionally fine-looking young man. He turned to the Elder in charge of the congregation and said to him: " I commit that young man into your charge and into your care, and I call this congregation to witness that I do so." The Elder took the young man into his own house and cared for him and instructed him, and the day came when the young man was baptised and received into the Church. But very soon afterwards he fell in with vicious and evil friends and embarked on such a career of crime that he ended up by becoming the leader of a band of murdering and pillaging brigands. Some time afterwards John returned to the congregation. He said to the Elder: " Restore to me the trust which I and the Lord committed to you and to the Church of which you are in charge." At first the Elder did not understand of what John was speaking. " I mean," said John, " that I am asking you for the soul of the young man whom I entrusted to you." " Alas! " said the Elder, " he is dead." " Dead? " said John. " He is dead to God," said the Elder. " He fell from grace; he was forced to flee from the city for his crimes and now he is a brigand in the mountains." Straightway John went to the mountains. Deliberately he allowed himself to be captured by the robber band. They brought him before the young man who was now the chief of the robber band, and, in his shame, the young man tried to run away from him. John, though an old man, pursued him. " My son," he cried, " are you running away from your father? I am feeble and far-advanced in age; have pity on me, my son; fear not; there is yet hope of salvation for you. I will stand for you before the Lord Christ. If need be I will gladly die for you as He died for me. Stop, stay, believe! It is Christ who has sent me to you." The appeal broke the heart of the young man. He stopped, threw away his weapons, and wept. Together he and John came down the mountainside, and the young man was brought back into the Church and into the Christian way. There we see the love and the courage of John still in operation.

Eusebius (3: 28) tells another story of John which he got from the works of Irenaeus. We have seen that one of the leaders of the Gnostic heresy was a man called Cerinthus. "The apostle John once entered a bath to bathe; but, when he learned that Cerinthus was within, he sprang from his place and rushed out of the door, for he could not bear to remain under the same roof with him. He advised those who were with him to do the same. 'Let us flee,' he said, 'lest the bath fall, for Cerinthus, the enemy of the truth, is within.'" There we have another glimpse of the temper of John. Boanerges was not quite dead.

Cassian tells another famous story about John. One day he was found playing with a tame partridge. A narrower and a more rigid brother rebuked him for thus wasting his time, whereat John answered: "The bow that is always bent will soon cease to shoot straight."

It is Jerome who tells the story of the last words of John. When John was dying, his disciples asked him if he had any last message to leave them. "Little children," he said, "love one another." Again and again he repeated it; and they asked him if that was all he had to say. "It is enough," he said, "for it is the Lord's command."

Such then is our information about John; and he emerges a figure of fiery temper, of wide ambition, of undoubted courage, and, in the end, of gentle love.

The Beloved Disciple

If we have been following our references closely we will have noticed one thing. All the references, all our information about John, come from the first three gospels. It is the astonishing fact that the Fourth Gospel never

mentions the apostle John from beginning to end. But
the Fourth Gospel does mention two other people. First,
it speaks of *the disciple whom Jesus loved*. There are four
mentions of this disciple. He is leaning on Jesus' breast
at the Last Supper (*John* 13: 23-25); it is into the care
of the beloved disciple that Jesus committed Mary as
He died upon His Cross (19: 25-27); it was Peter and
the disciple whom Jesus loved whom Mary Magdalene
met on her return from the empty tomb on the first Easter
morning (20: 2); he is present at the last resurrection
appearance of Jesus by the lake-side (21: 20). Second,
the Fourth Gospel has a kind of character whom we might
call the *witness*. As the Fourth Gospel tells of the spear
thrust into the side of Jesus and the issue of the water and
the blood, there comes the comment: " And he that
saw it bare record, and his record is true; and he knoweth
that he saith true, that ye might believe " (19: 34, 35).
At the end of the gospel there comes the statement that
it was the beloved disciple who testified of these things
" and we know that his testimony is true " (21: 24).

Now here we are faced with rather a strange thing. In
the Fourth Gospel John is never mentioned, but the
beloved disciple is; and in addition there is a witness
of some kind to the whole story. It has never really been
doubted in tradition that the beloved disciple is John.
A few have tried to identify the beloved disciple with
Lazarus, for Jesus is said to have loved Lazarus (*John*
11 : 3, 5), or with the Rich Young Ruler, of whom it is
said that Jesus, looking on him, loved him (*Mark* 10: 21).
But although the gospel never says so in so many words,
tradition has always identified the beloved disciple with
John, and there is no real need to doubt the identification.

But a very real point arises—suppose John himself
actually did the writing of the gospel, would he really be
likely to speak of himself as the disciple whom Jesus
loved? Would he really be likely to pick himself out like
this, and, as it were, to say: " I was His favourite; He

loved me best of all "? It is surely very unlikely that John would confer such a title on himself. If it was conferred on him by others, it is a lovely title; if it was conferred on him by himself, it comes perilously near to an almost incredible self-conceit.

Is there any way then that the gospel can be John's own eye-witness story, and yet that at the same time it may have been actually written down by someone else?

The Production of the Church

In our search for the truth we may begin by noting one of the outstanding and unique features of the Fourth Gospel. The most remarkable thing about the Fourth Gospel is the long speeches of Jesus. Often these speeches are whole chapters long; they are entirely unlike the way in which Jesus is portrayed as speaking in the other three gospels. The Fourth Gospel, as we have seen, was written about the year A.D. 100, that is, about seventy years after the crucifixion. Can it be possible that these are verbatim speeches of Jesus? Is it possible after these seventy years to look on them as word for word reports of what Jesus said? Or, can we explain them in some way that is perhaps even a greater way than that? We must begin by holding in our minds the fact of the speeches and the question which they inevitably raise.

And now we have something to add to that. It so happens that in the writings of the early Church we have a whole series of accounts of the way in which the Fourth Gospel came to be written. The earliest account is that of Irenaeus who was bishop of Lyons about A.D. 177; and Irenaeus was himself a pupil of Polycarp, who in turn had actually been a pupil of John. There is therefore a direct link between Irenaeus and John. Irenaeus writes:

" John, the disciple of the Lord, who also leant upon His breast, himself also *published* the gospel in Ephesus, when he was living in Asia."

The suggestive thing there is that Irenaeus does not merely say that John *wrote* the gospel; he says that John *published* (*exedōke*) the gospel in Ephesus. The word that Irenaeus uses makes it sound, not like the private publication of some personal memoir; it makes it sound like the public issue of some almost official document.

The next account is that of Clement of Alexandria who was head of the great school of Alexandria about A.D. 230. He writes:

> " Last of all, John perceiving that the bodily facts had been made plain in the gospel, *being urged by his friends*, composed a spiritual gospel."

The important thing here is the phrase *being urged by his friends*. It begins to become clear that the Fourth Gospel is far more than one man's personal production, that there is a group, a community, a Church behind it. Still on the same lines, there is a tenth century manuscript called the *Codex Toletanus* which prefaces the New Testament books with short descriptions. It prefaces the Fourth Gospel with this statement:

> " The apostle John, whom the Lord Jesus loved most, last of all wrote this gospel, *at the request of the bishops of Asia*, against Cerinthus and other heretics."

Once again we have the same idea—that behind the Fourth Gospel there is the authority of a group and of a Church.

We now turn to a very important document. It is known as the Muratorian Canon. It is so called after a scholar Muratori who discovered it. It is the first list of New Testament books which the Church ever issued. It was compiled in Rome about A.D. 170. Not only does it list the New Testament books, but it also gives short accounts of the origin and nature and contents of each one of them. Its account of the way in which the Fourth Gospel came to be written is extremely important and extremely illuminating.

" At the request of his fellow-disciples and of his bishops, John, one of the disciples, said: ' Fast with me for three days from this time and whatsoever shall be revealed to each of us, whether it be favourable to my writing or not, let us relate it to one another.' On the same night it was revealed to Andrew that John should relate all things, *aided by the revision of all.*"

It is obvious that we cannot accept all that statement, because it is not possible that Andrew, the apostle, was in Ephesus in A.D. 100; but the point is that here it is stated as clearly as possible that, while the authority and the mind and the memory behind the Fourth Gospel is that of John, it is nonetheless very clearly and definitely the product, not of one man, but of a group and a community.

And now we can see something of what happened. About the year A.D. 100 there was a group of men in Ephesus whose leader was John. They revered him as a saint and they loved him as a father. He must have been almost a hundred years old. Before he died, they thought most wisely that it would be a great thing if the aged saint and apostle set down his memories of the years when he had been with Jesus. But in the end they did far more than that. We can think of them sitting down and reliving the old days. One would say: " Do you remember how Jesus said . . .? " And John would say: " Yes, and now we know that He meant . . . " In other words this group was not only writing down what Jesus *said*; that would have been a mere feat of memory; they were writing down what Jesus *meant*; that was the guidance of the Holy Spirit. John had thought about every word that Jesus had said; he had thought under the guidance of the Holy Spirit who was so real to him. W. M. Macgregor has a sermon entitled: " What Jesus becomes to a man who has known Him long." That is a perfect description of the Jesus of the Fourth Gospel. A. H. N. Green-Armytage puts the thing perfectly in his book *John who saw. Mark,* he says, suits the *missionary* with his clear-cut account of the facts of Jesus' life; *Matthew* suits the *teacher* with his systematic account of the teaching of Jesus; *Luke* suits the *parish minister or priest* with his wide sympathy and his picture of Jesus as the Friend of all; but *John* is the gospel of the *contemplative*. He goes on to speak of the apparent contrast between *Mark* and *John*. " The two gospels are in a sense the same gospel. Only, where St. Mark saw things plainly, bluntly, literally, St. John saw them subtly, profoundly, spiritually. We might say that John lit St. Mark's pages by the lantern of a lifetime's meditation." Wordsworth defined Poetry as "Emotions recollected in tranquillity " that is a perfect description of the Fourth Gospel. That is why *John* is unquestionably the greatest of all the gospels. Its aim is, not to give us what Jesus said like a newspaper report, but to give us what Jesus meant. In it the Risen Christ still speaks. *John* is not so much *The Gospel according to St. John* ; it is rather The *Gospel according to the Holy Spirit*. It was not John of Ephesus who wrote the Fourth Gospel; it was the Holy Spirit who wrote it through John.

The Penman of the Gospel

But we have one question still to ask. We have seen that we can be quite sure that the mind and the memory behind the Fourth Gospel is that of John the apostle; but we have also seen that behind it there is a witness who was the actual writer, in the sense that he was the actual penman. Can we find out who he was? We know from what the early Church writers tell us that there were actually two Johns in Ephesus at the same time. There was John the apostle, but there was another John, who was known as John the Elder. Papias, who loved to collect all that he could find about the history of the New Testament and the story of Jesus, gives us some very interesting information. He was Bishop of Hierapolis, which is quite near Ephesus, and his dates are from about A.D. 70 to about A.D. 145. That is to say, he was actually a contemporary of John. He writes how he tried to find out " what

Andrew said or what Peter said, or what was said by Philip, by Thomas, or by James, or by John, or by Matthew, or by any other of the disciples of the Lord; and what things Aristion and *the Elder John*, the disciples of the Lord, say." In Ephesus there was the *apostle* John, and the *Elder* John; and the Elder John was so well-loved a figure that he was actually known as *The Elder* par excellence. He clearly had a unique place in the Church. Both Eusebius and Dionysius the Great tell us that even to their own days in Ephesus there were two famous tombs, the one of John the Apostle, and the other of John the Elder. Now let us turn to the two little letters, *Second John* and *Third John*. The *Letters* come from the same hand as the gospel, and how do they begin ? *The Second Letter begins*: " The Elder unto the elect lady and her children " (2 *John* 1). *The Third Letter* begins: " The Elder unto the well-beloved Gaius " (3 *John* 1). Here we have our solution. The actual penman of the letters was John the Elder; the mind and memory behind them was the aged John the Apostle, the master whom John the Elder always thought of and described as " the disciple whom Jesus loved."

The Precious Gospel

The more we know about the Fourth Gospel the more precious it becomes. For seventy years John had thought of Jesus. Day by day the Holy Spirit had opened out to John the meaning of what Jesus said. So when John was near the century of life, and when his days were numbered, he and his friends sat down to remember. So John the Elder held the pen to write for his master John the Apostle; and the last of the apostles set down, not only what he had heard Jesus say, but also now what he knew Jesus had meant. He remembered how Jesus had said: " I have many things to say to you, but you cannot bear them now; but when the Spirit of Truth comes, He will guide you into all truth " (*John* 16: 12, 13). There were many things which seventy years ago he had not understood;

there were many things which in the seventy years the Spirit of Truth had revealed to him. These things John set down even as the eternal glory was dawning upon him. So then when we read this gospel let us remember that we are reading the gospel which of all the gospels is most the work of the Holy Spirit, speaking to us of the things which Jesus meant, speaking through the mind and memory of John the Apostle, and by the pen of John the Elder. Behind this gospel there is the whole Church at Ephesus, the whole company of the saints, the last of the apostles, the Holy Spirit, the Risen Christ Himself.

JOHN

THE WORD

THE WORD BECAME FLESH

John I: 1-18

When the world had its beginning, the Word was already there; and the Word was with God; and the Word was God. This Word was in the beginning with God. He was the agent through whom all things were made; and there is not a single thing which exists in this world which came into being without Him. In Him was life and the life was the light of men; and the light shines in the darkness, because the darkness has never been able to conquer it. There emerged a man sent from God whose name was John. He came as a witness, in order to bear witness to the light, that through Him all might believe. He himself was not the light; his function was to bear witness to the light. He was the real light, who, in His coming into the world, gives light to every man. He was in the world, and, although the world was made by Him, the world did not recognize Him. It was into His own home that He came, and yet His own people did not receive Him. To all those who did receive Him, to those who believe in His name, He gave the right to become the children of God. These were born, not of blood, nor of any human impulse, nor of any man's will, but their birth was of God. So the Word became a person, and took up His abode in our being, full of grace and truth; and we beheld His glory, glory such as an only son receives from his father. John was His witness, for he cried: " This is He of whom I said to you, He who comes after me has been advanced before me, because He was before me. On His fulness we all of us have drawn, and we have received grace upon grace, because it was the law which was given by Moses, but grace and truth came through Jesus Christ. No one has ever seen God. It is the unique one, He who is God, He who is in the bosom of the Father, who has told us all about God."

We shall go on to study this passage in short sections and in detail; but, before we do so, we must try to understand what John was seeking to say when he described Jesus as *The Word*.

THE WORD BECAME FLESH

The first chapter of the Fourth Gospel is one of the greatest adventures of religious thought ever achieved by the mind of man. Before we begin to study it in detail, let us try to see what John was trying to do when he wrote it.

It was not long before the Christian Church was confronted with a very basic problem. The Church had begun in Judaism. In the beginning all its members had been Jews. By human descent Jesus was a Jew, and, to all intents and purposes, except for brief visits to the districts of Tyre and Sidon, and to the Decapolis, Jesus was never outside Palestine. Christianity began amongst the Jews; and therefore inevitably it spoke in the Jewish language and used Jewish categories of thought. But although Christianity was cradled in Judaism it very soon went out into the wider world. Within thirty years of Jesus' death, by A.D. 60, Christianity had travelled all over Asia Minor and Greece and had arrived in Rome. By A.D. 60 there must have been a hundred thousand Greeks in the Church for every Jew who was a Christian. Jewish ideas were completely strange to the Greeks. To take but one outstanding example, the Greeks had never heard of a Messiah. The very centre of Jewish expectation, the coming of the Messiah, was an idea that was quite alien to the Greeks. The very category in which the Jewish Christians conceived and presented Jesus meant nothing to a Greek. Here then was the problem—how was Christianity to be presented to the Greek world? Lecky, the historian, once said that the progress and spread of any idea depends, not only on the strength and force of the idea, but on the predisposition to receive it of the age to which it is presented.

The task of the Christian Church was to create in the Greek world a predisposition to receive the Christian message. As E. J. Goodspeed put it, the question was, "Must a Greek who was interested in Christianity be routed through Jewish Messianic ideas and through Jewish ways of thinking, or could some new approach be found which would speak out of his background to his mind and heart?" The problem was how to present Christianity and Christ in such a way that a Greek would understand.

Round about the year A.D. 100 there was a man in Ephesus who was fascinated by that problem. His name was John. He lived in a Greek city. He dealt with Greeks to whom Jewish ideas were strange and unintelligible and even uncouth. How could he find a way to present Christianity to these Greeks in their own thought and in their own language and in a way that they would welcome and understand? Suddenly the solution of the problem flashed upon him. In both Greek and Jewish thought there existed the conception of *The Word*. Here was something which could be worked out to meet the double world of Greek and Jew. Here was something which belonged to the heritage of both races, something that both could understand.

Let us then begin by looking at the two backgrounds of the conception of *The Word*.

The Jewish Background.

In the Jewish background four strands all contributed something to the idea of the word.

(1) To the Jew a word was far more than a mere sound; a word was something which had an active and independent existence and which actually did things. As Professor John Paterson has put it: "The spoken word to the Hebrew was fearfully alive. . . . It was a unit of energy charged with power. It flies like a bullet to its billet." For that very reason the Hebrew was sparing of words. The Hebrew speech has fewer than 10,000 words; the

Greek speech has 200,000. A modern poet tells how once the doer of an heroic deed was unable to tell it to his fellow-tribesmen for lack of words. Whereupon there arose a man " afflicted with the necessary magic of words," and he told the story in terms so vivid and so moving that " the words became alive and walked up and down in the hearts of his hearers." The words of the poet became a power. History has many an example of that kind of thing. When John Knox preached in the days of the Reformation in Scotland it was said that the voice of that one man put more courage into the hearts of his hearers than ten thousand trumpets braying in their ears. His words did things to people. In the days of the French Revolution Rouget de Lisle wrote the *Marseillaise* and that song sent men marching to revolution. The words did things. In the days of the Second World War, when this country was bereft alike of allies and of weapons, the words of the Prime Minister, Sir Winston Churchill, as he broadcast to the nation, did things to people. It was even more so in the East, and still is. To the eastern people a word is not merely a sound; it is a power which does things. Professor Paterson recalls an incident of which Sir George Adam Smith tells. Once when Sir George Adam Smith was travelling in the desert in the East, a group of Moslems gave his party the customary greeting: " Peace be upon you." At the moment they failed to notice that he was a Christian. When they discovered that they had spoken a blessing to an infidel, they hurried back to ask for the blessing back again. The word was like a thing which could be sent out to do things and which could be brought back again. Will Carleton, the poet, expresses something like that:

> " Boys flying kites haul in their white-winged birds;
> You can't do that way when you're flying words:
> ' Careful with fire,' is good advice we know,
> ' Careful with words,' is ten times doubly so.
> Thoughts unexpressed may sometimes fall back dead,
> But God Himself can't kill them when they're said.'

We can well understand how to the Eastern peoples words had an independent, power-filled existence.

(ii) Of that general idea of the power of words the Old Testament is full. Once Isaac had been deceived into blessing Jacob instead of Esau, nothing that he could do could take that word of blessing back again (*Genesis* 27). The word had gone out and had begun to act and nothing could stop it. In particular we see the Word of God in action in the Creation story. At every stage of it we read: "And God said . . . " (*Genesis* 1: 3, 6, 11). The Word of God is the creating power. Again and again we get this idea of the creative, acting, dynamic Word of God. "By the word of God were the heavens made" (*Psalm* 33: 6) "He sent His word and healed them" (*Psalm* 107: 20) "He sent forth His commandment upon earth; His word runneth very swiftly" (*Psalm* 147: 15). "So shall my word be that goeth forth out of my mouth; it shall not return unto me void, but it shall accomplish that which I please, and it shall prosper in the thing whereto I sent it" (*Isaiah* 55: 11). "Is not my word like as a fire? And like a hammer that breaketh the rock in pieces?" (*Jeremiah* 23: 29). "Thou spakest from the beginning of creation, even the first day, and saidst thus: 'Let heaven and earth be made.' And Thy word was a perfect work" (2 *Esdras* 6: 38). The writer of the *Book of Wisdom* addresses God as the one, "who hast made all things with Thy word" (*Wisdom* 9: 1). Everywhere in the Old Testament there is this idea of the powerful, creative word. Even men's words have a kind of dynamic activity; how much more must it be so with God?

(iii) There came into Hebrew religious life something which greatly accentuated the development of this idea of the Word of God. For a hundred years and more before the coming of Jesus Hebrew was a forgotten language. The Old Testament was written in Hebrew, but the Jews no longer knew Hebrew. The scholars knew it, but not

5

the ordinary people. The ordinary people spoke a development of Hebrew called Aramaic. Aramaic is to Hebrew
somewhat as modern English is to Anglo-Saxon. Since
that was so the scriptures of the Old Testament had to
be translated into this language that the people could
understand, and these translations were called the *Targums*.
In the synagogue the scriptures were read in the original
Hebrew, but after they had been read, they were translated
into the Aramaic which the people spoke and it was the
Targums which were used as translations. Now the
Targums were produced in a time when men were fascinated
by the transcendence of God. That is to say, they were
produced in a time when men could think of nothing but
the distance and the difference of God. Because of that
the men who made the translations which are in the
Targums were very much afraid of attributing human
thoughts and human feelings and human actions and
reactions to God. To put it in technical language, they
made every effort to avoid *anthropomorphism* in speaking
of God. That is to say, they did everything possible to
avoid attributing human feelings and actions to God. Now
the Old Testament regularly speaks of God in a human way;
and wherever a thing like that occurred in the Old Testament the *Targums* substitute *The word of God* for the
name of God. Let us see how this custom worked. In
Exodus 19: 17 we read that " Moses brought forth the
people out of the camp *to meet with God.*" The *Targums*
thought that that was too human a way to speak of God,
and said that Moses brought the people out of the camp
to meet the *Word of God.* In *Exodus* 31: 13 we read that
God said to the people that the Sabbath " is a sign between
me and you throughout your generations." That is far
too human a way to speak for the *Targums,* and so they
say that the Sabbath is a sign " between *my* Word and
you." *Deuteronomy* 9: 3 says that God is a consuming
fire, but the *Targums* translate it that *the* Word of God
ˢs a consuming fire. *Isaiah* 48: 13 has a great picture of

creation: " Mine hand hath laid the foundation of the earth; and my right hand hath spanned the heavens." That is much too human a picture of God for the *Targums*, and they make God say: " By *my Word* I have founded the earth; and by my strength I have hung up the heavens." Even so wonderful a passage as *Deuteronomy* 33: 27 which speaks of God's " everlasting arms " is changed, and becomes: " The eternal God is thy refuge, and by His word the world was created." In the Jonathan *Targum* this phrase *the Word of God* occurs no fewer than about three hundred and twenty times. It is quite true that it is simply a periphrasis for the name of God, that the translators simply used it when they wished to avoid attributing human thoughts and actions to God; but the fact remains that the phrase *the Word of God* became one of the commonest forms of Jewish expression. It was a phrase which any devout Jew would hear and recognize because he heard it so often in the synagogue when scripture was read. Every Jew was used to speaking of *the Memra, the Word* of God.

(iv) At this stage we have to take note of a fact that is basic for the development of this idea of the Word. The Greek term for *Word* is *Logos*; but *Logos* does not only mean *Word*; it also means *Reason*. For John, and for all the great thinkers who made use of this idea, these two meanings were always closely intertwined. Whenever they used the word *Logos* the twin ideas of the Word of God and the Reason of God were in their minds. Now the Jews had a type of literature called *The Wisdom Literature*. This *Wisdom Literature* was the concentrated wisdom of sages and wise men. It is not usually speculative and philosophical; it is usually practical wisdom for the living and the management of life. In the Old Testament itself the great example of Wisdom Literature is the *Book of Proverbs*. In the *Book of Proverbs* there are certain passages which give a mysterious and creative and life-giving and eternal power to *Wisdom (Sophia)*. In these

7

passages Wisdom has been, as it were, personified, and Wisdom is thought of as the eternal agent and instrument and co-worker of God. There are three main passages. The first is *Proverbs* 3: 13-26. Out of that passage we may specially note:

> " She is a tree of *life* to them that lay hold upon her; and happy is everyone that retaineth her. *The Lord by Wisdom* hath founded the earth; by understanding hath He established the heavens. By His knowledge the depths are broken up, and the clouds drop down the dew " (*Proverbs* 3: 18-20).

Now we remember that *Logos* means *Word*, and *Logos* means *Reason*. We have already seen how the Jews thought of the powerful and the creative word of God. Here we see the other side beginning to emerge. *Wisdom* is God's agent in enlightenment and in creation. And *Wisdom* and *Reason* are very much the same thing. So here we see the other side of the word *Logos* beginning to emerge. We have seen how important that term was in the sense of *Word*; now we see that it is beginning to be important in the sense of *Wisdom* or *Reason*. The second important passage is *Proverbs* 4: 5-13. In it we may notice:

> " Take fast hold of instruction; let her not go; for she is thy life."

The *Word* is the *light* of men and *Wisdom* is the *light* of men. The two ideas are amalgamating with each other rapidly now. The most important passage of all is in *Proverbs* 8: 1—9: 2. In it we may specially note:

> " The Lord possessed me (Wisdom is speaking) in the beginning of His way, before His works of old: I was from everlasting, from the beginning, or ever the earth was. When there was no depth I was brought forth, when there were no fountains abounding with water. Before the mountains were settled, before the hills, was I brought forth, while as yet He had not made the earth or the fields, nor the highest part of the dust of the world. When He prepared the heavens, I was there; when He set a compass upon the face of the depth; when He established the

8

clouds above, when He strengthened the fountains
of the deep; when He gave to the sea His decree,
that the waters should not pass His commandment,
when He appointed the foundations of the earth;
then was I by Him as one brought up with Him;
and I was daily His delight, rejoicing always before
Him " (*Proverbs* 8: 22-30).

Now when we read that passage there is echo after echo
of what John says of the *Word*, the *Logos* in the first
chapter of the Fourth Gospel. *Wisdom* had that eternal
existence, that light-giving function, that creative power
which John attributed to the *Word*, the *Logos*, with which
he identified Jesus Christ.

The development of this idea of *Wisdom* did not top
here. In between the Old and the New Testament, men
went on writing and producing this kind of writing which
is called Wisdom Literature. It had so much concentrated
wisdom in it; it drew so much from the experience of
wise men that it was a priceless guide for life. In particular
two very great books were written, books which are included
in the *Apocrypha*, and which are books which it will do
any man's soul good to read. (*a*) The first is the book
which is called *The Wisdom of Jesus, the son of Sirach*,
or, as it is better known, *Ecclesiasticus*. It too makes much
of this great conception of the creative and eternal wisdom
of God.

" The sand of the sea, and the drops of the rain,
And the days of eternity who shall number?
The height of the heaven and the breadth of the earth
And the deep and wisdom, who shall search them out?
Wisdom hath been created before all things,
And the understanding of prudence from everlasting "
(*Ecclesiasticus* 1: 1-10).

I came forth from the mouth of the Most High,
And covered the earth as a mist.
I dwelt in high places,
And my throne is in the pillar of the cloud.
Alone I compassed the circuit of the heaven,
And walked in the depth of the abyss "
(*Ecclesiasticus* 24: 3-5).

> " He created me from the beginning of the world,
> And to the end I shall not fail "
> > *(Ecclesiasticus* 24: 9).

Here again we find wisdom as the eternal, creative power which was at God's side in the days of creation and the beginning of time.

(b) *Ecclesiasticus* was written in Palestine about the year 100 B.C.; but at almost the same time an equally great book was written in Alexandria in Egypt. It is called *The Wisdom of Solomon*. In this book there is the greatest of all pictures of *Wisdom*. *Wisdom* is the treasure which men use to become the friends of God (7: 14). *Wisdom* is the artificer of all things (7: 22). She is the breath of the power of God and a pure effluence flowing from the Almighty (7: 25). She can do all things and she makes all things new (7: 27). But the writer of this book does more than talk about *Wisdom*; he equates *Wisdom* and the *Word*. To him the two ideas were the same. He could talk of the *Wisdom of God* and the *Word of God* in the same sentence and with the same meaning. When he prays to God, his address to God is:

> " O God of my fathers, and Lord of mercy, who hast made all things with *Thy Word*, and ordained man through *Thy Wisdom* " (9: 2).

He can speak of *The Word* almost as John was to speak:

> " For while all things were in quiet silence, and that night was in the midst of her swift course, *Thine Almighty Word* leaped down from heaven out of Thy royal throne, as a fierce man of war into the midst of a land of destruction, and brought Thine unfeigned commandment as a sharp sword, and standing up filled all things with death; and it touched the heaven but it stood upon the earth " (18: 14-16).

To the writer of the *Book of Wisdom*, *Wisdom* was God's eternal, creative, illuminating power; *Wisdom* and *The Word* were one and the same. It was *Wisdom* and *The Word* who were God's instruments and agents in creation, and

10

who ever bring the will of God to the mind and heart of man.

So when John was searching for a way in which he could commend Christianity he found in his own faith and in the record of his own people the idea of *The Word*, the ordinary word which is in itself, not merely a sound, but a dynamic thing, the *Word* of God by which God created the world, the *Word* of the Targums which expressed the very idea of the action of God, the *Wisdom* of the Wisdom Literature which was the eternal creative and illuminating power of God. So John said: " If you wish to see that *Word* of God, if you wish to see the creative power of God, if you wish to see that *Word* which brought the world into existence and which gives light and life to every man, *look at Jesus Christ*. In Him the *Word* of God came among you."

The Greek Background.

But we began by seeing that John's problem was not the problem of presenting Christianity to the Jewish world; it was the presenting of Christianity to the Greek world. How then did this idea of the *Word* fit into Greek thought? In Greek thought the idea of the *Word* was there waiting to be used. In Greek thought the idea of the *Word* began away back about 560 B.C., and, strangely enough, it began in Ephesus where the Fourth Gospel was also written. Away back in 560 B.C. there was an Ephesian philosopher called Heraclitus. His basic idea was that everything in this world is in a state of flux. Everything is changing from day to day and from moment to moment. His famous illustration was that it is impossible to step twice into the same river. You step into a river once; you step out again; you step in again; but you do not step into the same water again, for the river has flowed on and it is a different river. To Heraclitus everything was like that, everything was in a constantly changing state of flux. But if that be so, why is life not a complete chaos? How can there be any sense in a world where there is constant, never-ceasing, continuous flux and change? The answer of Heraclitus was: all this chance and flux is not haphazard; it is controlled and ordered; it is following a continuous pattern all the time; and that which controls the pattern is the *Logos*, the *Word*, the *Reason* of God. To Heraclitus, the *Logos*, the *Word* was the principle of order under which the universe continued to exist. But Heraclitus went further than that. He held that not only is there a pattern in the physical world; there is also a pattern in the world of events. He held that nothing moves with aimless feet, that in all life and in all the events of life there is a purpose, a plan, a scheme and a design. And what is it that controls events? Once again, the answer is, the controlling power is the *Logos*, the *Word*, the *Reason* of God. But Heraclitus took the matter even nearer home than that. What is it that in us individually tells us the difference between right and wrong? What is it that makes us able to think and to reason? What enables us to choose aright and to recognize the truth when we see it? Once again Heraclitus gives the same answer, that which gives a man reason and knowledge of the truth and the ability to judge and discern between right and wrong is the *Logos*, the *Word*, the *Reason* of God dwelling within him. Heraclitus held that in the world of nature and events " all things happen according to the *Logos*," and that in the individual man " the *Logos* is the judge of truth." To Heraclitus the *Logos* was nothing less than the mind of God controlling this world and controlling every man.

Once the Greeks had discovered this idea they never let it go. It fascinated them. Especially it fascinated the Stoics. The Stoics were always left in wondering amazement at the order of this world. Now order always implies a mind. Where there is order and arrangement and design and pattern there must be a mind which worked out and which controls that order. The Stoics asked the question: " What keeps the stars in their courses? What makes the tides ebb and flow? What makes day and night come in unalterable order? What brings the seasons round at their appointed times? " And the Stoics answered: " All things are controlled by the *Logos*, the *Word*, the *Reason* of God. The *Logos* is the power which puts sense into the world, the power which makes the world an order instead of a chaos, the power which set the world going and keeps it going in its perfect order. " The *Logos*," said the Stoics, " pervades all things."

There is still another name in the Greek world at which we must look. In Alexandria there was a Jew called Philo. Philo had made it the business of his life to study the wisdom of two worlds, the Jewish and the Greek world. No man ever knew the Jewish scriptures as he knew them; and no Jew ever knew the greatness of Greek thought as Philo knew it. He too knew and used and loved this idea of the *Logos*, the *Word*, the *Reason* of God. He held that the *Logos* was the oldest thing in the world and that the *Logos* was the instrument through which God had made the world. He said that the *Logos* is the thought of God stamped upon the universe; he talks about the *Logos* by which God made the world and all things; he says that God, the pilot of the universe, holds the *Logos* as a tiller, and with it steers all things. He says that man's mind is stamped also with the *Logos*, that the *Logos* is that which gives a man reason, the power to think and the power to know. He said that the *Logos* is the intermediary between the world and God, between the begotten and the unbegotten, that the *Logos* is the priest which sets the soul before God.

So Greek thought knew all about the *Logos*; it saw in the *Logos* the creating and the guiding and the directing power of God, the power which made the universe and which keeps the universe going. So John came to the Greeks and he said: " For centuries you have been thinking and writing and dreaming about the *Logos*, the power which made the world, the power which keeps the order of the world, the power by which men think and reason and know, the power by which men come into contact with God. Jesus is that *Logos* come down to earth." " The Word," said John, " became flesh." We could put it in another way—" The Mind of God became a person."

Both Jew and Greek

Slowly the Jews and Greeks had thought their way to the conception of the *Logos*, the *Word*, the *Reason* of God, the mind of God which made the world and which makes sense of the world. So John went out to Jews and Greeks to tell them that in Jesus Christ this creating, illuminating, controlling, sustaining mind of God had come to earth. He came to tell them that men need no longer guess and grope; all that they had to do was to look at Jesus and see the Mind of God.

THE ETERNAL WORD

John I: I

> When the world had its beginning, the Word was already there; and the Word was with God; and the Word was God. This Word was in the beginning with God.

THE beginning of John's Gospel is of such importance and of such depth of meaning that we must study it almost verse by verse. It is John's great thought that Jesus is none other than God's creative and life-giving and -light giving Word, that Jesus is the power of God which created the world and the reason of God which sustains the world come to earth in a human and bodily form.

Here at the beginning John says three things about the Word; and that is to say that He says three things about Jesus.

14

(i) **The** Word was already there at the very beginning of things. John's thought is going back to the very beginning of the Bible. " In the beginning God created the heaven and the earth " (*Genesis* I: I). What John is saying is this—the Word is not one of the created things; the Word was there *before creation*. The Word is not part of the world which came into being in time; the Word is part of eternity and was there with God before time and before the world began. This thought of John has a technical name in theology. John was thinking of what is known as *the pre-existence of Christ*. In many ways this idea of pre-existence is very difficult, if not altogether impossible, to grasp. But it does mean one very simple, very practical, and very tremendous thing. If the Word was with God before time began, if God's Word is part of the eternal scheme of things, it means that *God was always like Jesus.* Sometimes we tend to think of God as just and holy and stern and avenging; and we tend to think that something that Jesus did changed God's anger into love, and altered God's attitude to men. The New Testament knows nothing of that idea. The whole New Testament tells us, and this passage of John specially tells us, that God has always been like Jesus. What Jesus did was to open a window in time that we might see the eternal and unchanging love of God. But we may well ask, "If you say that, what about some of the things that we read in the Old Testament? What about the passages which speak about commandments of God to wipe out whole cities, and to destroy men, women and children? What of the anger and the destructiveness and the jealousy of God that we sometimes read of in the older parts of Scripture?" The answer to that question is this—it is not God who has changed; it is men's knowledge of God that has changed. Men wrote these things because they did not know any better. That was the stage to which their knowledge of God had reached. When a child is learning any subject, he has got to learn it stage by stage. He does not begin with full knowledge; he begins with what he can grasp and he goes on to more and more. When he begins algebra he does not begin with the binomial theorem; he begins with simple equations; and he goes through stage after stage until his knowledge grows. It was that way with men and God. They could only grasp and understand little parts of God. It was only when Jesus came that men saw fully and completely what God has *always* been like. It is told that a little girl was once confronted with some of the more bloodthirsty and savage parts of the Old Testament. Her comment was: " But that happened before God became a Christian! " If we may put it so with all reverence, when John says that the Word was always there, before the beginning of things, he is saying that God was always a Christian. He is telling us that God was and is and ever shall be always like Jesus; but men could never know and realise that until Jesus came.

(ii) John goes on to say that *the Word was with God.* What does he mean by that? He means that always there has been the closest and the most intimate connection between the Word and God. Let us put that in another and a simpler way—there has always been the most intimate connection between Jesus and God. Now that means that there is no one who can tell us what God is like, what God's will is for us, what God's love and heart and mind are like, as Jesus can. Let us take a simple human analogy. If we want to know what someone really thinks and feels about something, and if we are unable to approach the person ourselves, we do not go to someone who is a mere acquaintance of that person, to someone who has known him only for a very short time; we go to someone whom we know to be an intimate friend of many years' standing. We know that the intimate friend of many years will really be able to interpret the mind and the heart of the other person to us. It is something like that that John is saying about Jesus. He is saying that Jesus has always been with God. Let us use **very** human language because it is the only language that we can use. John is saying that Jesus is so intimate with God that God has no secrets from Jesus; and that, therefore, Jesus is the one person in all the universe who can reveal to us what God is like, and how God feels towards us.

(iii) Finally John says that *the Word was God*. There is no doubt that this is a difficult saying for us to understand, and it is difficult because Greek, in which John wrote, had a different way of saying things from the way in which English speaks. When Greek uses a noun it almost always uses the definite article with it. The Greek for God is *theos*, and the definite article is *ho*. When Greek speaks about God it does not simply say *theos*; it says *ho theos*. Now when Greek does not use the definite article with a noun that noun becomes much more like an adjective; it describes the character, the quality of the person. John did not say that the Word was *ho theos*; that would have been to say that the Word was *identical* with God; he says that the Word was *theos*—without the definite article—which means that the Word was, as we might say, of the very same character and quality and essence and being as God. When John said *the Word was God* he was not saying that Jesus is identical with God; he was saying that Jesus is so perfectly the same as God in mind, in heart, in being that in Jesus we perfectly see what God is like.

So right at the beginning of his Gospel John lays it down that in Jesus, and in Jesus alone, there is perfectly revealed to men all that God always was and always will be, and all that God feels towards and desires for men.

THE CREATOR OF ALL THINGS

John I: 3

He was the agent through whom all things were made; and there is not a single thing which exists in this world which came into being without Him.

IT may seem strange to us that John so stresses the way in which the world was created. And it may seem strange that he so definitely connects Jesus with the work of creation. But John had to do this because of a certain tendency in the thought of his day.

In the time of John there was a kind of heresy called *Gnosticism.* The characteristic of Gnosticism was that it was an intellectual and philosophical approach to Christianity. To the Gnostics the simple beliefs of the ordinary Christian were not enough. The Gnostics tried to construct a philosophic system out of Christianity. The Gnostics were troubled about the existence of sin and evil and sorrow and suffering in this world, so they worked out a theory and a philosophy to explain it. The theory was this. In the beginning two things existed— the one was God and the other was matter. The Gnostics held that matter was always there. Matter was the raw material out of which the world was made and formed and moulded. The Gnostic held that this original matter was flawed and imperfect. That is to say, from the beginning the material out of which the world was made was imperfect. To put it in modern language, the world got off to a bad start. It was made of material which had the seeds and germs of evil and corruption in it. But the Gnostics went further than that. God, they said, is pure spirit, and pure spirit is so pure that it can never touch matter at all. Still less can it touch matter which is essentially flawed and imperfect. Therefore it was not possible for God to carry out the work of creation Himself. So, according to the Gnostics, what God did was this. God put out from Himself a series of emanations. Each emanation was further and further away from God. As the emanations got further and further away from God, they knew less and less about God. About halfway down the series there was an emanation which knew nothing at all about God and which was quite ignorant of Him. Beyond that stage the emanations began to be not only ignorant of but

18

actually hostile to God. Finally in the series there was an emanation which was so distant from God that it was totally ignorant of God and totally hostile to God—and that emanation was the power which created the world, because it was so distant from God that it was possible for it to touch this flawed and evil matter. To the Gnostics the creator God was a God who was utterly divorced from and utterly at enmity with the real God. The Gnostics took one step further. They identified the creator God with the God of the Old Testament; and they held that the God of the Old Testament was quite different from, quite ignorant of and quite hostile to the God who was the God and Father of Jesus Christ. In the time of John this kind of belief was widespread. Men believed that the world was evil and that an evil God had created it. It is to combat this teaching that John here lays down two basic Christian truths. In point of fact the connection of Jesus with creation is repeatedly laid down in the New Testament, just because of this background of thought which divorced God from the world in which we live. In *Colossians* 1: 16 Paul writes: " For by Him were all things created that are in heaven and that are in earth. . . . All things were created by Him and for Him." In I *Corinthians* 8: 6 he writes of the Lord Jesus Christ " by whom are all things." The writer to the Hebrews speaks of the one who was the Son, " by whom also God made the worlds " (*Hebrews* 1: 2). John and the other New Testament writers who spoke like this were stressing two great truths.

(i) Christianity has always believed in what is called *creation out of nothing*. We do not believe that in His creation of the world God had to work with alien and evil matter. We do not believe that the world began with an essential flaw in it. We do not believe that the world began with God and something else. It is our belief that behind everything there is God and God alone.

(ii) Christianity has always believed that this is *God's world*. So far from being so detached from the world that He could have nothing to do with it, God is intimately involved in the world. The Gnostics tried to put the blame for the evil of the world on the shoulders of the creator of the world. Christianity believes that what is wrong with the world is due to nothing other than to man's sin. But even though sin has injured the world and kept it from being what it might have been, we can never despise the world, and we can never hate the world, because this is essentially God's world. If we believe this it gives us a new sense of the value of the world and a new sense of responsibility to the world. There is a story of a child who dwelt in the back streets of a great city, and who was taken for a day in the country. When she saw the blue-bells in the woods, she asked: " Do you think God would mind if I plucked some of His flowers? " This is God's world; because of that nothing is out of His control; and because of that we must use all things in the memory that they belong to God. The Christian does not belittle the world by thinking that it was created by an ignorant and a hostile God; he glorifies the world by remembering that everywhere God is behind it and in it all the time; he believes that the Christ who recreates the world was the co-worker of God when the world was first created, and that, in the act of redemption, God is seeking to win back that which was always His own.

LIFE AND LIGHT

John I: 4

In Him was life and the life was the light of men.

IN a great piece of music the composer often begins by stating the themes which he is going to work out and elaborate in the course of the whole work. That is what John does here. In the Fourth Gospel *life* and *light* are two of the great basic words on which the gospel is built up. They are two of the main themes which it is the aim of the gospel to develop and to expound. Let us look at them in detail.

The Fourth Gospel begins and ends with *life*. Here at the very beginning we read that in Jesus was *life*; and at the very end we read that John's aim in writing the Gospel was that men might "believe that Jesus is the Christ, the Son of God, and that believing ye might have *life* through His name" (*John* 20: 31). The word is continually on the lips of Jesus. It is the wistful regret of Jesus that men will not come to Him that they might have *life* (5: 40). It is Jesus' claim that He came that men might have *life* and that they might have it more abundantly (10: 10). He claims that He gives men *life* and that they will never perish because no one will pluck them out of His hand (10: 28). It is His claim that He is the Way, the Truth and the *Life* (14: 6). In the Gospel the word *life* (*zōē*) occurs more than thirty-five times, and the verb *to live* or *to have life* (*zēn*) more than fifteen times. What then does John mean by *life*?

(i) Quite simply he means that *life* is the opposite of destruction, condemnation and death. God sent His Son that the man who believes should not perish but have everlasting *life* (3: 16). The man who hears and believes has everlasting *life* and will not come into condemnation (5: 24). There is a contrast between the resurrection to *life* and the resurrection to *condemnation* (5: 29). Those to whom Jesus gives *life* will never perish (10: 28). There is in Jesus that which gives a man security in this life and in the life to come. Until we accept Jesus and take Him as our Saviour and enthrone Him as our King we cannot be said to live at all. The man who lives a Christless life *exists*, but he does not know what *life* is. Jesus is the one person who can make life worth living, and in whose company death is only the prelude to still fuller life.

(ii) But John is quite sure that, although Jesus is the bringer of this *life*, the source, the author and the giver of life is God. Again and again John uses the phrase *the living God,* as indeed the whole Bible repeatedly does. It is the will of the Father who sent Jesus that everyone who sees Jesus and believes on Him should have life (6: 40). Jesus is the giver of life because the Father has set His own seal of approval upon Him (6: 27). He gives life to as many as God has given Him (17: 2). At the back of it all there is God. It is as if God was saying: " I created men that they should have real life; through their sin they have ceased to live, and they only exist; I have sent them my Son to enable them to know what real life is."

(iii) We must ask what this life is. Again and again the Fourth Gospel uses the phrase *eternal life.* We shall discuss the full meaning of that phrase later on. At present we must note this. The word John uses for *eternal* is *aiōnios.* Now clearly whatever else *eternal* life is, it is not simply life which lasts for ever. It is obvious that a life which lasted for ever could be a most terrible curse; often the one thing for which men have longed is release from life. In eternal life there must be more than *duration* of life; there must be a certain *quality* of life. Life is not desirable unless it is a certain kind of life. Now here we have the clue. *Aiōnios* is the adjective which is repeatedly used to describe God. In the true sense of the word *only* God is *aiōnios, eternal;* therefore *eternal life is that life which God lives.* What Jesus offers us from God is God's own life. Eternal life is a life which knows something of the serenity and the power of the life of God Himself. When Jesus came offering men *eternal life,* He was inviting men to enter into the very life of God Himself.

(iv) How, then, can we enter into that life? We enter into that life *by believing in Jesus Christ.* The word *to believe* (*pisteuein*) occurs in the Fourth Gospel no fewer than seventy times. " He that believeth on the Son shall have everlasting life " (3: 36). " He that believeth on me," says Jesus, " has everlasting life " (6: 47). It is God's will that men should see the Son, and believe on Him, and have everlasting life (5: 24). What does John mean by *to believe*? He means two things. (*a*) He means that we must be convinced that Jesus is really and truly the Son of God. He means that we must make up our minds about Jesus. After all, if Jesus is only a man, there is no reason why we should give Him the utter and implicit obedience that He demands. We have to think out for ourselves who Jesus was. We have to look at Him, learn about Him, study Him, think about Him until we are driven to the conclusion that this is none other than the Son of God. (*b*) But there is more than intellectual belief in this. To believe in Jesus means to take Jesus at His word. It means to accept His commandments as absolutely binding, to believe without question that what He says is true, to act on the conviction that we cannot do anything else than take Him at His word. For John, belief has three steps in it. First, it means the conviction of the mind that Jesus is the Son of God. Second, it means the trust of the heart that everything that Jesus says is true. Third, it means the basing of every action in life on the unshakable assurance that we must take Jesus at His word. When we do that we stop existing and begin living. We know what *Life*, with a capital L, really means.

LIFE AND LIGHT

John I: 4 (*continued*)

> In Him was life and the life was the light of men.

THE second of the great Johannine keywords which we meet here is the word *Light*. This word *light* occurs in the Fourth Gospel no fewer than twenty-one times. Jesus, as John says here, is the *light* of men. The function of John the Baptist was to point men to that *light* which was in Christ. Twice Jesus calls Himself the *Light* of the world (8: 12; 9: 5). This *light* can be in men (11: 10), so that they can become children of the *light* (12: 36), "I am come," said Jesus, "a light unto the world"

(12: 46). Let us see if we can understand something of this idea of the *light* which Jesus brings into the world. Three things stand out.

(i) The *light* which Jesus brings is the *light* which puts chaos to flight. In the creation story God moved upon the dark, formless chaos which was before the world began and said: " Let there be light " (*Genesis* 1: 3). The new-created light of God routed the empty chaos into which it came. So Jesus was *the light which shines in the darkness* (1: 5). Jesus is the one person who can save life from becoming a chaos. Left to ourselves we are at the mercy of our passions, our desires, our fears, our dreads. When Jesus dawns upon life, then light comes. One of the oldest fears in the world is the fear of the dark. Life is dark, full of nameless, instinctive dreads, until Jesus comes. There is a story of a child who was to sleep in a strange house. His hostess, thinking to be kind, offered to leave the light on when he went to bed. Politely he declined the offer with thanks. " I thought," said his hostess, " that you might be afraid of the dark." " O, no," said the lad, " you see, it's God's dark." With Jesus the night is light about us as the day.

(ii) The *light* which Jesus brings is a revealing *light*. It is the condemnation of men that they loved the darkness rather than the *light*; and they did so because their deeds were evil; and they hated the *light* lest their deeds should be reproved (3: 19, 20). The *light* which Jesus brings is something which shows things as they are. It strips away the disguises and the concealments; it shows things in all their nakedness; it shows them in their true character and their true values. Long ago the Cynics said that men hate the truth for the truth is like the light to sore eyes. In Cædmon's poem there is a strange picture. It is a picture of the last day and in the centre of the scene there is the Cross; and from the Cross there flows a strange blood-red light, and the mysterious quality of that light is such that it shows things as they are. The externals,

24

the disguises, the outer wrappings and trappings are stripped away; and everything stands revealed in the naked and awful loneliness of what it essentially is. We never see ourselves until we see ourselves through the eyes of Jesus. We never see what our lives are like until we see them in the light of Jesus. Jesus often drives us to God by revealing us to ourselves.

(iii) The *light* which Jesus brings is a guiding *light*. If a man does not possess that *light* he walks in darkness and he does not know where he is going (12: 36). When a man receives that *light* and believes in it, he walks no more in darkness (12: 46). One of the features of the gospel stories which no one can miss is the number of people who came running to Jesus asking: " What am I to do? " When Jesus comes into life the time of guessing and of groping is ended, the time of doubt and uncertainty and vacillation is gone. The path that was dark becomes light; the decision that was wrapped in a night of uncertainty is illumined. Without Jesus we are like men groping on an unknown road in a black-out. With Him the way is clear.

THE HOSTILE DARK

John 1: 5

And the light shines in the darkness, and the darkness did not put it out.

HERE we meet still another of John's key-words—the word *darkness* (*skotos, skotia*). This word darkness occurs seven times in the gospel. To John there was a *darkness* in the world that was as real as the *light*.

(i) The *darkness* is hostile to the *light*. The light shines in the *darkness*, but, however hard the *darkness* tries, it cannot extinguish it. Sinning man loves the *darkness* and hates the light, because the light shows up too many things. It may well be that in John's mind there was a borrowed thought here. John, as we know, was prepared to go out and to take in new ideas, if by so doing he could present and commend the Christian message to men. The great eastern religion of Zoroastrianism, the Persian religion, had at this time a very great influence on men's thoughts. It believed that there were two great opposing powers in the universe, the god of the light and the god of the dark, Ahriman and Ormuzd. This whole universe was a battle-ground in this eternal, cosmic conflict between the light and the dark; and all that mattered in life was the side which a man chose. So John is saying: " Into this world there comes Jesus, the light of the world; there is a darkness which would seek to eliminate Him, to banish Him from life, to extinguish Him. But there is a power in Jesus that is undefeatable. The darkness can hate Him, but it can never get rid of Him." As it has been truly said: " Not all the darkness in the world can extinguish the littlest flame." The unconquerable light will in the end defeat the hostile dark. John is saying: " Choose your side in the eternal conflict and choose aright."

(ii) The *darkness* stands for the natural sphere of all those who hate the good. It is men whose deeds are evil who fear the light (3: 19, 20). The man who has something to hide hates the light and loves the dark; but it is impossible to hide anything from God. The searchlight of God sweeps the shadows and illuminates the skulking evils of the world.

(iii) There are certain passages where the *darkness* seems to stand for *ignorance*, especially for that wilful ignorance which refuses the light of Jesus Christ. Jesus said: " I am the light of the world; he that followeth me shall not walk in *darkness* " (8: 12). He says to His disciples that the light will be with them only for so short a time; let them walk in it; if they do not, the *darkness* comes and a man who walks in *darkness* does not know where he is going (12: 35). He says that He came with His light that men should not abide in *darkness* (12: 46). Without Jesus Christ a man cannot find or see the way.

He is like a blindfolded man, or even like a blind man. Without Jesus Christ life goes lost. It was Goethe who cried out for: " Light, more light! " It was one of the old Scots leaders who said to his friends towards the end: " Light the candle that I may see to die." Jesus is the light which shows a man the road, and which lights the road at every step of the way.

There are times when John uses this word *darkness* symbolically. He uses it at times to mean more than merely the dark of a literal and an earthly night. He tells of the miracle of Jesus walking on the water. He tells how the disciples had embarked on their boat and how they were crossing the lake without Jesus; and then he says, " *And it was now dark,* and Jesus was not come to them " (6: 17). Without the presence of Jesus there was nothing but the threatening dark. He tells of the Resurrection morning and of the hours before those who had loved Jesus realized that He had risen from the dead. He begins the story: " The first day of the week cometh Mary Magdalene, *when it was yet dark* " (20: 1). She was living at the moment in a world from which she thought that Jesus had been eliminated, and a world like that was dark. John tells the story of the Last Supper. In it he tells how Judas received the sop, and how he then went out to do his terrible work and to arrange for the betrayal of Jesus; and, as he tells the story, John says with a kind of terrible symbolism: " He then having received the sop went immediately out; *and it was night* " (13: 30). Judas was going out into the night of a life which had betrayed Christ.

To John the Christless life was life in the dark. The *darkness* stands for life without Christ, and especially for life which has turned its back on Christ.

Before we leave this passage there is one other thing to note. The word which we have translated *put out* is in Greek *katalambanein*. This word can have three meanings. (*a*) It could mean that the darkness never *understood* the light. There is a sense in which the man of the world simply cannot understand the demands of Christ and the way which Christ offers him. To him it seems sheer foolishness. A man cannot understand Christ until he first submits to Christ. (b) It could mean the darkness never *overcame* the light. *Katalambanein* can mean *to pursue until one overtakes and so lays hold on and overcomes*. This could mean that the darkness of the world had done everything possible to eliminate Jesus Christ, even to crucifying Him, but it could never destroy Him. This could be a reference to the crucified and conquering Christ. (c) It can be used of *extinguishing a fire or flame*. That is the sense in which we have taken it here. Although men did all they could to obscure and extinguish the light of God in Christ, they could not quench it. In every generation the light of Christ still shines in spite of the efforts of men to extinguish the flame.

THE WITNESS TO JESUS CHRIST

John I: 6-9

> There emerged a man sent from God whose name was John. He came as a witness, in order to bear witness to the light, that through Him all might believe. He himself was not the light; his function was to bear witness to the light.

IT is a strange fact that in the Fourth Gospel every reference to John the Baptist is a reference of depreciation. There is an explanation of that fact. John was a prophetic voice; for four hundred years the voice of prophecy had been silent, and in John that voice spoke again. It seems that there were certain people who were so fascinated by John that they gave to him a higher place than he ought to have. There are, in fact, indications that there was actually a sect who put John the Baptist in the highest place. We find an echo of them in *Acts* 19: 3, 4. In Ephesus Paul came upon certain people who knew nothing but the baptism of John. It was not that the Fourth Gospel

wished to criticise John or that it under-rated his importance. It was simply that John knew that there were certain
people who gave John the Baptist a place that encroached
upon the place of Jesus Himself. So all through the Fourth
Gospel John is careful to point out again and again that the
place of John the Baptist in the scheme of things was
high, but that nonetheless it was still subordinate to the
place of Jesus Christ. Here he is careful to say that John
was not that light, but only a witness to the light (1: 8).
He shows us John denying that he was the Christ, or even
that he was the great prophet whom Moses had promised
(1: 20). When the Jews came to John and told him that
Jesus had begun His career as a teacher they must have
expected John to resent this intrusion. But the Fourth
Gospel shows us John denying that the first place was his,
and declaring that he must decrease while Jesus increased
(3: 25-30). It is pointed out that Jesus was more successful
in His appeal to men than John was (4: 1). It is pointed
out that even the people said that John was not able to
do the things that Jesus did (10: 41). Somewhere in
the Church there was a group of men who wished to give
John the Baptist too high a place. John the Baptist
himself gave no encouragement to that; he did everything
to discourage it. But the Fourth Gospel knew that that
tendency was there, and took steps to guard against it.
It can still happen that men may worship a preacher
rather than Christ. It can still happen that men's eyes
may be fixed upon the herald rather than upon the King
of whom he is the messenger. John the Baptist was not
in the least to blame for what had happened; but John
the Evangelist was determined to see that none should
shoulder Christ from out the topmost niche.

It is more important to note that in this passage we
come upon another of the great key-words of the Fourth
Gospel. That is the word *witness*. The Fourth Gospel
presents us with witness after witness to the supreme

place of Jesus Christ. In the Fourth Gospel there are eight witnesses to the unique position of Jesus.

(i) There is the witness of the *Father*. Jesus said: " The Father Himself, which hath sent me, hath borne witness of me " (5: 37). " The Father that sent me beareth witness of me " (8: 18). What did Jesus mean by this? He meant two things. He meant something which affected *Himself*. In His heart the inner voice of God spoke, and that voice of God left Him in no doubt as to who He was and what He was sent to do. Jesus did not regard Himself as having Himself chosen His task. His inner conviction was that none other than God had sent Him into the world to live and to die for men. He meant something which affected *men*. When a man is confronted with Christ there comes to him an inner conviction that this is none other than the Son of God. Father Tyrrell has said that the world can never get away from that " strange man upon the Cross." That inner power which always brings our eyes back to Christ even when we wish to forget Him, that inner voice which tells us that this Jesus is none other than the Son of God, and the Saviour of the world is the witness of God within our souls.

(ii) There is the witness of *Jesus Himself*. " I am one," He said, " that beareth witness of myself " (8: 18). " Though I bear record of myself," He said, " yet is my record true " (8: 14). What does this mean? It means that it was what Jesus was that was His best witness. Jesus claimed to be the light and the life and the truth and the way. He claimed to be the Son of God and to be one with the Father. He claimed to be the Saviour and the Master of all men. Unless His life and His character had been what they were, such claims would have been merely shocking and blasphemous. What Jesus was in Himself was the best witness that His claims were true.

(iii) There is the witness of *His works*. He said: " The works that the Father hath given me to do . . . bear witness of me " (5: 36). " The works that I do in my Father's

name, they bear witness of me " (10: 25). He tells Philip
of His complete identity with the Father, and then goes
on to say: " Believe me for the very works' sake " (14: 11).
One of the condemnations of men is that they have seen
His works, and have not believed (15: 24). We must
note one thing—when John spoke of the works of Jesus,
he was not speaking *only* of the miracles of Jesus; he
was thinking of Jesus' whole life. He was thinking not
only of the great outstanding moments, but of the life
that Jesus lived every minute of the day. No man could
have done the mighty works that Jesus did unless He
was closer to God than any other man ever was; but,
equally, no man could have lived that life of love and pity
compassion and forgiveness, service and help in the life
of the everyday unless He had been in God and God in
Him. It is not by working miracles that we can prove that
we belong to Christ, but by living a Christ-like life every
moment of every day. It is in the ordinary things of life
that we show that we belong to Him.

(iv) There is the witness which *the Scriptures* bear to
Him. Jesus said: " Search the scriptures, for in them
ye think ye have eternal life; and they are they which
testify of me " (5: 39). " If ye had believed Moses, you
would have believed me; for he wrote of me " (5: 46).
It is Philip's conviction that he has found Him of whom
Moses and the law and the prophets wrote (1: 45). All
through the history of Israel men had dreamed of the
day when God's Messiah would come. They had drawn
their pictures and set down their ideas of Him. And now
in Jesus all these dreams and pictures and hopes were
finally and fully realised and fulfilled. He for whom the
world was waiting had come.

(v) There is the witness of *the last of the prophets*, John the
Baptist. " He came for a witness to bear witness of that
light " (1: 7, 8). John bore witness that he saw the Spirit
descending upon Jesus. The one in whom the prophetic

31

witness culminated was the one who bore witness to Jesus to whom all the prophetic witness pointed.

(vi) There is the witness of *those with whom Jesus came into contact.* The woman of Samaria bore witness to the insight and to the power of Jesus (4: 39). The man born blind bore witness to Jesus' healing power (9: 25, 38). The people who witnessed Jesus' miracles told of their wonder at the things He did (12: 17). There is a legend which tells how the Sanhedrin sought for witnesses when Jesus was on trial. There came a crowd of people saying: " I was a leper and He healed me "; " I was blind and He opened my eyes "; " I was deaf and He made me able to hear." That was precisely the kind of witness that the Sanhedrin did not want. But in every age and in every generation there have always been a great crowd of those who were ready to bear witness to what Christ had done for their souls.

(vii) There is the witness of *the disciples and especially of the writer of the gospel himself.* It was Jesus' commission to His disciples: " Ye also shall bear witness because ye have been with me from the beginning " (15: 27). The writer of the gospel is a personal witness and guarantor of the things which he relates. Of the crucifixion he writes: " He that saw it bears witness, and his witness is true " (19: 35). " This," he says, " is the disciple which bears witness to these things, and wrote these things " (21: 24). The story he tells is no carried story, no second-hand tale. His gospel is the story of what he had seen and experienced himself. The best kind of witness of all is the witness which can say: " This is true, because I know it from my own experience."

(viii) There is the witness of *the Holy Spirit.* " When the Comforter is come . . . even the Spirit of truth . . . He will bear witness of me " (15: 26). In the *First Epistle* John writes: " It is the Spirit that beareth witness, for the Spirit is truth " (I *John* 5: 6). To the Jew the Spirit had two functions. The Spirit brought God's truth to men, and the Spirit enabled men to recognize that truth when they saw it. It is the work of the Spirit within our hearts which enables us to recognize Jesus for what He is and to trust Him for what He can do.

John wrote his gospel to put before men the unanswerable witness that Jesus Christ is the mind of God fully revealed to men.

THE LIGHT OF EVERY MAN

John I: 9

> He was the real light, who, in His coming into the world, gives light to every man.

IN this verse John uses a very significant word to describe Jesus. He says that Jesus was the *real* light. In Greek there are two words which are very like each other. The Authorised Version uses the word *true* to translate both of them; but they have a different shade of meaning. The first word is *alēthēs*. *Alēthēs* means *true* as opposed to *false*; it is the word that would be used of a statement which is true. The other word is *alēthinos*. *Alēthinos* means *real* or *genuine* as opposed to unreal. So what John is saying is that Jesus is the real light come to enlighten and to illumine men. Before Jesus came there were other lights which men followed. Some were flickers of the truth; some were faint glimpses of reality; some were will o' the wisps which men followed, and which led men out into the dark and left them there. It is still the case. There are still the partial lights; and there are still the false lights; and men still follow them. Jesus is the only genuine light, the real light to guide men on their way.

John says that Jesus, by His coming into the world, brought the real light to men. The coming of Jesus was like a blaze of light. It was like the coming of the dawn. A traveller tells how once in Italy he was standing on a hill overlooking the Bay of Naples. It was so pitch dark

33

that nothing could be seen; then all of a sudden there came a lightning flash and everything, in every detail, was suddenly lit up and illumined. When Jesus came into this world He came like a light in the dark.

(i) His coming dissipated the shadows of *doubt*. Until He came men could only guess about God. " It is difficult to find out about God," said one of the Greeks, " and when you have found out about Him it is impossible to tell anyone else about Him." To the pagan, God either dwelt in the shadows that no man can penetrate or in the light that no man can approach. But when Jesus came men saw full-displayed what God is like. The shadows and the mists of the dark were gone. The days of guessing were at an end; there was no more need for a wistful agnosticism. The light had come.

(ii) His coming dissipated the shadows of *despair*. Jesus came to a world that was in despair. " Men," as Seneca said, " are conscious of their helplessness in necessary things." They were longing for a hand let down to let them up. " They hate their sins but cannot leave them." Men despaired of ever making themselves or the world what they knew they and it ought to be. But with the coming of Jesus a new power, a new dynamic came into life. He came not only with knowledge but with power. He came not only to show men the right way but to enable them to walk in it. He gave them not only instruction; He gave them a presence in which all the impossible things had become possible. The darkness of pessimism and despair were gone for ever.

(iii) His coming dissipated the darkness of *death*. The ancient world feared death. Men have always been in bondage to the fear of death. At the best, death was annihilation and the soul of man shuddered at the thought of it. At the worst, death was torture by whatever gods there be and the soul of man was afraid. But Jesus by His coming, by His life, His death, His Resurrection showed men that death was only the way to a larger life. The darkness of death was gone. Stevenson has a scene in one of his stories in which he draws the picture of a young man who has almost miraculously escaped in a duel in which he was certain he would be killed. As he walked away still alive his heart was singing: " The bitterness of death is past." Because of Jesus the bitterness of death is past for every man.

But, still further, Jesus is the light who lights *every* man who comes into the world. The ancient world was exclusive. The Jew hated the Gentile and held that the Gentiles were created for no other purpose than to be fuel for the fires of hell. True, there was a lonely prophet who saw that Israel's destiny was to be a light to the Gentiles (*Isaiah* 42: 6; 49: 6) but that was a destiny which Israel has always definitely refused. The Greek world never dreamed that knowledge was for every man. The Roman world looked down on the barbarians, the lesser breeds without the law. But Jesus Christ came to be a light to *every* man. Only the God who is the God and Father of our Lord Jesus Christ has a heart big enough to hold all the world.

UNRECOGNIZED

John I: 10, 11

> He was in the world, and, although the world came into being through Him, the world did not recognize Him. It was into His own home that He came, and His own people did not welcome Him.

WHEN John wrote this passage two thoughts were in his mind.

(i) He was thinking of the time before Jesus Christ came into the world in the body. Long before Jesus came into the world in the body, from the beginning of time, ever since the world came into being, God's *Logos*, God's *Word* has been active in the world. In the beginning God's creating, dynamic *Word* brought the world into being;

and ever since it is the *Word*, the *Logos*, the *Reason* of God which has made the world an ordered whole and which has made man a thinking being. If men had only had the sense to see Him, the *Logos*, the *Word* was always visible and recognizable in the universe. The Westminster Confession of Faith begins by saying that " the lights of nature, and the works of creation and providence do so far manifest the goodness, wisdom and power of God as to leave men inexcusable." Long ago Paul had said that the visible things of the world were so designed by God as to lead men's thoughts to the invisible things, and that if men had looked with open eyes and an understanding heart at the world their thoughts would have been inevitably led to the creator of the world (*Romans* 1: 19, 20). The world has always been such that, looked at in the right way, it would lead men's minds to God. Theology has always made a distinction between *natural* theology and *revealed* theology. Revealed theology deals with the truths that came to us directly from God in the words of the prophets, the pages of His Book, and supremely in Jesus Christ. Natural theology deals with the truths that man could discover by the exercise of his own mind and intellect on the world in which he lives. How, then, can we see God's *Word*, God's *Logos*, God's *Reason*, God's *Mind* in the world in which we live?

(a) We must look *outwards*. It was always a basic Greek thought that where there is order there must be a mind. When we look at the world we see an amazing order. The planets keep to their appointed courses. The tides observe their appointed times. Seed time and harvest, summer and winter, day and night come in their appointed order. Clearly there is order in nature, and, therefore, equally clearly there must be a mind behind it all. Further, that mind must be greater than any human mind because it achieves results that the human mind can never achieve. No man can make day into night, or night into day; no man can make a seed that will have in it the power of growth; no man can make a living thing. Therefore the mind in nature is far above the human mind in man. If then in the world there is order, there must be mind; and if in that order there are things which are beyond the mind of man to do, then the mind behind the order of nature must be a mind above and beyond the mind of man—and straightway we have reached God. To look outwards upon the world is to come face to face with the God who made the world.

(*b*) We must look *upwards*. Of all things which demonstrate the amazing order of the universe nothing demonstrates it so much as the movement of the world. Astronomers tell us that there are as many stars as there are grains of sand upon the seashore. If we may put it in human terms, think of the traffic problem of the heavens. And yet the heavenly bodies keep their appointed courses and travel their appointed way. An astronomer is able to forecast to the minute and to the inch when and where a certain planet will appear. An astronomer can tell us when and where an eclipse of the sun will happen hundreds of years from now, and he can tell us to the second how long it will last. It has been said that " no astronomer can be an atheist." When we look upwards we see God.

(*c*) We must look *inwards*. Where did we get the power to think, to reason and to know? Where did we get our knowledge of right and of wrong? Why does even the most uncontrolled and evil-ridden man know in his heart of hearts when he is doing a wrong thing? Kant said long ago that two things convinced him of the existence of God—the starry heavens above him and the moral law within him. We neither gave ourselves life, nor did we give ourselves the reason which guides and directs life. It must have come from some power outside ourselves. Where do remorse and regret and the sense of guilt come from? Why can we never do what we like and be at peace? When we look inwards we find what Marcus Aurelius called " the god within," and what Seneca called " the holy spirit which sits within our souls." No man can explain himself apart from God.

(*d*) We must look *backwards*. Froude, the great historian, said that the whole of history is a demonstration of the moral law in action. Empires rise and empires collapse. As Kipling wrote:

> " Lo, all our pomp of yesterday
> Is one with Nineveh and Tyre! "

And it is the demonstrable fact of history that moral degeneration and national collapse go hand in hand. " No nation," said George Bernard Shaw, " has ever outlived the loss of its gods." All history is the practical demonstration in events that there is a God.

So, then, even if Jesus Christ had never come into this world in a bodily form, it would still have been possible for men to see God's *Word*, God's *Logos*, God's *Reason* in action in this world. But, although the action of the *Word* was there for all to see, men never recognized Him.

UNRECOGNIZED

John I: 10, 11 (*continued*)

> He was in the world, and, although the world came into being through Him, the world did not recognize Him. It was into His own home that He came, and His own people did not welcome Him.

(ii) In the end God's creating and directing *Word* did come into this world in the form of the man Jesus. John says that the *Word* came to His own home, and His own people gave Him no welcome. What does he mean by that?

What John means is that when God's *Word* entered this world, He did not come to Rome or to Greece or to Egypt or to the Eastern Empires. *He came to Palestine.* And Palestine was specially God's land, and the Jews were specially God's people. The land of Palestine and the nations of the Jews belonged to God as no other land and no other people did.

The very titles by which the Old Testament calls the
land and the people show that. Palestine is repeatedly
called *the holy land* (*Zechariah* 2: 12; 2 *Maccabees* 1: 7;
Wisdom 12: 3). It is called *the Lord's land*; God speaks
of it as *His land* (*Hosea* 9: 3; *Jeremiah* 2: 7; 16: 18;
Leviticus 25: 23). The Jewish nation is called *God's
peculiar treasure* (*Exodus* 19: 5; *Psalm* 135: 4). The Jews
are called *God's special people* (*Deuteronomy* 7: 6). They
are called God's *peculiar people* (*Deuteronomy* 14: 2;
26: 18). They are called *the Lord's portion* (*Deuteronomy*
32: 9).

When Jesus came He came to a land which was peculiarly
God's land and a people who were peculiarly God's people.
He ought to have been coming to a nation that would
welcome Him with open arms; the door should have
been wide open for Him; He should have been welcomed
like a wayfarer coming home; or, even more, like a king
coming to his own—*and He was rejected.* He was welcomed
with hate and not with adoration.

Here there is the tragedy of a people being prepared
for a task, and then refusing that task. It may be that in
this life parents plan and save and sacrifice to give a son
or a daughter a chance in life, to prepare that son or
daughter for some special task and opportunity—and
then when the chance comes, the one for whom so much
sacrifice was made refuses to grasp the opportunity, or
fails miserably when confronted with the challenge.
Therein is tragedy. And that is what happened to God.

It would be quite wrong to think that God prepared
only the Jewish people. God is preparing every man and
woman and child in this world for some task that God
has prepared for them. A novelist tells of a girl who
refused to touch the soiling things. When she was asked
why, she said: " Some day something fine is going to come
into my life, and when it comes I want to be ready for it."
But the tragedy is that so many people refuse the task
that God has for them. We may put it in another way—

a way that strikes home—there are so few people who become what they have it in them to be. It may be through lethargy and laziness, it may be through timidity and cowardice, it may be through lack of discipline and self-indulgence, it may be through the involvement in second-bests and byways. The world is full of people who have never realised the possibilities which are in them. We need not think of the task which God has in store for us in terms of some great act or achievement of which all men will know. It may be to fit a child for life; it may be at some crucial moment to speak that word and exert that influence which will stop someone ruining life; it may be to do some quite small job superlatively well; it may be something which will touch the lives of many by our hands, our voices or our minds. The fact remains that God is preparing us by all the experiences of life for *something*; and the fact remains that there are so many who refuse the task when it comes, and who never even realise that they are refusing it.

There is all the pathos in the world in the simple saying: " He came to His own home—and His own people gave Him no welcome." It happened to Jesus Christ long ago—and it is happening yet.

CHILDREN OF GOD

John I: 12, 13

> To all those who did receive Him, to those who believe in His name, He gave the right to become the children of God. These were born not of blood, nor of any human impulse, nor of any man's will, but their birth was of God.

NOT everyone rejected Jesus when He came; there were some who did receive Him and welcome Him; and to them Jesus gave the right to become children of God.

There is a sense in which a man is not naturally a child of God. There is a sense in which he has to *become* a child of God. We may think of this in human terms, because human terms are the only terms in which we can think of it. There are two kinds of sons. There is the son who never does anything else but use his home. All through his youth he takes everything that the home has to offer and gives nothing in return. His father may work and sacrifice to give him his chance in life, and he takes it as a right, and never realises what he is taking and makes no effort to deserve it or repay it. When he leaves home, he makes no attempt to keep in touch with the home. The home has served his purpose and he is finished with it. He realises no bond to be maintained and no debt to be paid. Such a son is his father's son; to his father he owes his existence; and to his father he owes what he is; but between him and the father there is no bond of love and intimacy and union. The father has given all in love; but the son has given nothing in return. On the other hand there is the son who all his life realises what his father is doing and has done for him. He takes every opportunity to show his gratitude by trying to be the son his father would wish him to be; as the years go on he grows closer and closer to his father; the relationship of father and son becomes the relationship of fellowship and friendship. Even when he leaves home the bond is still there and he is still conscious of a debt that can never be repaid. In the one case the son grows further and further away from the father; in the other case he grows nearer and nearer the father. Both these sons are sons, but the sonship is very different. The second has *become* a son in a way that the first never was. We may illustrate this kind of relationship from another, but a kindred, sphere. The name of a certain younger man was mentioned to a famous teacher, whose student the younger man claimed to be. The older man answered: " He may have attended my lectures, but he was not one of my students." There is all the world of a difference between sitting in a teacher's class room and being one of his students. There can be contact without communion; there can be relationship without fellowship. All men are the sons of God in the sense that all men owe to God the creation and the preservation of their lives; but only some men *become* the sons of God in the real depth and intimacy of the true father and son relationship.

It is the claim of John that men can only enter into that true and real sonship through Jesus Christ. When John says that it does not come from blood, John is using Jewish thought, for the Jews believed that a physical son was born from the union of the seed of the father with the blood of the mother; this sonship does not come from any human impulse or desire or from any act of the human will; it comes entirely from God. We cannot make ourselves sons of God; we have to enter into a relationship which God offers us. No man can ever enter into friendship with God by his own will and power; there is a great gulf fixed between the human and the divine. Man can only enter into friendship with God when God Himself opens the way. Again let us think in human terms. A commoner cannot approach a king with the offer of friendship; if there is ever to be such a friendship it must depend entirely on the approach of the king. It is so with us and God. We cannot by will or achievement enter into the relationship of fellowship with God, for we are men and God is God. We can only enter into it when God, in His totally undeserved grace, condescends in love to open the way to Himself.

But there is a human side to this. What God offers man has to appropriate. A human father may offer his son his love, his advice, his friendship, and the son may refuse it and prefer to take his own way. It is so with God; God offers us *the right* to become sons, but we need not accept that right.

We do accept it through believing in the name of Jesus Christ. What does that mean? Hebrew thought and language had a way of using the expression *the name*

42

which is strange to us. By *the name* Jewish thought did not so much mean the name by which a person was called, as the nature of that person in so far as it is revealed and known. For instance, in *Psalm 9: 10* the psalmist says: "They that know *Thy name* will put their trust in Thee." Clearly that does not mean that those who know that God is called Jehovah will trust Him; it means that those who know God's character, God's nature, who know what God is like, will be ready and willing to trust Him for everything. In *Psalm 20: 7* the psalmist says: "Some trust in chariots and some in horses: but we will remember *the name* of the Lord our God." Clearly that does not mean that we will remember that God is called Jehovah. It means that some people will put their trust in human aids, but we will put our trust in God because we know what God is like. To trust in the name of Jesus therefore means to put our trust in what Jesus is. Jesus was the embodiment of kindness and love and gentleness and service. It is John's great central doctrine that in Jesus we see the very mind of God, the attitude of God to men. If we believe that, then we also believe that God is like Jesus, as kind, as loving as Jesus was. To believe in the name of Jesus is to believe that God is like Jesus; and it is only when we believe that, that we can submit ourselves to God and become His children. Unless we had seen in Jesus what God is like we would never even have dared to think of ourselves as being able to become the children of God. It is what Jesus is that opens to us the possibility of becoming the children of God.

THE WORD BECAME FLESH

John 1: 14

So the Word of God became a person, and took up His abode in our being, full of grace and truth; and we looked with our own eyes upon His glory, glory like the glory which an only son receives from a father.

HERE we come to the sentence for the sake of which John wrote the Fourth Gospel. He has thought and talked about the Word of God, that powerful creative dynamic word which was the agent and the cause of creation, that guiding, directing, controlling Word which puts order into the universe and mind into man. These were ideas which were known and familiar to both Jew and Greek. Now he says the most startling and incredible thing that he could have said. He said quite simply: "This Word which created the world, this Reason which controls the order of the world, has become a person, and with our own eyes we saw Him." The word that John uses for *seeing* this Word is *theasthai*; that word is used in the New Testament more than twenty times, and it is always used of *actual physical sight*. This is no spiritual vision seen with the eye of the soul or of the mind. John declares that this Word actually came to earth in the form of a man, and was seen by human eyes. He says: "If you want to see what this creating Word, this controlling Reason is like, look at Jesus of Nazareth."

This is where John parted with all thought which had gone before him. This was the entirely new thing which John brought to the Greek world for which he was writing. Augustine afterwards said that in his pre-Christian days he had read and studied the great pagan philosophers and their writings, and that he had read many things, but he had never read that the Word became flesh. To a Greek this was the impossible thing. The one thing that no Greek would ever have dreamed of was that God could take a body. To the Greek the body was an evil, a prison-house in which the soul was shackled, a tomb in which the spirit was confined. Plutarch, the wise old Greek, did not even believe that God could control the happenings of this world directly; He had to do it by deputies and intermediaries, for, as Plutarch saw it, it was nothing less than blasphemy to involve God in the affairs of the world. Philo could never have said it. He said: "The life of God has not descended to us; nor has it come as far as the necessities of the body." The great Roman Stoic Emperor, Marcus Aurelius, despised the body in comparison with the spirit. " Therefore despise the flesh—blood and bones and a net-work, a twisted skein of nerves and veins and arteries." " The composition of the whole body is under corruption." Here was the shatteringly new thing—that God could and would become a human person, that God could enter into this life that we live, that eternity could appear in time, that somehow the Creator could appear in creation in such a way that men's eyes could actually see Him.

So staggeringly new and unheard-of was this conception of God in a human form that it is not surprising that there were some even in the Church who could not believe it. What John says is that the Word became *sarx*. Now *sarx* is the very word that Paul uses over and over again to describe what he called *the flesh*, human nature in all its weakness and in all its liability to sin. The very thought of taking this word and applying it to the Word, to God, was something that their minds staggered at. So there arose in the Church a body of people called *Docetists*. *Dokein* is the Greek word for *to seem to be*. These people held that Jesus in fact was only a phantom, an appearance, that His human body was not a real body, that He was only a walking spirit like a ghost, that He could not really feel hunger and weariness, sorrow and pain, that He was in fact a disembodied spirit in the apparent form of a man. John dealt with these people much more directly in his First Letter. " Hereby know we the Spirit of God. Every spirit that confesseth that Jesus Christ is come *in the flesh* is of God; and every spirit that confesseth not that Jesus Christ is come in the flesh is not of God; and this is the spirit of Antichrist " (I *John* 4: 2, 3). It is true that this heresy was born of a kind of mistaken reverence. It was born of the spirit that was afraid to say that Jesus was really, fully and truly human. To John it was a spirit that contradicted the whole Christian gospel.

It may well be that we are often so eager to conserve the fact that Jesus was fully God that we tend to forget the fact that He was fully man. *The Word became flesh—* here, perhaps as nowhere else in the New Testament, we have the full manhood of Jesus gloriously proclaimed. In Jesus we see the creating Word of God, the controlling Reason of God, taking manhood upon Himself. In Jesus we see God living life as God would have lived it if God had been a man. Suppose we said nothing else about Jesus we could still say that He shows us how God would live this life that we have to live.

THE WORD BECAME FLESH

John I: 14 (continued)

> So the Word of God became a person, and took up His abode in our being, full of grace and truth; and we looked with our own eyes upon His glory, glory like the glory which an only son receives from a father.

IT might well be held that this is the greatest single verse in the whole New Testament; we must therefore spend much time upon it that we may enter the more fully into its riches.

We have already seen how John has certain great words which haunt his mind and dominate his thought and are the themes out of which his whole message is elaborated. Here we have three more of these words.

(i) The first is the word *grace*. This word grace has always two basic ideas in it. (*a*) It always has the idea of something completely undeserved and unmerited. It always has the idea of something that we could never have earned, or won, or achieved, or attained for ourselves. The fact that God came to earth to live and to die for men is not something which humanity deserved; it is an act of pure love on the part of God. The word grace emphasises at one and the same time the helpless poverty of man and the limitless kindness of the love of God. (b) It always has the idea of beauty in it. In modern Greek the word means *charm*. In Jesus we see the sheer winsomeness of God. Men had thought of God in terms of might and majesty and power and judgment. They had thought of the power of God which could crush all opposition and defeat all rebellion; but in Jesus men are confronted with the sheer loveliness of the love of God.

(ii) The second is the word *truth*. This word *truth* is one of the dominant notes of the Fourth Gospel. As we go through the gospel we will meet it again and again. Here we can only briefly and summarily gather together what John has to say about Jesus and the truth.

(a) Jesus is the embodiment of the truth. He said: " I am the truth " (14: 6). To see truth we must look at Jesus. Here is something infinitely precious for every simple mind and soul. There are very few people who can grasp abstract ideas. Most people think in pictures, not in abstractions. We could think and argue for ever and we would very likely be no nearer arriving at a definition of beauty. But if we can point at a beautiful person, we can say that *is* beauty and the thing becomes clear. Ever since men began to think about God they have been trying to define just who and what God is—and their puny minds get no nearer a definition. But we can cease our thinking and look at Jesus Christ, and we can say: " That is what God is like." Jesus did not come to *talk* to men about God; He came to *show* men what God is like, so that the simplest mind might know God as intimately as the mind of the greatest philosopher.

(b) Jesus is the communicator of the truth. Jesus told His disciples that if they continued with Him they would know the truth (8: 31). He told Pilate that His object in coming into this world was to witness to the truth (18: 37). Men will flock to a teacher or preacher who can really give them guidance for this tangled business of thinking and living. Jesus is the one who, amidst the shadows, makes things clear; who, at the many cross-roads of life, shows us the right way; who, in the baffling moments of decision, enables us to choose aright; who, amidst the many voices which clamour for our allegiance, tells us what to believe.

(c) Even when Jesus left this earth in the body, He left us His Spirit to tell us the truth and to guide us into the truth. His Spirit is the Spirit of truth (14: 17; 15: 26; 16: 13). Jesus did not leave us only a book of instruction and a body of teaching. We do not need to search through some unintelligible text-book to find out what to do. Still, to this day, we can ask Him what to do, for His Spirit is with us every step of the way.

(d) The truth is that which makes us free (8: 32). There is always a certain liberating quality in the truth. A child often gets queer, mistaken notions about things when he thinks about them himself. And often he becomes afraid. When he is told the truth he is emancipated from his fears. A man may fear that he is ill; he goes to the doctor; even if the verdict is bad he is at least liberated from the vague fears which haunted his mind. The truth which Jesus brings liberates us from estrangement from God; it liberates us from frustration in life; it liberates us from our own fears and weaknesses and defeats. Jesus Christ is the greatest liberator on earth.

(e) The truth can be resented. They sought to kill Jesus because He told them the truth (8: 40). The truth may well condemn a man; it may well show him how far wrong he was. " Truth," said the Cynics, " can be like the light to sore eyes." The Cynics declared that the teacher who never annoyed anyone never did anyone any good. But one fact remains—men may shut their ears and their minds to the truth; they may kill the man who tells them the truth—but the truth remains. No man ever destroyed the truth by refusing to listen to the voice that told him the truth. And the truth will catch up with him in the end.

(*f*) The truth can be disbelieved (8: 45). There are two main reasons why men disbelieve the truth. They may disbelieve it because it is too good to be true; or they may disbelieve it because they are so fastened to their half-truths that they will not let them go. In many cases the half-truths are the worst enemies of the whole truths.

(*g*) The truth is not something abstract; it is something which must be done (3: 21). The truth is something which must be known with the mind, accepted with the heart, and enacted in life.

THE WORD BECAME FLESH

John 1: 14 (*continued*)

> So the Word of God became a person, and took up His abode in our being, full of grace and truth; and we looked with our own eyes upon His glory, glory like the glory which an only son receives from a father.

THIS is one of the verses of scripture of which a lifetime of study and thought could not exhaust the truth. So we must yet again look at it. We have already looked at two of the great theme words that are in it; now we must look at the third—the word *glory*. Again and again John uses this word glory in connection with Jesus Christ. We shall first look at what John says about the glory of Christ, and then we shall go on to see if we can understand a little of what he means.

(i) The life of Jesus Christ was a manifestation of glory. When He performed the miracle of the water and the wine at Cana of Galilee, John says that He manifested forth His glory (2: 11). To look at Jesus and to experience His power and love was to enter into a new glory.

(ii) The glory which He manifests is the glory of God. It is not from men that He receives glory (5: 41). He seeks not His own glory but the glory of Him who sent Him (7: 18). It is His Father who glorifies Him (8: 50, 54). It is the glory of God that Martha will see in the raising of Lazarus (11: 4). The raising of Lazarus is for the glory of God, that the Son may be glorified thereby (11: 4). The glory that was on Jesus, that clung about Him, that shone through Him, that acted in Him is the glory of God.

(iii) And yet that glory was uniquely His own. At the end He prays that God will glorify Him with the glory that He had before the world began (17: 5). He shines with no borrowed radiance; His glory is His and His by right.

(iv) The glory which is His He has transmitted to His disciples. The glory which God gave Him He has given to them (17: 22). It is as if Jesus shared in the glory of God and the disciple shares in the glory of Christ. It would be to say that the coming of Jesus is the coming of God's glory among men.

Now what does John mean by all this? To answer that we must turn to the Old Testament. To the Jew the idea of the *Shechinah* was very dear. The *Shechinah* means *that which dwells*; and it is the word which is used for the visible presence of God among men. Repeatedly in the Old Testament we come across the idea that there were certain times when God's glory was visible among men. In the desert, before the giving of the manna, the children of Israel " looked toward the wilderness, and, behold, the glory of the Lord appeared in the cloud " (*Exodus* 16: 10). Before the giving of the Ten Commandments, " the glory of the Lord abode upon Mount Sinai " (*Exodus* 24: 16). When the Tabernacle had been erected and equipped, " the glory of the Lord filled the tabernacle " (*Exodus* 40: 34). When Solomon's Temple was dedicated the priests could not enter in to minister " for the glory of the Lord had filled the house of the Lord " (1 *Kings* 8: 11). When Isaiah had his vision in the Temple, he heard the angelic choir singing that " the whole earth is full of His glory " (*Isaiah* 6: 3). Ezekiel in his ecstasy saw " the likeness of the glory of the Lord " (*Ezekiel* 1: 28). In the Old Testament the glory of the Lord came at times when God was very near and very close.

The glory of the Lord means quite simply the presence of God. John uses a homely illustration. A father gives to his eldest son his own authority, his own honour. The heir apparent to the throne, the king's heir, his eldest son, is invested with all the royal glory of his father. It was so with Jesus. When Jesus came to this earth men saw in Him the splendour of God, and at the heart of that splendour is love. When Jesus came to this earth men saw the wonder of God, and the wonder was love. When Jesus came men saw that God's glory and God's love were one and the same thing. The glory of God is not the glory of a despotic eastern tyrant, but that splendour of love before which we fall, not in abject terror, but lost in wonder, love and praise.

THE INEXHAUSTIBLE FULNESS

John 1: 15-17

> John was His witness and his statement still sounds out: " This is He of whom I said to you, He who comes after me has been advanced before me, because He was before me." On His fulness we all of us have drawn, and from Him we have received grace upon grace, for it was the law which was given by Moses, but grace and truth came through Jesus Christ.

WE have already seen that the Fourth Gospel was written in a situation where it was necessary to make sure that John the Baptist did not occupy an exaggerated position in men's thoughts. So John begins this passage with a saying of John the Baptist which gives to Jesus the first and only place.

John the Baptist says of Jesus: " He who comes after me was before me." He may mean more than one thing by that. (a) Jesus was actually six months younger in age than John, and John may be saying quite simply: "He who is my junior has been advanced beyond me." (b) John may be saying: "I was in the field before Jesus; I occupied the centre of the stage before He did; my hand was laid to the work before His was; but all that I was doing was to prepare the way for His coming; I was only the advance guard of the main force and the herald of the king." (c) It may be that John is thinking in terms much more deep than that. He may be thinking not in terms of time but of eternity. He may be thinking and remembering that Jesus is the one who existed before the world began, and beside whom any human figure has no standing at all. It may be that all three ideas were in John's mind. It was not John who had exaggerated his own position; that was the mistake that some of his followers had made. To John the topmost place belonged to Jesus Christ.

This passage then goes on to say three great things about Jesus.

(i) On His fulness we all have drawn. The word that John uses for *fulness* is a great word; it is the word *plērōma*, and it means the sum total of all that is in God. It is a word which Paul uses often. In *Colossians* 1: 19 he says that all *plērōma* dwelt in Christ. In *Colossians* 2: 9 he says in Christ there dwelt the *plērōma* of deity in a bodily form. He meant that in Jesus there dwelt the totality of the wisdom, the power, the love of God. Just because of that Jesus is inexhaustible. A man can go to Jesus with any need and find that need supplied. A man can go to Jesus with any ideal and find that ideal realised. In Jesus the man in love with beauty will find the supreme beauty. In Jesus the man to whom life is the search for knowledge will find the supreme revelation. In Jesus the man who needs courage will find the pattern and the secret of being brave. In Jesus the man who feels that he cannot cope with life will find the Master of life and the power to live.

In Jesus the man who is conscious of his sin will find the forgiveness for his sin and the power to be good. In Jesus the *plērōma*, the fulness of God, all that is in God, what Westcott called "the spring of divine life," becomes available to men.

(ii) From Him we have received grace upon grace. Literally the Greek means *grace instead of grace*. What does that strange phrase mean? (*a*) It may mean that in Christ we have found one wonder leading to another. One of the old missionaries came to one of the ancient Pictish kings. The king asked him what he might expect if he became a Christian. The missionary answered: "You will find wonder upon wonder and every one of them true." Sometimes when we travel a very lovely road, vista after vista opens to us. At every view we think that nothing could be lovelier, and then we turn another corner and a new and even greater loveliness opens before us. When a man enters on the study of some great subject, like music or poetry or art, he never gets to the end of it. Always there are fresh experiences of beauty waiting for him. It is so with Christ. The more we know of Him, the more wonderful He becomes. The longer we live with Him the more loveliness we discover. The more we think about Him and with Him the wider the horizon of truth becomes. This phrase may be John's way of expressing the limitlessness of Christ. It may be his way of saying that the man who companies with Christ will find new wonders dawning upon his soul and enlightening his mind and enchaining his heart every day. (*b*) It may be that we ought to take this expression quite literally. In Christ we find *grace instead of grace*. The different ages and the different situations in life demand a different kind of grace. We need one grace in the days of prosperity and another in the days of adversity. We need one grace in the sunlit days of youth and another when the shadows of age begin to lengthen upon life. The Church needs one grace in the days of persecution and another when

53

the days of acceptance have come. We need one grace when we feel that we are on the top of things and another when we are depressed and discouraged and near to despair. We need one grace to bear our own burdens and another to bear one another's burdens. We need one grace when we are sure of things and another when there seems nothing certain left in the world. The grace of God is never a static but always a dynamic thing. It never fails to meet the situation. One need invades life and one grace comes with it. That need passes and another need assaults us and with the other need another grace comes. All through life we are constantly receiving grace instead of grace, for the grace of Christ is triumphantly adequate to deal with any situation.

(iii) The law was given by Moses, but grace and truth came through Jesus Christ. In the old way of life, life was governed by law. A man had to do a thing whether he liked it or not, and whether he knew the reason for it or not; but with the coming of Jesus we no longer seek to obey the law of God like slaves; we seek to answer the love of God like sons. It is through Jesus Christ that God the law-giver has become God the Father, that God the judge has become God the lover of the souls of men.

THE REVELATION OF GOD

John I: 18

> No one has ever seen God. It is the unique one, He who is God, He who is in the bosom of the Father, who has told us all about God.

WHEN John said that no man has ever seen God everyone in the ancient world would have fully agreed with him. In the ancient world men were fascinated and depressed and frustrated by what they regarded as the infinite distance and the utter unknowability of God. In the Old Testament God is represented as saying to Moses: " Thou canst not see my face; for there shall no man see me and live " (*Exodus* 33: 20). When God reminds the people of the giving of the law, He says: " Ye heard the voice of the words but saw no similitude; only you heard a voice " (*Deuteronomy* 4: 12). No one in the Old Testament would have thought it possible to see God. The great Greek thinkers felt in exactly the same way. Xenophanes had said: " Guesswork is over all." Plato had said: " Never man and God can meet." Celsus had laughed at the way that the Christians called God Father, because " God is away beyond everything." At the best, Apuleius said, men could catch a glimpse of God as a lightning flash lights up a dark night—one split second of illumination, and then the dark. As Glover said: " Whatever God was, He was far from being within the reach of ordinary men." There might be very very rare moments of ecstasy when men caught a glimpse of what they called " Absolute Being," but ordinary men were the prisoners of ignorance and fancy. There would have been none to disagree with John when he said that no man has ever seen God.

But John does not stop there; he goes on to make the startling and tremendous statement that Jesus has fully revealed to men what God is like. What has come to men is what J. H. Bernard calls " the exhibition to the world of God in Christ." Here again the keynote of John's gospel sounds: " If you want to see what God is like, look at Jesus Christ."

Why should it be that Jesus can do what no one else has ever done? Wherein lies His power to reveal God to men? John says three things about Jesus.

(i) Jesus is *unique*. The Greek word is *monogenēs*, which the Authorised Version translates *only-begotten*. It is true that that is what *monogenēs* literally means; but long before this it had lost its purely physical sense, and it had come to have two special meanings. It had come to mean *unique* and *specially beloved*. Obviously an only son has a unique place and a unique love in his father's heart. So this word came to express *uniqueness* more than anything else. It is the conviction of the New Testament that Jesus is unique, that there is no one like Him, that He can do for men what no one else can do. He alone is the one who can bring God to men and bring men to God.

(ii) Jesus is *God*. Here we have the very same form of expression as we had in the first verse of the chapter. This does not mean that Jesus is identical with God; it does mean that in mind and character and being Jesus is one with God. In this case it might be better if we thought of it as meaning that Jesus is divine. To see Him is to see what God is.

(iii) Jesus is *in the bosom of the Father*. To be in the bosom of someone is the Hebrew phrase which expresses the deepest intimacy possible in human life. It is used of mother and child; it is used of husband and wife; a man speaks of the wife of his bosom (*Numbers* 11: 12; *Deuteronomy* 13: 6); it is used of two friends who are in complete communion with one another. When John used this phrase about Jesus, he meant that between Jesus and God there is complete and total and uninterrupted intimacy. It is because Jesus is so intimate with God, that He is one with God, that He can reveal God to men.

In Jesus Christ the distant, unknowable, invisible, unreachable God has come to men; and God can never be a stranger to us again.

THE WITNESS OF JOHN

John 1: 19-28

This is the witness of John, when the Jews sent priests and Levites to him from Jerusalem to ask him: " Who are you? " He quite definitely affirmed and stated: " I am not the Messiah." So they asked him: " What then are we to think? Are you Elijah? " He said: " I am not." " Are you the promised prophet? " He answered: " No." So they said to him: " Who are you? Tell us, so that we can give an answer to those who sent us. What claim do you make for yourself?" He said: "I am the voice of one crying in the wilderness, 'Make the Lord's road straight,' as Isaiah the prophet said." Now they had been sent by the Pharisees. So they asked him and said to him: "If you are neither the Messiah, nor Elijah, nor the promised prophet, why then do you baptize?" John answered: "I baptize with water. But there is one standing among you, whom you do not know, I mean the one who is coming after me, the straps of whose sandals I am not worthy to unloose." These things happened at Bethany, on the far side of Jordan, where John was baptizing.

WITH this passage John begins the narrative part of his gospel. In the prologue he has shown what he intends to do; he is writing his gospel to demonstrate that Jesus is the Mind, the Reason, the Word of God come into this world in the form of a human person. Having set down his central thought, he now begins the story of the life of Jesus.

No one is so careful of details of time as John is. Starting from this passage and going on to 2: 11 he tells step by step the story of the first momentous week in the public life of Jesus. The events of the first day are in 1: 19-28; the story of the second day is 1: 29-34; the third day is unfolded in 1: 35-39. The three verses 1: 40-42 tell the story of the fourth day. The events of the fifth day are told in 1: 43-51. The sixth day is left a blank. And the events of the last day of the week are told in 2: 1-11. In all this section John is taking us day by day through a series of notable events which mark this first week of the public ministry of Jesus. No other gospel is so careful to insert the marks of the time sequence as the Fourth Gospel is.

Further, in this same section from 1: 19 to 2: 11 the Fourth Gospel gives us three different kinds of witness to Jesus. In three different ways he gives us three witnesses to the greatness and the uniqueness of Jesus. (i) There is the witness of John the Baptist (1: 19-34). (ii) There is the witness of those who accepted Jesus as their Master, and who became His disciples (1: 41-51). (iii) There is the witness of Jesus' own wonderful powers (2: 1-11). John is setting Jesus before us in three different contexts, and in each context he is showing us the supreme wonder of Jesus.

We have already seen that the Fourth Gospel had to take account of a situation in which John the Baptist was given a position far higher than he himself had claimed. As late as A.D. 250 the *Clementine Recognitions* tell us that " there were some of John's disciples who preached about him as if their master was the Messiah." In this passage the Fourth Gospel shows us that that was a view and a claim that John the Baptist himself would have entirely and definitely repudiated.

Let us now turn to the passage itself. Right at the beginning of it we come upon a characteristic of the Fourth Gospel. It is emissaries of the *Jews* who come to cross-question John. This word *Jews* (*Ioudaioi*) occurs in the Fourth Gospel no fewer than seventy times; and always the Jews are the opposition. They are the people who have set themselves against Jesus. The mention of the *Jews* brings the opposition thus early upon the stage. The Fourth Gospel is two things. First, as we have seen, it is the exhibition of God in Jesus Christ. But, second, it is equally the story of the rejection of Jesus Christ by the Jews. The gospel is at one and the same time the story of God's offer and man's refusal, the story of God's love and man's sin, the story of Jesus Christ's invitation and man's rejection of it. The Fourth Gospel is the gospel in which love and warning are uniquely and vividly combined.

The deputation which came to interview John was composed of two kinds of people. First, there were the priests and the Levites. Their interest was very natural, for John was the son of Zacharias, and Zacharias was a priest (*Luke* 1: 5). In Judaism the only qualification for the priesthood was descent. If a man was not a descendant of Aaron nothing could make him a priest; if he was a descendant of Aaron nothing could stop him being a priest. Therefore in the eyes of the authorities, John the Baptist was in fact a priest, and it was very natural that the priests should come to find out why a priest was behaving in such an unusual way. Second, there were emissaries of the Pharisees. Now it may well be that behind them there was the Sanhedrin. One of the functions of the Sanhedrin was to deal with any man who was suspected of being a false prophet. John was a preacher to whom the people were flocking out in hordes. The Sanhedrin may well have felt it to be their duty to check up on this man in case he was a false prophet.

The whole thing shows us how suspicious orthodoxy was of anything unusual. John did not conform to the normal idea of a priest; and he did not conform to the normal idea of a preacher; and therefore the ecclesiastical authorities of the day looked upon him askance. The Church always runs the danger of condemning a new way of doing things just because it is new. In one sense there is hardly any institution in the world which resents change so much as the Church does. The Church has often rejected a great teacher, and has often refused some great adventure simply because it wished to be left alone, and suspected all things new.

THE WITNESS OF JOHN

John 1: 19-28 (*continued*)

THE emissaries of the orthodox could think of three things that John might claim to be.

(i) They asked him if he was the Messiah. The Jews were waiting, and are waiting to this day, for the Messiah. Any captive people waits for its deliverer. The Jews believed themselves to be God's chosen people; they could not doubt that sooner or later God would intervene to save His people. There was no one idea of the Messiah. Some people expected one who would bring peace over all the earth. Some expected one who would bring in the reign of righteousness. Most expected one who would be a great national champion to lead the armies of the Jews as conquerors over all the world. Some expected a supernatural figure straight from God. Still more expected a prince to rise from David's line. Frequently Messianic pretenders arose and caused rebellions. The time of Jesus was an excited age. It was natural to ask John if he claimed to be the Messiah; but John completely rejected that claim; but he rejected it with a certain hint. In the Greek the word I is stressed by its position. It is as if John said: "I am not the Messiah, but, if you only knew, the Messiah is here."

(ii) They asked him if he was Elijah. It was the Jewish belief that, before the Messiah came, Elijah would return to herald His coming and to prepare the world to receive Him. Particularly, Elijah was to come to arrange all disputes. He would settle what things and what people were clean and unclean; he would settle who were Jews and who were not Jews; he would bring together again families which were estranged. So much so did the Jews believe this that the traditional law said that money and property whose owners were disputed, or anything found whose owner was unknown, must wait " until Elijah comes." The belief that Elijah would come before the Messiah goes back to *Malachi* 4: 5. It was even believed that Elijah would anoint the Messiah to His kingly office, as all kings were anointed, and that he would raise the dead to share in the new kingdom; but John denied that any such honour was his.

(iii) They asked him if he was the expected and promised prophet. It was sometimes believed that Isaiah and, especially, Jeremiah would return at the coming of the

Messiah. But this is really a reference to the assurance which Moses gave to the people in *Deuteronomy* 18: 15: "The Lord thy God will raise up unto thee a Prophet from the midst of thee, of thy brethren, like unto me; unto him shall ye hearken." That was a promise that no Jew ever forgot. They waited for the emergence of the prophet who would be the greatest of all prophets, and longed for his coming, the prophet who would be *The Prophet par excellence*. But once again John denied that that honour was his.

So they asked him who he was; his answer was that he was nothing but a voice bidding men prepare the way for the King. The quotation is from *Isaiah* 40: 3. All the gospels cite this text about John (*Mark* 1: 3; *Matthew* 3: 3; *Luke* 3: 4). The idea behind it is this. Eastern roads were not surfaced and metalled. They were mere tracks. When a king was about to visit a province, when a conqueror was about to travel through his domains, the roads were smoothed and straightened out and put in order. What John was saying is: " I am nobody; I am only a voice telling you to get ready for the coming of the King." John was saying: " Get yourselves ready, for the King is on the way."

John was what every true preacher and teacher ought to be—he was only a voice, a pointer to the King. The last thing that he wanted men to do was to look at him; he wanted them to forget him and to see only the King.

But the Pharisees were puzzled about one thing—what right had John to baptize? If he had been the Messiah, or even Elijah or the prophet, he might have baptized. Isaiah had written: " So shall He sprinkle many nations " (*Isaiah* 52: 15). Ezekiel had said: " Then will I sprinkle clean water upon you, and ye shall be clean " (*Ezekiel* 36: 25). Zechariah had said: " In that day there shall be a fountain opened to the house of David

and to the inhabitants of Jerusalem for sin and for uncleanness " (*Zechariah* 13: 1). But why should John baptize?
And what made it still more strange was this. Baptism
at the hands of men was not for Israelites at all. It was
proselytes, incomers from other faiths, who were baptized.
An Israelite was never baptized; he was God's already;
he did not need to be washed; but *Gentiles* who came
in from heathen faiths had to be washed in baptism. John
was making Israelites do what only Gentiles had to do.
He was suggesting that *the chosen people had to be cleansed.*
That was indeed precisely what John believed. But he
did not answer directly.

He said: " I am only baptizing with water; but there
is One among you—you don't recognize Him—and I
am not worthy to untie the straps of His shoes." John
could not have given himself a more menial office. To
untie the straps of sandals was slaves' work. There was a
Rabbinic saying which said that a disciple might do for
his master anything that a servant did, *except* only to
untie his sandals. That was too menial a service for even
a disciple to render. So John said: " One is coming whose
slave I am not fit to be." We are to understand that by
this time the baptism of Jesus had taken place at which
John had recognized Jesus. So here John is saying the same
again. He is saying: " The King is coming. And, for
His coming, you need to be cleansed as much as any
Gentile. Prepare yourself for the entry into history of the
King."

John's function was to be only the preparer of the way.
Any greatness he had came from the greatness of the one
whose coming he foretold. John is the great example of
the man prepared to obliterate himself in order that Jesus
Christ may be seen. He was only, as he saw it, a finger-post
pointing to Christ. God give us grace to forget ourselves
and to remember only Christ.

THE LAMB OF GOD

John 1: 29-31

> On the next day, John saw Jesus as He was coming towards him, and said: " See! The Lamb of God who is taking away the sin of the world! This is He of whom I said to you: ' There is a man who is coming after me, who has been advanced before me, because He was before me.' Even I did not know Him. All the same, the reason that I came baptizing with water is that He might be shown forth to Israel."

HERE we come to the second day of this momentous week in the life of Jesus. By this time His baptism and His temptations were past and He was about to set His hand to the work which He came into the world to do. And once again the Fourth Gospel shows us John paying his spontaneous tribute to Jesus. He calls Jesus by that tremendous title which has become woven into the very language of devotion—*The Lamb of God*. What was John thinking about and what was in his mind when he used that title? There are at least four pictures which may well all contribute something to it.

(i) It may well have been that John was thinking of the Passover Lamb. The Passover Feast was not very far away (*John* 2: 13). The old story of the Passover was that it was the blood of the slain lamb which protected the houses of the Israelites on the night when they left Egypt (*Exodus* 12: 11-13). On that night when the Angel of Death walked abroad and smote the first-born of the Egyptians, the Israelites were to smear their doorposts with the blood of the slain lamb, and the angel would see that blood and pass over that house. It was the blood of the lamb which delivered them from destruction. It has been suggested that even as John the Baptist saw Jesus, there passed by flocks of lambs, being driven up to Jerusalem from the country districts, to serve as sacrificial lambs for the Passover Feast. It was the blood of the Passover lamb which delivered the Israelites in Egypt from destruction and death; and it may be that John was saying: " There is the one true sacrifice who can deliver you from death." Paul too thought of Jesus as the Passover lamb (I *Corinthians* 5: 7). There is a deliverance that only Jesus Christ can win for us.

(ii) John was the son of a priest. He would know all the ritual of the Temple and its sacrifices. Now every morning and every evening in life a lamb was sacrificed in the Temple for the sins of the people (*Exodus* 29: 38-42). So long as the Temple stood this daily sacrifice was made. Even when the people were starving in war and in siege they never omitted to offer the lamb until in A.D. 70 the Temple was destroyed. It may be that John is saying: " In the Temple a lamb is offered every night and every morning for the sins of the people; but in this Jesus alone is the only sacrifice which can deliver men from sin."

(iii) There are two great pictures of the lamb in the prophets. Jeremiah writes: " But I was like a lamb or an ox that is brought to the slaughter " (*Jeremiah* 11: 19). And Isaiah has the great picture of the one who was brought " as a lamb to the slaughter " (*Isaiah* 53: 7). Both these great prophets had the vision of one who by His sufferings and His sacrifice, meekly and lovingly borne, would redeem His people. Maybe John is saying: " Your prophets dreamed of the one who was to love and suffer and die for the people; that one is come." It is certainly true that in later times the picture of *Isaiah* 53 became to the Church one of the most precious forecasts of Jesus in all the Old Testament. It may be that John the Baptist was the first to see it so.

(iv) But there is a fourth picture which would be very familiar to the Jews, although it is very strange to us. In the time between the Old and New Testament there were the days of the great struggles in which the Maccabees fought and died and conquered. In those days the lamb, and especially the horned lamb, was the symbol of a great conqueror. Judas Maccabaeus is so described, as are Samuel and David and Solomon. The lamb—strange as it may sound to us—stood for the conquering champion of God. It may well be that this is no picture of gentle and helpless weakness, but rather a picture of conquering majesty and power. Jesus was the champion of God who fought with sin and mastered it, the one who defeated and abolished sin in single contest.

There is sheer wonder in this phrase, the Lamb of God. It haunted the writer of the Revelation. Twenty-nine times he used it in his book. It became one of the most precious titles of Christ. In one word it sums up the love, the sacrifice, the suffering and the triumph of Christ.

John says that he did not know Jesus. Now John was a relation of Jesus (*Luke* I: 36), and he must have been acquainted with Jesus. What John is saying is not that he did not know *who* Jesus was, but that he did not know *what* Jesus was. It had suddenly been revealed to John that this Jesus was none other than the Son of God.

Once again, John makes clear what his only function was. His only function was to point men to Christ. He was nothing and Christ was everything. He claimed no greatness and no place for himself; he was only the man who, as it were, drew back the curtain, and left Jesus occupying the lonely centre of the stage.

THE COMING OF THE SPIRIT

John I: 32, 34

> So John bore his witness. " With my own eyes," he said, " I saw the Spirit coming down from heaven, as it might have been a dove, and the Spirit remained upon Him. And I did not know Him. But it was He who sent me to baptize with water who said to me: ' The one on whom you see the Spirit coming down and remaining is the one who baptizes with the Holy Spirit.' And I saw it happen; and my witness stands that this is the Son of God."

65

SOMETHING had happened at the baptism of Jesus which had convinced John beyond all doubt that Jesus was the Son of God. As the fathers of the Church saw centuries ago, it was something which only the eye of the mind and soul could see. But John saw it and he was convinced.

In Palestine the dove was a sacred bird. It was not hunted and it was not eaten. Philo noticed the number of doves at Ascalon, because it was not permitted to catch and kill them, and they were tame. In *Genesis* 1: 2 we read of the creative Spirit of God moving upon the face of the waters. The Rabbis used to say that the Spirit of God moved and fluttered like a dove over the ancient chaos breathing order and beauty into it. The picture of the dove was one which the Jews knew and loved.

It was at the baptism that the Spirit came upon Jesus with power. Now we must remember that at this time the *Christian* doctrine and realisation of the Spirit had not yet come into being. We have to wait for the last chapters of John's gospel and for Pentecost for that to emerge. When John the Baptist spoke of the Spirit coming upon Jesus, he must have been thinking in *Jewish* terms. What then was the Jewish idea of the Spirit?

The Jewish word for Spirit is *ruach*, which is the word which means *wind*. To the Jew there were always three basic ideas of the Spirit. The Spirit was *power*, power like a mighty rushing wind; the Spirit was *life*, the very centre and soul and essence of life, the very dynamic of the existence of man; the Spirit was *God*; the power and the life of the Spirit were beyond mere human achievement and attainment. The coming of the Spirit into a man's life was the coming of God. Above all it was the Spirit who controlled and inspired the prophets. " I am full of power by the Spirit of the Lord and of judgment and of might to declare unto Jacob his transgression and unto Israel his sin " (*Micah* 3: 8). God speaks to Isaiah of " My Spirit which is upon thee and my words which I have put into thy mouth " (*Isaiah* 59: 21). " The Spirit of the

Lord is upon me because the Lord hath appointed me to preach good tidings " (*Isaiah* 61: 1). " A new heart will I give you and a new spirit will I put within you. . . . I will put my Spirit within you " (*Ezekiel* 36: 26, 27). We may say that the Spirit of God did three things for the man on whom He came. First, He brought to men the truth of God. Second, He gave men the power to recognize that truth when they saw it. Third, He gave them the ability and the courage to preach that truth to men. To the Jew the Spirit was God coming into a man's life. Now at the baptism in the most unique way the Spirit came upon Jesus. And He came upon Him in a different way from that in which He ever came on any other person. Most men have what might be called spasmodic experiences of the Spirit. They have their moments of dazzling illumination, of extraordinary power, of superhuman courage. But these moments come and go. But twice (verses 32, 33) John goes out of his way to point out that the Spirit *stayed, abode, dwelt* on Jesus. Here was no momentary inspiration. In Jesus uniquely the Spirit took up His permanent abode. That is still another way of saying that the Mind and the Power of God were uniquely in Jesus.

Here we can learn a great deal of what the word *baptism* means. The Greek verb *baptizein* means *to dip* or *to submerge*. It can be used of clothes being *dipped* in dye; it can be used of a ship *submerged* beneath the waves; it can be used of a person who is so drunk that he is *soaked* in drink. When John says that Jesus will baptize men with the Holy Spirit, he means that Jesus can bring God's Spirit to us in such a way that we are soaked in it, that life is permeated with it, that we are saturated with the Spirit of God, that our mind, our life, our being is flooded with the Spirit of God. Now what did this baptism mean for John? John's own baptism meant two things. (i) It meant *cleansing*. It meant that a man was being washed from the impurities that clung to him. (ii) It meant *dedication.* It meant that he went out to a new and a different and a better life. But Jesus' baptism was *a baptism of the Spirit.* When we remember the Jewish conception of the Spirit we can say certain things. When the Spirit takes possession of a man certain things happen.

(i) His life is *illumined.* There comes to him the knowledge of God. The will of God becomes clear. He knows what God's purpose is, what life means, where duty lies. Some of God's wisdom and light has come into him.

(ii) His life is *strengthened.* Knowledge without power is a haunting and frustrating thing. But the Spirit gives us, not only knowledge to know the right, but also strength and power to do the right. The Spirit gives us a triumphant adequacy to cope with life.

(iii) His life is *purified.* Christ's baptism with the Spirit was to be a baptism of *fire* (Matthew 3: 11; Luke 3: 16). The dross of evil things, the alloy of the lower things, the base admixture is cleansed and burned away, until a man is clean and pure.

Often our prayers for the Spirit are a kind of theological and liturgical formality; but when we know that for which we are praying, our prayers for the Spirit become the desperate cry of the human heart.

THE FIRST DISCIPLES

John 1: 35-39

> On the next day John was again standing with two of his disciples. John looked at Jesus as He walked. " See! " he said, " The Lamb of God! " And the two disciples heard him speaking and followed Jesus. Jesus turned and saw them following Him. " What are you looking for?" He said to them. " Rabbi " (the word means Teacher), they said to Him, " where are you staying? " He said to them: " Come and see! " They came and saw where He was staying, and they stayed with Him throughout that day. And it was about four o'clock in the afternoon.

NEVER was a passage of scripture fuller of little revealing touches than this.

Once again we see John the Baptist pointing beyond himself. He must have known very well that to speak to his disciples about Jesus like that was to invite them to leave him and to transfer their loyalty to this new and greater teacher; and yet he did it. There was no jealousy in John. He had come to attach men, not to himself, but to Christ. There is no harder task than to take the second place when once the first place was enjoyed. But once Jesus had emerged on the scene John never had any other thought than to send men to Him.

So the two disciples of John followed Jesus. It may well be that they were too shy to approach Him directly, and that they followed respectfully some distance behind. And then Jesus did something which was and is entirely characteristic of Him. He turned and spoke to them. That is to say, He met them half way. He made things easier for them. He opened the door that they might come in. Here we have the symbol of the divine initiative. It is always God who takes the first step. When the human mind begins to seek and the human heart begins to long, God comes to meet us far more than half way. God does not leave a man to search and search until he comes to Himself; God goes out to meet the man. As Augustine said, we could not even have begun to seek for God unless God had already found us. When we go to God we do not go to one who hides Himself and keeps us at a distance; we go to one who stands waiting for us, and who even takes the initiative by coming to meet us on the road.

Jesus began by asking these two men the most fundamental question in life. " What are you looking for? " He asked them. It was very relevant to ask that question in Palestine in the time of Jesus. Were they legalists, looking only for subtle and recondite conversations about the little details of the Law, as the Scribes and Pharisees did? Where they ambitious time-servers looking for a place and power, as the Sadducees did? Were they nationalists looking for a political demagogue and a military commander who would smash the occupying power of Rome, as the Zealots did? Were they humble men of prayer and waiting, seeking for God and for His will, as the Quiet in the Land did? Or were they simply puzzled, bewildered men and sinners seeking for light on the road of life and forgiveness from God? It would be well if every now and again in life, we were to ask ourselves: " What am I looking for? What am I trying to extract from life? What's my aim and goal? If I am honest, what, in the depth of my heart, am i really trying to get out of life? " There are some who are searching for *security*. They would like a position which is safe, money enough to meet the needs of life and to put some past for the time when work is done, a material security which will take away the essential worry about material things. It is not a wrong aim, but it is a low aim, and an inadequate thing to which to direct all life; for, in the last analysis, there is no safe security in the uncertainty of the chances and the changes of this life. There are some who are searching for what they would call a *career*, for power, for prominence, for prestige, for a place to fit the talents and the abilities they believe themselves to have, for an opportunity to do the work they believe themselves capable of doing. Again it is not a bad aim. If it be directed by motives of personal ambition it can be a bad aim; if it be directed by motives of the service of our fellow men it can be a high aim. But it is not enough, for its horizon is limited by time and by the world. There are some who are searching for some kind of *peace*, for something to enable them to live at peace with themselves, and at peace with God, and at peace with men. That is the search for God; that is the aim that only Jesus Christ can meet and supply.

The answer of John's disciples was that they wished to know where Jesus stayed. They called him *Rabbi*; that is a Hebrew word which literally means *My great one*.

It was the title of respect given by students and seekers after knowledge to their teachers and to wise men. John, who wrote the gospel, was writing for Greeks. He knew they would not recognize that Hebrew word, so he translates it for them by the Greek word *didaskalos*, which means *teacher*. It was not mere curiosity which made these two ask this question. What they meant was that they did not wish only to speak to Jesus on the road, in the passing, as chance acquaintances might stop and exchange a few words. They wished to enter in and linger long with Him, and talk out their problems and their troubles. The man who would be Jesus' disciple can never be satisfied with a passing word with Jesus. He wants to meet Jesus, not as an acquaintance in the passing, but as a friend in His own house.

Jesus' answer was: "Come and see!" The Jewish Rabbis had a way of using that phrase in their teaching. They would say: "Do you want to know the answer to this question? Do you want to know the solution to this problem? Come and see, and we will think about it together." When Jesus said: "Come and see!" He was inviting those two, not only to come and talk, but to come and find the things that He alone could open out to them.

So John who wrote the gospel finishes the paragraph— "It was about four o'clock in the afternoon." It may very well be that he finishes that way because he was one of the two himself. He could tell you the hour of the day, the very stone of the road he was standing on when he met Jesus. At four o'clock on a spring afternoon in Galilee, life became a new thing for John. When a man really meets Christ he will no more forget that day and hour than he will forget the day of his birth. It marks the dividing line between the time when he did not know and the time when he came to know Jesus Christ.

SHARING THE GLORY

John I: 40-42

> Andrew, Simon Peter's brother, was one of the two who had heard John speaking about Jesus, and who had followed Him. First thing in the morning, he went and found his own brother Simon. "We have found the Messiah," he said to him. (The word *Messiah* means the same as the word *Christ*). He brought him to Jesus. Jesus looked intently at him. "You are Simon, Jona's son," He said. "You will be called Cephas." *Cephas* is the same name as *Peter* and means a *rock*.

THE Authorised Version has it that Andrew " *first* findeth his own brother Simon." In the Greek manuscripts there are two readings. Some manuscripts have the word *prōton*, which means *first*, and that is the reading that the Authorised Version has translated. Other manuscripts have *prōi*, which means *early in the morning*. In our translation we have taken the second reading because it suits the story better to regard this event of our passage as taking place on the next day. We have seen that John is giving us the story of the first momentous week in Jesus' life, and that story fits better if we take Andrew's finding of Peter to have happened on the next day.

In this passage again John has explained a Hebrew word in order to help the Greeks, for whom he wrote, to understand better. *Messiah* and *Christ* are the same word. *Messiah* is Hebrew and *Christ* is Greek; both mean *anointed*. In the ancient world, as to-day in our own country, kings were anointed with oil at their coronation. And *Messiah* and *Christos* both mean *God's Anointed King*.

We do not possess a great deal of information about Andrew, but even the little that we do know of him perfectly paints his character. Andrew is one of the most attractive characters in the apostolic band. He has two outstanding characteristics.

(i) Andrew was characteristically the man who was
prepared to take the second place. Again and again Andrew
is identified as *Simon Peter's brother*. It is clear that Andrew
lived under the shadow of Peter. People might not know
who Andrew was, but everyone knew who Peter was;
and when men spoke of Andrew they described him as
Peter's brother. Andrew was not one of the inner circle
of the disciples. When Jesus healed Jairus's daughter,
when He went up to the Mount of Transfiguration, when
He underwent His temptation in Gethsemane, it was
Peter, James and John whom He took with Him. It
would have been so easy for Andrew to resent this. Was
he not one of the first two disciples who ever followed
Jesus? Did Peter not owe his meeting with Jesus to
Andrew? Might Andrew not reasonably have expected
and demanded a foremost place in the apostolic band?
But all that never even occurred to Andrew. He was
quite content to stand back and to let his more famous
brother have the limelight; he was quite content to play
a humble part in the company of the Twelve. To Andrew,
matters of precedence and place and honour mattered
nothing at all. All that mattered was to be with Jesus and
to serve Him as he could. Andrew is the patron saint of
all who humbly and loyally and ungrudgingly take the
second place.

(ii) Andrew is characteristically the man who was
always introducing others to Jesus. There are only
three times in the gospel story when Andrew is brought
into the centre of the stage. There is this incident here,
in which Andrew brings Peter to Jesus. There is the
incident in *John* 6: 8, 9 when Andrew brought to Jesus
the boy with the five loaves and two small fishes. And there
is the incident in *John* 12: 22 when Andrew brought
the enquiring Greeks into the presence of Jesus. It was
Andrew's great joy to bring others to Jesus. He stands
out as the man whose one desire was to share the glory.
He is the man with the missionary heart. Having himself

found the friendship of Jesus, he spent all life in introducing others to that friendship. Andrew is our great example in that he could not keep Jesus to himself.

When Andrew brought Peter to Jesus, Jesus looked at Peter. The word that is used of that look is *emblepein*. This word describes a concentrated, intent gaze. It describes the gaze which does not only see the superficial things that lie on the surface, but which reads a man's heart. When Jesus saw Simon, as he was then called, he said to him: "Your name is Simon; but you are going to be called Cephas, which means a rock." In the ancient world nearly everyone had two names. Greek was the universal language of that world and nearly everyone had a name in his own native tongue, by which he was known to his friends and his family circle, and he had a name in the Greek tongue, by which he was known in the business and the commercial and the wider world. Sometimes the one name was a translation of the other. *Peter* is the *Greek* and *Cephas* is the *Aramaic* for a *rock*; *Thomas* was the *Aramaic* and *Didymus* was the Greek for a *twin*; *Tabitha* was the *Aramaic* and *Dorcas* was the *Greek* for a *gazelle*. Sometimes the Greek name was chosen because it sounded like the Aramaic name. A Jew who was called *Eliakim* or *Abel* in his own tongue might become *Alcimus* or *Apelles* to his Greek circle of acquaintances. So then *Peter* and *Cephas* are not different names; they are the same name in different languages.

In the Old Testament a change of name often denoted a new relationship with God. For instance, *Jacob* became *Israel* (*Genesis* 32: 28), and *Abram* became *Abraham* (*Genesis* 17: 5) when they entered into a new relationship with God. When a man enters into a new relationship with God, it is as if life began all over again and he became a new man, so that he needs a new name.

But the great thing about this story is that it tells us *how Jesus looks at men*. Jesus does not only see what a man *is*; He also sees what a man *can become*. He sees not only the *actualities* in a man; he also sees the *possibilities*. Jesus looked at Peter and He saw in him, not only a Galilaean fisherman; He saw one who had it in him to become the rock on which His Church would be built. Jesus sees us not only as we are, but as we can be; and He says to us: " Give your life to me, and I will make you what you have it in you to be." It is told that once someone came on Michael Angelo chipping away with his chisel at a huge shapeless piece of rock. He asked the sculptor what he was doing. " I am releasing the angel that is imprisoned in this marble," he answered. Jesus is the one who sees and who can release the hidden hero in every man.

THE SURRENDER OF NATHANAEL

John I: 43-51

On the next day Jesus determined to go away to Galilee; and there He found Philip. Jesus said to Him: " Follow me! " Now Philip came from Bethsaida, which was the town from which Andrew and Peter came. Philip went and found Nathanael and said to him: " We have found the One about whom Moses wrote in the law, and about whom the prophets spoke—I mean Jesus, the son of Joseph, the man from Nazareth." Nathanael said to him: " Can anything good come out of Nazareth? " Philip said to him: " Come and see! " When Jesus saw Nathanael coming towards Him, He said: " See! A man who is really an Israelite! A man in whom there is no guile! " Nathanael said to Him: " How do you know me? " " Before Philip called you," said Jesus, " I saw you when you were under the fig-tree." " Rabbi," answered Nathanael, " you are the Son of God; you are the King of Israel." Jesus answered: " Do you believe because I said to you, ' I saw you under the fig-tree '? You will see greater things than these." He said to him: " This is the truth I tell you—you will see the heavens opened, and the angels of God ascending and descending on the Son of Man."

AT this point in the story Jesus left the south and went north to Galilee. There, perhaps in Cana itself, He found and called Philip. Philip, like Andrew, could not keep the good news to himself. As Godet said: "One lighted torch serves to light another." So Philip went and found his friend Nathanael. He told him that he believed that he had discovered the long promised Messiah in Jesus, the man from Nazareth. Nathanael was contemptuous There was nothing in the Old Testament which foretold that God's Chosen One should come from Nazareth. Nazareth was a quite undistinguished place. Nathanael himself came from Cana, another Galilaean town, and, in the country places, jealousy between town and town, and rivalry between village and village, is notorious. Nathanael's reaction was to declare that Nazareth was not the kind of place that anything good was likely to come out of. Philip was wise. He did not argue. He said simply: "Come and see!"

Not very many people have ever been argued into Christianity. Very often our arguments do more harm than good. The only way to convince a man of the supremacy of Christ is to confront him with Christ. On the whole it is true to say that it is not argumentative and philosophical preaching and teaching which has won men for Christ; it is the presentation of the story of the Cross. There is a story which tells how, towards the end of the nineteenth century, Huxley, the great agnostic, was a member of a house-party at a country house. Sunday came round, and most of the members prepared to go to Church; but, very naturally, Huxley did not propose to go. Huxley approached a man known to have a simple and a radiant Christian faith. He said to him: "Suppose you don't go to Church to-day. Suppose you stay at home and you tell me quite simply what your Christian faith means to you and why you are a Christian." "But," said the man, "you could demolish my arguments in an instant. I'm not clever enough to argue with you." Huxley said gently: "I don't want to argue with you; I just want you to tell me simply what this Christ means to you." The man stayed at home and told Huxley most simply of his faith. When he had finished there were tears in the great agnostic's eyes. "I would give my right hand," he said, "if only I could believe that." It was not clever argument that touched Huxley's heart. He could have dealt efficiently and devastatingly with any argument that that simple Christian was likely to have produced. The simple presentation of Christ caught him by the heart. The best argument is to say to people: "Come and see!" But the trouble is we have to know Christ ourselves before we can invite others to come to Him. The only true evangelist is the man who himself knows Christ.

So Nathanael came; and Jesus could see into Nathanael's heart. "Here," said Jesus, "is a true and genuine Israelite, a man in whose heart there is no guile." That was a tribute that any devout Israelite would recognize. "Blessed is the man," said the Psalmist, "unto whom the Lord imputeth not iniquity, and in whose spirit there is no guile" (Psalm 32: 2). "He hath done no violence," said the prophet of the Servant of the Lord "neither was any deceit in his mouth" (Isaiah 53: 9). Nathanael was surprised that anyone could give a verdict like that on so short an acquaintance, and he demanded how Jesus could possibly know him. Jesus told him that He had already seen him under the fig-tree. What is the significance of that? In Jewish thought the fig-tree always stood for peace. Their idea of peace was when a man could be undisturbed under his own vine and his own fig-tree (cp. I Kings 4: 25; Micah 4: 4). Still further, the fig-tree was leafy and shady, and it was the custom to sit and meditate under the roof of its branches. No doubt that was what Nathanael had been doing. And no doubt as he sat under the fig-tree he had thought of and prayed for the day when God's Chosen One should come. No doubt he had been meditating on the promises of God. And now he felt that Jesus had seen into the very depths of his heart. It was not so much that Jesus had seen him under the fig-tree that surprised Nathanael; it was the fact that Jesus had read the thoughts of his inmost heart. So Nathanael said to himself: " Here is the man who understands my dreams! Here is the man who knows my prayers! Here is the man who has seen into my most intimate and secret longings, longings which I have never even dared to put into words! Here is the man who can translate the inarticulate sigh of my soul! This must be the Son of God, God's promised anointed one and no other." Nathanael capitulated for ever to the man who read and understood and satisfied his heart.

It may be that Jesus smiled. He quoted the old story of Jacob at Bethel who had seen the golden ladder leading up to heaven (*Genesis* 28: 12, 13). It was as if Jesus said: " Nathanael, I can do far more than read your heart. I can be for you and for all men the way, the ladder that leads to heaven." It is through Jesus and Jesus alone that the souls of men can mount the ladder which leads to heaven.

This passage presents us with one problem. Who was Nathanael? In the Fourth Gospel he is one of the first group of disciples; in the other three gospels he never appears at all, not even by name. What is the explanation? More than one explanation has been given.

(i) It has been suggested that Nathanael is not a real figure at all. That he is an ideal figure, and that he stands for all the real and the true Israelites who burst the bonds of national pride and prejudice and gave themselves to Jesus Christ. It is suggested that Nathanael is not a single individual, but that he stands for all true Israelites who had no guile and who received Jesus Christ.

(ii) On the same basis, it has been suggested that he stands either for Paul, or for the beloved disciple who is mentioned throughout the Fourth Gospel. Paul was the

great example of the Israelite who had accepted Christ.
The beloved disciple was the ideal disciple.   Again the
supposition is that Nathanael stands for an ideal; that
he is a type and not a person. If this were the only mention
of Nathanael that might be true; but Nathanael appears
again in *John* 21: 2 and there is no thought of him as an
ideal there.

(iii) He has been identified with Matthew, because both
Matthew and *Nathanael* mean *the gift of God*. We saw
that in those days most people had two names; but in
that case the one name was Greek and the other was
Jewish; and in this case both *Matthew* and *Nathanael* are
Jewish names.

(iv) There is a simpler explanation.   *Nathanael* was
brought to Jesus by *Philip*.   *Nathanael's* name is never
mentioned in the other three gospels; and in the Fourth
Gospel *Bartholomew's* name is never mentioned.   Now
first, in the list of the disciples in *Matthew* 10: 3 and
Mark 3: 18, *Philip* and *Bartholomew* come together, as
if it was natural and inevitable to connect them. Second,
Bartholomew is really a *second* name.   It means *Son of
Tholmai* or *Ptolemy*. *Bartholomew* must have had another
name, a first name; and it is at least possible that *Bartholomew* and *Nathanael* are the same person under different
names.   That certainly fits the facts.

Whatever else is true, it is true that Nathanael stands
for the Israelite whose heart was cleansed of pride and
prejudice, and who saw in Jesus the one who satisfied the
longing of his waiting, seeking heart.

THE NEW EXHILARATION

John 2: I-II

Two days after this there was a wedding in Cana of
Galilee; and Jesus' mother was there.   And Jesus
was invited to the wedding and so were His disciples.
When the wine had run short, Jesus' mother said to

Him: " They have no wine." Jesus said to her: " Lady, let me handle this in my own way. My hour has not yet come." His mother said to the servants: " Do whatever He tells you to do." There were six stone waterpots standing there—they were needed for the Jewish purifying customs—and each of them held about twenty or thirty gallons. Jesus said to them: " Fill the waterpots with water." They filled them up to the very brim. He said to them: " Draw from them now, and take what you draw to the steward in charge." They did so. When the steward had tasted the water which had become wine—he did not know where it came from, but the servants who had drawn the water knew—the steward called the bridegroom and said to him: " Everyone first sets before the guests the good wine, and then, when they have drunk their fill, he sets before them the inferior wine. You have kept the good wine until now."

Jesus did the first of His signs in Cana of Galilee, and displayed His glory; and His disciples believed on Him.

THE very richness of the Fourth Gospel presents those who would study it and him who would expound it with a problem. Always in the Fourth Gospel there are two things. There is a simple surface story that anyone can understand and re-tell; but there is also a wealth of deeper meaning for him who has the eagerness to search and the eye to see and the mind to understand. There is so much in a passage like this that we must take three days to study it. We shall look at it first of all quite simply to set it within its background and to see it come alive. We shall then look at certain of the things it tells us about Jesus and His work. And finally we shall look at the permanent truth which John is seeking to tell us in this story.

Cana of Galilee is so called to distinguish it from Cana in Coelo-Syria. It was a village quite near to Nazareth. Jerome, who stayed in Palestine, says that he saw it from Nazareth. In Cana there was a wedding feast and to that feast Mary went. The whole story tells us that Mary held a special place at that feast. She had something to do with the arrangements for she was worried when the wine ran done; and she had authority enough to order the servants to do whatever Jesus told them to do. Some of the later gospels which never got into the New Testament add certain details to this story. One of the Coptic gospels from Egypt tells us that Mary was a sister of the bride-groom's mother. There is an early set of Prefaces to the books of the New Testament called the Monarchian Prefaces which tell us that the bridegroom was no other than John himself, and that his mother was Salome, the sister of Mary. We do not know whether these extra details are true or not, but it is certain that the story is so vividly told that it is clearly an eye-witness account.

In the story Mary alone is mentioned, and there is no mention of Joseph. The explanation most probably is that by this time Joseph was dead. It would seem that Joseph died quite soon, and that the reason why Jesus spent eighteen long years in Nazareth was that Jesus had to take upon Himself the support of His mother and His family. It was only when His younger brothers and sisters were able to look after themselves and the home that He left home. Mary is mentioned alone here because by this time Joseph was dead.

The scene of the story is a village wedding feast. In Palestine a wedding was a really notable occasion. It was the Jewish law that the wedding of a virgin should take place on a Wednesday. This is interesting because it gives us a date from which to work back; and if this wedding took place on a Wednesday then it must have been the Sabbath day when Jesus first met Andrew and John and when they stayed the whole day with Him. In Palestine the wedding festivities lasted for far more than one day. The wedding ceremony itself took place late in the evening, after a feast. After the ceremony the young couple were conducted to their new home. By that time it would be dark and they were conducted through the village streets with the light of the flaming torches and with a canopy over their heads. They were taken by as long a road as possible so that as many people as possible would have the opportunity to wish them well. But in Palestine a newly married couple did not go away for their honeymoon; they stayed at home; and for a week they kept open house. They wore crowns and dressed in their bridal robes. They were treated like a king and queen; they were actually addressed as king and queen and their word was law. In a life where there was much poverty and constant hard work, this week of festivity and joy was one of the supreme occasions in life.

It was in a happy time like that that Jesus gladly shared. But something went wrong. It is very likely that the coming of Jesus caused something of a problem. He had been invited to the feast, but He had arrived, not alone, but with five disciples. Five extra people at the feast may well have caused complications; five unexpected guests would provide any festival with a problem, and the wine went done.

For a Jewish feast wine was essential. " Without wine," said the Rabbis, " there is no joy." It was not that people were drunken, but in the East wine was an essential. Drunkenness was in fact a great disgrace, and they actually drank their wine in a mixture composed of two parts of wine to three parts of water. At any time the failure of provisions would have been a problem, for hospitality in the East is a sacred duty, but for the provisions to fail at a wedding would be a terrible shame for the bride and the bridegroom. That indeed would have been a humiliation.

So Mary came to Jesus to tell Him that it was so. The Authorised Version translation of Jesus' reply makes it sound very discourteous. It makes Him say: " Woman, what have I to do with thee? " That is indeed a translation of the *words*, but it does not in any way give the *tone*. The phrase, " What have I to do with thee? " was a common conversational phrase. When it was uttered angrily and sharply it did indicate complete disagreement and reproach, but when it was spoken gently it indicated, not so much reproach, but misunderstanding. It means: " Don't worry; you don't quite understand what is going on; leave things to me, and I will settle them in my own way." When Jesus said this to Mary, He was simply telling her to leave things to Him, that He would have His own way of dealing with this situation. The word *Woman (gunai)* is also misleading. It sounds to us very rough and abrupt. But it is the same word as Jesus used when on the Cross He addressed Mary as He left her to the care of John (John 19: 26). In Homer it is the title by which Odysseus addresses Penelope, his well-loved wife. It is the title by which Augustus, the Roman Emperor, addressed Cleopatra, the famous Egyptian queen. So far from being a rough and discourteous way of address, it was a title of respect. We have no way of speaking in English which exactly renders it; but it is better to translate it *Lady* which gives at least the courtesy in it.

However Jesus spoke Mary was confident in Him. She told the servants to do as Jesus told them to do. At the door there were six great water jars. The word that is translated *firkin* represents the Hebrew measure called the *bath* which was a measure equivalent to between eight and nine gallons. They were very large; they would hold about twenty gallons of water apiece. John was writing his gospel for Greeks and so he explains that these jars were there to provide water for the purifying ceremonies of the Jews. Water would be required for two purposes. First, it would be required for cleansing the feet on entry to the house. The roads in Palestine were not surfaced. Sandals were merely a sole attached to the foot by straps. On a dry day the feet were covered by dust and on a wet day they were soiled with mud, and the water was used for cleansing them. Second, it would be required for the handwashing. Strict Jews washed the hands before a meal and between each course. First the hand was held upright and the water was poured over it in such a way that it ran right to the wrist; then the hand was held pointing down and the water was poured in such a way that it ran from the wrist to the finger-tips. This was done with each hand in turn; and then each palm was cleansed by rubbing it with the fist of the other hand. The Jewish ceremonial law insisted that this should be done, not only at the beginning of a meal, but also between each course; and if it was not done the hands were technically *unclean*. It was for this footwashing and handwashing that these great stone jars of water stood there.

Jesus commanded that the jars should be filled to the brim. John mentions that point to make it clear that nothing else but water was put into them. He then told them to draw out the water and to take it to the *architriklinos*, whom the Authorised Version calls *the ruler of the feast*. At their banquets the Romans had a toast-master called the *arbiter bibendi*, the arranger of the drinking. Sometimes one of the guests acted as a kind of master of ceremonies at a Jewish wedding. But our equivalent of the *architriklinos* is really the head-waiter. He was responsible for the seating of the guests and the correct running of the feast. When he tasted the water which had become wine he was astonished. He called the bridegroom—it was the bridegroom's parents who were responsible for the feast—and spoke jestingly. " Most people," he said, " serve the good wine first; and then, when the guests have drunk a good deal, and when their palates are dulled and when they are not in much of a condition to appreciate what they are drinking, they serve the inferior wine, but you have kept the best until now."

So it was at a village girl's wedding in a Galilaean village that Jesus first showed His glory; and it was there that His disciples caught another dazzling glimpse of what He was.

THE NEW EXHILARATION

John 2: I-II *(continued)*

THIS story is crammed with things which throw light on Jesus. We must note three general things about this wonderful deed which Jesus did.

(i) We must note *when* it happened. It happened at a wedding feast. Jesus was perfectly at home at a wedding feast. He was no severe, austere killjoy. He loved to share in the happy rejoicing of a wedding feast. There are certain religious people who shed a gloom wherever they go. There are certain people who are suspicious of all joy and happiness. To them religion is the thing of the black clothes, the lowered voice, the expulsion of social fellowship. They descend like a gloom wherever they go. It was said of Alice Freeman Palmer, the great teacher, by one of her scholars: " She made me feel as if I was bathed in sunshine." Jesus was like that. C. H. Spurgeon in his book *Lectures to my Students* has some wise, if caustic, sayings of advice. " Sepulchral tones may fit a man to be an undertaker, but Lazarus is not called out of his grave by hollow moans." " I know brethren who from head to foot, in garb, tone, manner, necktie and boots are so utterly *parsonic* that no particle of manhood is visible. . . . Some men appear to have a white cravat twisted round their souls, their manhood is throttled with that starched rag." " An individual who has no geniality about him had better be an undertaker, and bury the dead, for he will never succeed in influencing the living." " I commend cheerfulness to all who would win souls; not levity and frothiness, but a genial, happy spirit. There are more flies caught with honey than with vinegar, and there will be more souls led to heaven by a man who wears heaven in his face than by one who bears Tartarus in his looks." Jesus never counted it a crime to be happy. Why should His followers do so?

(ii) We must note *where* it happened. It happened in a humble home in a village in Galilee. This miracle was not wrought against the background of some great occasion and in the presence of vast crowds. It was wrought in a home. A. H. N. Green-Armytage in his book, *A Portrait of St. Luke,* speaks of how Luke delighted to show Jesus against a background of simple, homely things and people. In a vivid phrase he says that St. Luke's gospel " domesticated God "; it brought God right into the home circle and into the ordinary things of life. Jesus' action at Cana of Galilee shows what He thought of a home. As the Authorised Version has it, He " manifested forth His glory," and that manifestation of glory took place within a home. There is a strange paradox in the attitude of so many people to the place that they call home. They would admit at once that there is no more precious place in all the world; and yet, at the same time, they would also have to admit that in it they claim the right to be far more discourteous, far more boorish, far more selfish, far more impolite than they would dare to be in any society of strangers. There are many of us who treat the ones we love most in a way that we would never dare to treat a chance acquaintance. It is the tragic fact that it is so often strangers who see us at our best and those who live with us who see us at our worst. We ought ever to remember that it was in a humble home that Jesus manifested forth His glory. To Him a home was a place for which nothing but His best was good enough.

(iii) We must note *why* it happened. We have already seen that in the East hospitality was always a sacred duty. It would have brought embarrassed shame and humiliation to that home that day if the wine had run done. It was to save a humble Galilaean family from hurt and humiliation that Jesus put forth His power. It was in sympathy, in kindness, in understanding for simple folk that Jesus acted. Nearly everyone can do the big thing on the big occasion; but it takes Jesus to do the big thing on a simple, homely occasion like this.   There is a kind of natural human maliciousness which rather enjoys the misfortunes of others, and which delights to make a good story of them over the teacups.   But Jesus, the Lord of all life, and the King of Glory, used His power to save a simple Galilaean lad and lass from shame and humiliation.   It is just by such deeds of understanding, simple kindliness that we too can show that we are followers of Jesus Christ.

Still further, this story shows us very beautifully Mary's faith in Jesus.   In it we see two things about that faith.

(i) Instinctively Mary turned to Jesus whenever anything went wrong.   She knew her son.   It was not till He was thirty years old that Jesus had left home; and all these years Mary had lived with Him.   There is an old legend which tells of the days when Jesus was a little baby in the home in Nazareth.   It tells how in those days when people felt tired, and worried, and hot and bothered and upset, they would say: " Let us go and look at Mary's child," and they would go and look at Jesus, and somehow all their troubles rolled away.   It is still true that those who know Jesus intimately instinctively turn to Him when things go wrong—and they never find Him wanting.

(ii) Even when Mary did not understand what Jesus was going to do, even when it seemed that He had refused her request, Mary still believed in Him so much that she turned to the serving folk and told them to do whatever Jesus told them to do.   Mary had the faith which could trust even when it did not understand.   She did not know what Jesus was going to do, but she was quite sure that He would do the right thing.   In every life there come periods of darkness when we do not see the way.   In every life there come things which are such that we do not see why they came and we do not see the meaning of them. Happy is the man who in such a case still trusts even when he cannot understand.

Still further, this story tells us something about Jesus. In answer to Mary He said: " My hour has not yet come."

THE GOSPEL OF JOHN

All through the gospel story Jesus talks about *His hour.*
In *John* 7: 6, 8 it is the hour of His emergence as the
Messiah. In *John* 12: 23 and 17: 1, and in *Matthew* 26: 18,
45 and in *Mark* 14: 41 it is the hour of His crucifixion
and His death. All through His life Jesus knew that He
had come into this world for a definite purpose and a
definite task. He saw His life, not in terms of His wishes,
but in terms of God's purpose for Himself. He saw His
life, not against the shifting background of time, but
against the steady background of eternity. All through
His life He went steadily towards that hour for which He
knew that He had come into the world. It is not only
Jesus who came into this world to fulfil the purpose of
God. As someone has said: " Every man is a dream
and an idea of God." And we too must think, not of our
own wishes and our own desires, but of the purpose for
which God sent us into His world.

THE NEW EXHILARATION

John 2: 1-11 (*continued*)

AND now we must think of the deep and the permanent
truth which John is seeking to teach us when he tells us
this story.

We must remember that John was writing out of a
double background. He was a Jew and he was writing
for Jews; but his great object was to write the story of
Jesus in such a way that it would come home also to the
Greeks.

Let us look at it first of all from the *Jewish* point of
view. We must always remember that beneath John's
simple stories there is a deeper meaning which is only
open to those who have eyes to see. In all his gospel John
never wrote an unnecessary or an unmeaning detail.
Everything means something and everything points beyond.

There were six stone waterpots; and at the command of Jesus the water in them turned to wine. Now according to the Jews, *seven* is the number which is absolute and complete and perfect; and *six* is the number which is incomplete, unfinished and imperfect. The six stone waterpots stand for all the imperfections of the Jewish law. Jesus came to do away with the imperfections of the law, and to put in their place the new wine of the gospel of His grace. Jesus, by His coming, turned the imperfection of the law into the perfection of grace. There is another thing to note in this connection. Remember that every detail in a story told by John is meaningful. There were six waterpots; each held between twenty and thirty gallons of water. Jesus turned the water into wine. That would give anything up to one hundred and eighty gallons of wine. Simply to state that fact is to show that John did not mean the story to be taken with crude literalness. What John did mean to say is this, that when the grace of Jesus comes to men there is enough and to spare for all. No wedding party on earth could drink one hundred and eighty gallons of wine. No need on earth can exhaust the grace of Christ. There is a glorious superabundance in the grace of Christ. John is telling us that in Jesus the imperfections have become perfection, and the grace has become illimitable, sufficient and more than sufficient for every need.

Let us look at it now from the Greek point of view. Now it so happens that the Greeks actually possessed stories like this. Dionysos was the Greek god of wine. Pausanias was a Greek who wrote a description of his country and of its ancient ceremonies. In his description of Elis, he describes an old ceremony and belief like this: " Between the market-place and the Menius is an old theatre and a sanctuary of Dionysos; the image is by Praxiteles. No god is more revered by the Eleans than Dionysos is, and they say that he attends their festival of the Thyia. The place where they hold the festival called

the Thyia is about a mile from the city. Three empty
kettles are taken into the building and deposited there
by the priests in the presence of the citizens and of any
strangers who may happen to be staying in the country.
On the doors of the buildings the priests, and all who
choose to do so, put their seals. Next day they are free
to examine the seals, and on entering the building they
find the kettles full of wine. I was not there myself at
the time of the festival, but the most respectable men
of Elis, and strangers too, swore that the facts were as
I have said." So the Greeks too had their stories like this;
and it is as if John said to them: " You have your stories
and your legends about your gods. They are only stories,
and you know that they are not really true. But Jesus
has come to do what you have always dreamed that your
gods could do. He has come to make the things you longed
for come true."

So to the Jews John said: " Jesus has come to turn the
imperfection of the law into the perfection of grace."
And to the Greeks John said: " Jesus has come really
and truly to do the things you only dreamed the gods
could do."

Now we can see what John is teaching us. Every story
John tells us, not of something that Jesus did
once and never did again, but of something which Jesus
is for ever and eternally doing. John tells us, not of things
that Jesus once did in Palestine, but of things that Jesus
still does to-day. And what John wants us to see here is
not that Jesus once on a day turned some waterpots of
water into wine; he wants us to see that whenever Jesus
comes into life, there comes a new quality which is like
turning water into wine. Without Jesus life is dull, and
stale, and flat; when Jesus comes into life, life becomes
vivid and sparkling and exciting. Without Jesus life is
drab and uninteresting; with Jesus life is thrilling and
wonderful and exhilarating. When Sir Wilfred Grenfell
was appealing for volunteers for his work in Labrador,

he said that he could not promise them much money, but he could promise that if they came out to do the work he could offer them they would have the time of their lives. That is what Jesus promises us. Remember that John was writing seventy years after Jesus was crucified. For seventy years he had thought and meditated and remembered, until he saw meanings and significances that he had not seen at the time. When John told this story he was remembering what life with Jesus was like; and he said, " Wherever Jesus went, whenever He came into life, and whenever He comes into life, it is like water turning into wine." This story is John saying to *us*: " If you want the new exhilaration, become a follower of Jesus Christ, and then there will come a change in your life which will be like water turning into wine."

THE ANGER OF JESUS

John 2: 12-16

> After this Jesus went down to Capernaum with His mother and His brothers and His disciples; and they stayed there for a short time.
> The Passover Feast of the Jews was near, and Jesus went up to Jerusalem. In the Temple He found those who were selling oxen and sheep and doves, and the money-changers sitting at their tables. He made a scourge of cords and drove them all out of the Temple, and the sheep and the oxen as well. He scattered the coins of the exchangers, and overturned their tables. He said to those who were selling doves: " Take these away and stop making my Father's house a house of trade."

AFTER the wedding feast at Cana of Galilee Jesus and His friends returned for a short visit to Capernaum. It is a strange thing that to this day the exact site of Capernaum is by no means certain. It is generally identified with either Tel Hum or Khan Minyeh which are on the north shore of the Sea of Galilee. Cana is about twenty miles from these places, and they came down because Cana is up in the Galilaean highlands and Capernaum is on the shore of the lake.

Shortly after this Jesus set out to observe the Passover Feast at Jerusalem. The Passover Feast fell on the 15th Nisan, which is about the middle of April; and, according to the law, it was obligatory for every male Jew who lived within twenty miles of Jerusalem to attend the feast.

Here we have a very interesting thing. We find that at first sight John has a quite different chronology of the life of Jesus from the chronology of the other three gospels. In the other three gospels Jesus is depicted as going to Jerusalem only once. The Passover Feast at which He was crucified is the only Passover Feast which they mention, and the only visit to Jerusalem that they mention except the visit to the Temple when Jesus was a boy. But in John's gospel we find Jesus making frequent visits to Jerusalem. John tells us of no fewer than three Passovers—this present one, the one in *John* 6: 4 and the one in *John* 11: 55. In addition to that, according to John's story, Jesus was in Jerusalem for an unnamed feast in 5: 1; for the Feast of Tabernacles in 7: 2, 10; and for the Feast of the Dedication in 10: 22. In fact, according to John's story, Jesus comes to Jerusalem in 10: 22 and never leaves it again. Now the Feast of the Dedication is in winter (*John* 10: 22); it is actually in December, and the Passover Feast is in mid-April, and so John's story seems to show that Jesus' last visit to Jerusalem lasted, not for a few days, but for some months. In point of fact in the other three gospels the main ministry of Jesus is in Galilee; in John's gospel Jesus is only in Galilee for brief periods (2: 1-12; 4: 43—5: 1; 6: 1—7: 14), and His main ministry is in Jerusalem. The truth is that there is no real contradiction here at all. John and the other three writers of the gospels are telling the story from different points of view. They do not contradict each other; they complement each other. Matthew,

Mark and Luke concentrate on the ministry in Galilee; John concentrates on the ministry in Jerusalem. Although the other three writers only tell us of one visit to Jerusalem and one Passover there, they imply that there must have been many other visits. At His last visit they show us Jesus mourning over Jerusalem: " O Jerusalem, Jerusalem, thou that killest the prophets, and stonest them which are sent unto thee, how often would I have gathered thy children together, even as a hen gathereth her chickens under her wings, and ye would not! " (*Matthew* 23: 37). Jesus could never have spoken like that unless He had made repeated appeals to Jerusalem; He could not have spoken like that if the visit at which He was crucified was His first visit to the city. If we are wise, we will not talk about the contradictions between the Fourth Gospel and the other three; we will not set them against each other, but we will use them both to get as complete a picture of the life of Jesus as possible.

But there is a real difficulty which we must face. This passage tells us of the incident which is known as the Cleansing of the Temple. Here John sets it right at the *beginning* of the ministry of Jesus, while the other three gospel writers set it right at the *end* (*Matthew* 21: 12, 13; *Mark* 11: 15-17; *Luke* 19: 45, 46). This definitely needs explanation. Various explanations have been put forward. (i) It has been suggested that Jesus cleansed the Temple twice, once at the beginning and once at the end of His ministry. That is not very likely, because if Jesus had done this staggering thing once, it is very unlikely that He would ever have had the chance to do it again. His reappearance in the Temple would have been a sign for such precautions to be taken that a repetition of it would not have been possible. (ii) It is suggested that John is right in placing this action at the beginning of Jesus' ministry and that the other three gospel writers are wrong. But the incident fits in much better at the end of Jesus' ministry. It is the natural succession to the blazing courage of the Triumphal

Entry and the inevitable prelude to the Crucifixion. If we have to choose between John's dating of this incident and the dating of the other three writers, we must choose the dating of the three. (iii) It is suggested that when John died he left his gospel not completely finished; that he left the various incidents written out on separate sheets of papyrus and not bound up together. It is then suggested that the sheet containing the account of this incident got out of place, and was inserted near the beginning of the manuscript instead of near the end. That is quite possible, but it involves assuming that the person who arranged the manuscript did not know the correct order, which is difficult to believe when he must have known at least some of the other gospels. (iv) We must always remember one thing—John, as someone has said, is more interested in the truth than in the facts. He is not interested in writing a chronological biography of Jesus. He is supremely interested in showing Jesus as the Son of God, and the Messiah. It is very probable that John was thinking back to the great prophecies and forecasts of the coming of the Messiah. " And the Lord whom ye seek shall suddenly come to His Temple, even the messenger of the covenant whom ye delight in; behold He shall come, saith the Lord of Hosts. But who may abide the day of His coming? and who shall stand when He appeareth? for he is like a refiner's fire, and like fuller's soap. . . . He shall purify the sons of Levi . . . that they may offer unto the Lord an offering in righteousness. Then shall the offering of Judah and Jerusalem be pleasant unto the Lord, as in the days of old, and as in former years " (*Malachi* 3: 1-4). John had these tremendous prophecies ringing in his mind. He was not interested to tell men *when* Jesus cleansed the Temple; he was supremely interested in telling men that Jesus *did* cleanse the Temple, because that cleansing was the act of the promised Messiah of God. All the likelihood is that John put this tremendous incident here to set in the very forefront of his story of

94

Jesus the great fact that Jesus was the Messiah of God who came to cleanse the worship of men and to open the door to God. It is not the date that John is interested in; the date does not matter; his great concern is to show men the fact that Jesus' actions prove Him to be the promised one of God. Right at the beginning John shows us Jesus acting as God's Messiah must act.

THE ANGER OF JESUS

John 2: 12-16 (continued)

Now let us see why Jesus acted as He did. The anger of Jesus is a terrifying thing; the picture of the Christ with the whip is an awe-inspiring sight. We must see what moved Jesus to this white-hot anger in the Temple Courts.

The Passover was the greatest of all the Jewish feasts. As we have already seen, the law laid it down that every adult male Jew who lived within twenty miles of Jerusalem was bound to attend it. But it was not only the Jews in Palestine who came to the Passover Feast. By this time the Jews were scattered all over the world, but the Jews never forgot their ancestral faith and their ancestral land, and it was the dream and aim of every Jew, no matter in what land he stayed, to celebrate at least one Passover in Jerusalem. Astonishing as it may sound, it is likely that as many as two and a quarter million Jews sometimes assembled in the Holy City to keep the Passover. Now there was one tax that every Jew over nineteen years of age must pay. That was the Temple tax. It was necessary that all should pay that tax so that the Temple sacrifices and the Temple ritual might be carried out day by day. The tax was one half-shekel. We must always remember, when we are thinking of sums of money, that at this time a working man's wage was about eightpence per day. The value of a half-shekel was about one shilling and twopence. It was, therefore, equivalent to almost two days' wages. For all ordinary purposes in Palestine all kinds of currencies were valid. Silver coins from Rome and Greece and Egypt and Tyre and Sidon and Palestine itself all circulated and were all valid. But this Temple tax had to be paid either in Galilaean shekels or in shekels of the sanctuary. These were Jewish coins, and could be used as a gift to the Temple; the other currencies were foreign; they were therefore polluted and unclean; they might be used to pay ordinary debts, but not a debt to God. Now pilgrims arrived from all over the world with all kinds of coins. So in the Temple courts there sat the *money-changers*. If their trade had been straightforward and honest they would have been fulfilling an honest and a necessary purpose. But what in fact they did was this—they charged one ma'ah, a coin worth about twopence, for every half-shekel they changed, and they charged another ma'ah on every half-shekel of change they had to give if a larger coin was tendered. So, if a man came with a coin the value of which was two shekels, he had to pay twopence to get it changed, and three other twopences to get his change of three half-shekels. In other words the money-changers made eightpence out of him—and eightpence was one day's wage. The wealth which accrued from the Temple tax and from this method of money-changing was fantastic. The annual revenue of the Temple from the Temple tax has been estimated at £75,000, and the annual profit of the money-changers at £9,000. It is the case that when Crassus captured Jerusalem and raided the Temple treasury in 54 B.C. he took from it £2,500,000 without coming near to exhausting it. The fact that the money-changers received some discount when they changed the coins of the pilgrims was not in itself wrong. The *Talmud* laid it down: "It is necessary that everyone should have half a shekel to pay for himself. Therefore when he comes to the exchange to change a shekel for two half-shekels he is obliged to allow the money-changer some gain." The word for this discount was *kollubos*, and the money-changers are called *kollubistai*. This word *kollubos* produced the comedy character name Kollybos in Greek and Collybus in Latin, which meant much the same as Shylock in English. What enraged Jesus was that the pilgrims to the Passover, who could ill afford it, were being fleeced at an exorbitant rate by the money-changers. It was a rampant and shameless social injustice—and what was worse, it was being done in the name of religion.

Besides the money-changers there were the sellers of oxen and sheep and doves. Frequently a visit to the Temple meant a sacrifice. Many a pilgrim would wish to offer thank-offering for a favourable journey to the Holy City; and most acts and events in life had their appropriate sacrifice. It might therefore seem to be a natural and helpful thing that the victims for the sacrifices could be bought in the Temple court. It might well have been so. But the law was that any animal offered in sacrifice must be perfect, flawless and unblemished. The Temple authorities had appointed inspectors (*mumcheh*) to examine the victims which were to be offered. The fee for inspection was two-pence. If a worshipper bought a victim outside the Temple, it was to all intents and purposes certain that that victim would be examined and rejected. Again that might not have mattered much, but, in point of fact, a pair of doves could cost as little as ninepence outside the Temple, and as much as fifteen shillings inside the Temple. Here again was bare-faced extortion at the expense of poor and humble pilgrims, who were practically blackmailed into buying their victims from the Temple booths if they wished to sacrifice at all. Once again it was a glaring social injustice aggravated by the fact that it was perpetrated in the name of pure religion.

It was that which moved Jesus to flaming anger. We are told that He took cords and made a whip. Jerome thinks that the very sight of Jesus made the whip unnecessary.

" A certain fiery and starry light shone from His eyes, and the majesty of the Godhead gleamed in His face." Jesus loved God, and just because He loved God, He loved God's children, and it was impossible for Him to stand passively by while the poor worshippers of Jerusalem were treated like that.

THE ANGER OF JESUS

John 2: 12-16 (continued)

WE have seen that it was the exploitation of the pilgrims by conscienceless men which moved Jesus to immediate wrath; but there were deep things behind this cleansing of the Temple. Let us see if we can penetrate to the even deeper reasons why Jesus took this drastic step.

No two of the evangelists give Jesus' words in precisely the same way. They all remembered their own version of what Jesus said. It is only by putting all the accounts together that we get a true picture of what Jesus said. So then let us set down the way in which the different gospel writers report the words of Jesus. Matthew gives Jesus' words as: " My house shall be called the house of prayer, but ye have made it a den of thieves " (*Matthew* 21: 13). Mark has it: " My house shall be called of all nations the house of prayer. But ye have made it a den of thieves " (*Mark* 11: 17). Luke has it: " My house is the house of prayer; but ye have made it a den of thieves " (*Luke* 19: 46). John has it: " Take these things hence; make not my Father's house a house of merchandise " (*John* 2: 16).

There were at least three reasons why Jesus acted as He did, and why anger was in His heart.

(i) He acted as He did because God's house was being desecrated. In tne Temple there was worship without reverence. Reverence is an instinctive thing. Edward Seago, the artist, tells how he took two gipsy children on

a visit to a cathedral in England. They were wild enough
children at ordinary times. But, he tells us, from the
moment they came into the cathedral they were strangely
still and quiet; all the way home they were unusually
solemn; and it was not until the evening time that they
returned to their normal boisterousness. Instinctive
reverence was in their uninstructed hearts. Worship
without reverence can be a terrible thing. It may be a
worship which is formalised and pushed through anyhow;
and the most dignified prayers on earth can be read like
a passage from an auctioneer's catalogue. It may be worship
which does not realize the holiness of God, and which
sounds as if, in H. H. Farmer's phrase, the worshipper
was "pally with the Deity." It may be worship in which
leader or congregation are completely unprepared. It
may be the use of the house of God for purposes and in a
way where reverence and the true function of God's house
is forgotten. In that Temple court at Jerusalem there would
be arguments about prices, disputes about coins that were
worn and thin, the clatter of the market place in the court
of the house of God. That particular way of irreverence
may not be common now, but there are other ways of
offering an irreverent worship to God.

(ii) It may well be that Jesus acted as He did in order
to show that the whole paraphernalia of animal sacrifice
was completely irrelevant. For centuries the prophets
had been saying exactly that. "To what purpose is the
multitude of your sacrifices unto me? said the Lord: I
am full of the burnt offering of rams, and the fat of fed
beasts; and I delight not in the blood of bullocks, or of
lambs, or of he-goats. . . . Bring no more vain oblations"
(*Isaiah* 1: 11-17). "I spake not unto your fathers nor
commanded them in the day that I brought them out of
the land of Egypt, concerning burnt-offerings or sacrifices"
(*Jeremiah* 7: 22). "They shall go with their flocks and
herds to seek the Lord but they shall not find Him"
(*Hosea* 5: 6). "They sacrifice flesh for the sacrifices of

mine offerings, and eat it; but the Lord accepteth them
not " (*Hosea* 8: 13). " Thou desirest not sacrifice else
would I give it; Thou delightest not in burnt-offering "
(*Psalm* 51: 16). Always there was this chorus of prophetic
voices telling men of the sheer irrelevancy of the burnt-
offerings and the animal sacrifices which smoked continuously upon the altar at Jerusalem. It may well be
that Jesus acted as He did to show that no sacrifice of
any animal can ever put a man right with God. We are
not totally free from this very tendency to-day. True,
we will not offer animal sacrifice to God. But we can
identify the service of God with the installation of stained
glass windows, the obtaining of a more sonorous organ,
the lavishing of money on stone and lime and carved wood,
while real worship is far away. It is not that these things
are to be condemned—far from it. They are often—thank
God—the lovely offerings of the loving heart. When they
are aids to true devotion they are God-blessed things;
but when they are substitutes for true devotion they make
God sick at heart.

(iii) But there is still another reason why Jesus may
have acted as He did. Mark has a curious little addition
which none of the other gospel writers has: " My house
shall be called *of all nations* the house of prayer " (*Mark*
11: 17). The Temple consisted of a series of courts leading
into the Temple proper and to the Holy Place. There was
first the Court of the Gentiles, then the Court of the Women,
then the Court of the Israelites, then the Court of the
Priests. Now all this buying and selling was going on
in the Court of the Gentiles. The Court of the Gentiles
was the only place into which a Gentile might come. A
Gentile might enter it, but, beyond that, access to him
was barred. So then if there was a Gentile whose heart
God had touched, he might come into the Court of the
Gentiles to think and meditate and pray and distantly
touch God. For him the Court of the Gentiles was the
only place of prayer he knew. And these Temple authorities

and these Jewish traders were making the Court of the
Gentiles into an uproar and a rabble where no man could
pray. The lowing of the oxen, the bleating of the sheep,
the cooing of the doves, the shouts of the hucksters, the
rattle of the coins, the voices raised in bargaining disputes—
all these things combined to make the Court of the Gentiles
a place where no man could worship. The conduct of the
Temple court shut out the seeking Gentile from the fringe
of the presence of God. It may well be that that was what
was most in Jesus' mind; it may well be that Mark alone
preserved the little phrase which means so much. Jesus
was moved to the depths of His heart because seeking
men were being shut out from the presence of God. Is
there anything in our Church life—a snobbishness, an
exclusiveness, a coldness, a lack of welcome, a tendency to
make the congregation into a closed club, an arrogance, a
fastidiousness—which keeps the seeking stranger out?
Let us remember the wrath of Jesus against those who
made it difficult and even impossible for the seeking
stranger to make contact with God.

THE NEW TEMPLE

John 2: 17-22

> His disciples remembered that there is a scripture
> which stands written: " The zeal of your house has
> devoured me." Then the Jews demanded of Him:
> " What sign do you show us to justify your acting
> in this way? " Jesus answered: " Destroy this
> Temple and in three days I will raise it up." Then the
> Jews said: " It has taken forty-six years to build
> the Temple so far, and are you going to raise it up
> in three days? " But He was speaking about the
> temple of His body. So when He was raised from the
> dead, His disciples remembered that He had said this,
> and they believed on the scripture and on the word
> which Jesus spoke.

IT was quite certain that an act like the cleansing of the Temple would produce an immediate reaction in those who saw it happening. It was not the kind of thing that anyone could look at with complete indifference. It was much too staggering for that.

Here we have two reactions. First, there is the reaction of the disciples. Their reaction was to remember the words of *Psalm* 69: 9. Now the point is that that Psalm was taken to refer to the Messiah. When the Messiah came He would be burned up with a zeal for the house of God. So when the verse from this Psalm leapt into their minds, that is just another way of saying that the conviction that Jesus was the Messiah seized the minds of the disciples even more deeply and more definitely. This action was an action which befitted none but the Messiah, and the disciples were surer than ever that Jesus was in fact The Anointed One of God.

Second, there was the reaction of the Jews. Their reaction was very natural. They demanded what right Jesus had to act like that and they demanded that He should at once prove His credentials by some sign. The point in their case is this. They acknowledged the act of Jesus to be the act of one who by the very act claimed to be the Messiah. Now it was always expected that when the Messiah came He would confirm and guarantee His claims by doing amazing and extraordinary things. False Messiahs did in fact arise and did promise to cleave the waters of Jordan in two, or to make the walls of the city collapse at a word. The popular idea of the Messiah was connected with wonders. So the Jews said: " By this act of yours you have publicly claimed to be the Messiah. Now show us some wonder which will prove your claim."

It is Jesus' reply that constitutes the great problem of this passage. What did Jesus really say? And what did Jesus really mean? It is always to be remembered that the last two verses of this passage, verses 21 and 22, are John's interpretation written long afterwards. He was inevitably reading into the passage ideas which were the product of seventy years of thinking about and experience of the Risen Christ. As Irenaeus said long ago: " No prophecy is fully understood until after the fulfilment of it." But what did Jesus originally say and what did Jesus originally mean?

There is no possible doubt that Jesus spoke words which were very like these, words which could be maliciously twisted into a destructive claim. When Jesus was on His trial the false witness that was borne against Him was: " This fellow said, I am able to destroy the temple of God, and to build it in three days " (*Matthew* 26: 61). The charge levelled against Stephen was: " We have heard him say that this Jesus of Nazareth shall destroy this place, and shall change the customs which Moses delivered us " (*Acts* 6: 14).

We must remember two things and we must put them together. First, Jesus certainly never said that He would destroy the physical material Temple, and that He would then rebuild it. Jesus in fact looked for the end of the Temple. He said to the woman of Samaria that the day was coming when men would worship God, neither in Mount Gerizim, nor in Jerusalem, but in spirit and in truth (*John* 4: 21). The second thing that we must remember is that the Cleansing of the Temple, as we have seen, may well have been Jesus' dramatic way of showing that the whole Temple worship with its ritual and its sacrifice was irrelevant and could do nothing to lead men to God. It is then clear that Jesus did expect that the Temple would pass away; that He in fact had come to render its worship unnecessary and obsolete; and that therefore He would never suggest that He would rebuild the Temple at all.

We must now turn to Mark's account of the charge against Jesus. As so often, we will find the little extra suggestive and illuminating phrase in Mark. As Mark relates the charge against Jesus, it ran: " I will destroy this Temple that is made with hands, and within three

days I will build another *made without hands*" (Mark
14: 58). Now clearly what Jesus really meant was that
His coming had put an end to all this man-made, man-
arranged way of worshipping God, and had put in its
place a spiritual worship; that He had put an end to all
this business of animal sacrifice and priestly ritual, and had
put in its place a direct approach of our spirit to the Spirit
of God which did not need an elaborate man-made Temple
and a ritual of incense and sacrifice offered by the hands
of men. The threat of Jesus was: " Your Temple worship,
your elaborate ritual, your lavish animal sacrifices are
at an end, because I have come." The promise of Jesus
was: " I will give you a way to come to God without all
this human elaboration and this human ritual. I have
come to destroy this Temple in Jerusalem and to make the
whole round earth the Temple where men can approach
and know the presence of the living God."

And the Jews saw that. It was in 19 B.C. that Herod
had begun to build that wondrous Temple; it was not
until A.D. 64 that the building was finally finished. It was
forty-six years since it had been started; it was to be
another twenty years before it was ended. And Jesus
shattered the Jews by telling them that all its magnificence
and all its splendour and all the money and the skill that
had been lavished on it were completely irrelevant; that
He had come to show men a way to come to God without
any Temple at all.

That must be what Jesus actually said; but in the years
to come John saw far more than that in Jesus' saying.
He saw in it nothing less than a prophecy of the Resurrection; *and John was right*. He was right for this basic
reason, that the whole round earth could never become
the temple of the living God until Jesus was released from
the body and was everywhere present; and until it was
true that He was with men everywhere, even unto the
end of the world. It is indeed the presence of the living,
risen Christ which makes the whole world into the Temple

of God. So John says that when they remembered, they saw in this a promise of the Resurrection. They did not see that at the time; they could not; it was only their own experience of the living Christ which one day showed to them the true depth of what Jesus said.

Finally John says that " they believed the scripture." To what scripture does he refer? He means that scripture which haunted the early Church—" Neither wilt Thou suffer Thy Holy One to see corruption." That is a quotation from *Psalm* 16: 10. Peter quoted it at Pentecost (*Acts* 2: 31); Paul quoted it at Antioch (*Acts* 13: 35). John quotes it here. It expressed the confidence of the Church in the power of God and in the Resurrection of Jesus Christ.

We have here a tremendous truth. We have here the truth that our contact with God, our entry into the presence of God, our approach to God is not dependent on anything that men's hands can build or men's minds devise. In the street, in the home, at business, on the hills, on the open road, in the Church we have our inner temple, the presence of the Risen Christ for ever with us throughout all the world.

THE SEARCHER OF THE HEARTS OF MEN

John 2: 23-25

> When He was in Jerusalem, at the Passover, at the Feast, many believed in His name, as they saw the signs which He did; but Jesus Himself would not entrust Himself to them, because He knew them all, and because He had no need that anyone should testify to Him what man is like, for He well knew what was in human nature.

JOHN does not relate the story of any wonder that Jesus did in Jerusalem at the Passover season; but Jesus did do wonders there; and there were many, who, when they saw His powers, believed in Him. The question which John is answering here is—if there were many who believed in Jesus in Jerusalem right at the very beginning, why did Jesus not there and then set up His standard, and publicly claim to be the Messiah, and openly declare Himself? The answer is that Jesus knew human nature only too well. He knew quite well that there were many to whom He was only a nine-days' wonder. He knew quite well that there were many who were only attracted by the sensational things that He did. He knew quite well that there were none who understood the way that He had chosen. He knew quite well that there were many who would have followed Him while He continued to produce miracles and wonders and signs, but, if He had begun to talk to them about service and self-denial, if He had begun to talk to them about self-surrender to the will of God, if He had begun to talk to them about a cross and about carrying a cross, they would have stared at Him with blank incomprehension and would have left Him on the spot. It is the great characteristic of Jesus that He did not want followers unless these followers clearly knew and definitely accepted that which was involved in following Him. He refused—in the modern phrase—to cash in on a moment's popularity. If He had entrusted Himself to the mob in Jerusalem they would have declared Him Messiah there and then, and would have waited for the kind of material action that they expected the Messiah to take. But Jesus was a leader who refused to ask men ever to accept Him until they knew what accepting meant. He insisted that a man should know what He was doing.

Jesus knew human nature. He knew the fickleness, the instability of the heart of man. He knew that a man can be swept away in a moment of emotion, and then back out when he discovers what decision really means. He knew how human nature hungers for sensations. He wanted, not a crowd of men cheering they knew not what, but a small company who knew what they were doing and who were prepared to follow to the end.

There is one thing that we must note in this passage, for we shall have occasion to mark it again and again. When John speaks of Jesus' miracles he calls them *signs*. The New Testament uses three different words for the wonderful works of God and of Jesus, and each of them has something to tell us about what a miracle really is. (i) It uses the word *teras*. *Teras* simply means an amazing, a staggering, a marvellous thing. It is a word with no moral significance at all. A conjuring trick might be a *teras*. A *teras* was simply an astonishing happening which left a man gasping with surprise. The New Testament never uses this word alone of the works of God or of Jesus. (ii) It uses the word *dunamis*. *Dunamis* literally means *power*. It is the word from which *dynamite* comes. It can be used of any kind of unusual and extraordinary power. It can be used of the power of growth, of the powers of nature, of the power of a drug, of the power of a man's genius. It always has the meaning of an effective power which does things, and which any man can recognize. (iii) It uses the word *sēmeion*, which means a *sign*. This is John's favourite word. To him a miracle was not simply an astonishing happening; it was not simply a deed of power; it was a sign. That is to say, it told men something of the person who did it; it revealed something of his character; it laid bare something of his nature; it was an action through which it was possible, better and more fully, to understand the character of the person who did it. To John the supreme thing about the miracles of Jesus was that *they told men something about the nature and the character of God*. The power of Jesus was used to heal the sick, to feed the hungry, to comfort the sorrowing; and the very fact that Jesus did use His power in that way was the proof that God cared for the sorrows and the needs and the pains of men. To John miracles were the signs of the love of God.

In any miracle, then, there are three things. There is the wonder which leaves men dazzled, astonished, aghast.

There is the power which is effective, which can deal with and mend a broken body, an unhinged mind, a bruised heart, a power which can do things. There is the sign which tells us of the love in the heart of the God who does such things for men.

THE MAN WHO CAME BY NIGHT

John 3: 1-6

> There was a man who was one of the Pharisees who was called Nicodemus, a ruler of the Jews. He came to Jesus by night and said to Him: " Rabbi, we know that you are a teacher who has come from God, for no one can do the signs which you do unless God is with him." Jesus answered him: " This is the truth I tell you—unless a man is reborn from above, he cannot see the Kingdom of God." Nicodemus said to Him: " How can a man be born when he is old? Surely he cannot enter into his mother's womb a second time and be born? " Jesus answered: " This is the truth I tell you—unless a man is born of water and the Spirit, he cannot enter into the Kingdom of God. That which is born from the flesh is flesh, and that which is born of the Spirit is spirit."

FOR the most part we see Jesus surrounded by the ordinary people, but here we see Him in contact with one of the aristocracy of Jerusalem. There are certain things that we know about Nicodemus.

(i) Nicodemus must have been wealthy. When Jesus died Nicodemus brought for His body " a mixture of myrrh and aloes about an hundred pound weight " (*John* 19: 39), and only a wealthy man could have brought that.

(ii) Nicodemus was a Pharisee. In many ways the Pharisees were the best people in the whole country. There were never more than 6,000 of them; they were what was known as a *chaburah*, or brotherhood. They entered into this brotherhood, by taking a pledge in front of three witnesses that they would spend all their lives observing every detail of the scribal law. What exactly did that mean? To the Jew the Law was the most sacred thing in all the world. The Law was the first five books of the Old Testament. They believed the Law to be the perfect word of God. To add one word to it or to take one word away from it was a deadly sin. Now if the Law is the perfect and complete word of God, that must mean that the Law contains everything that a man need know for the living of a good life. If it does not contain it explicitly it must contain it implicitly. If it is not there in so many words, it must be possible to deduce it. Now the Law as it stands consists of great, wide, noble principles which a man has to work out for himself. But for the later Jews that was not enough. They said: " The Law is complete; it contains everything necessary for the living of a good life; therefore in the Law there must be a rule and a regulation to govern every possible incident in every possible moment of life for every possible man." So they set to to extract from the great principles of the law an infinite number of rules and regulations to govern every conceivable situation in life. In other words they changed the law of the great principles into the legalism of by-laws and regulations.

The best example of what they did is to be seen in the Sabbath Law. In the Bible itself we are simply told that we must remember the Sabbath day to keep it holy, and that on that day no work must be done, either by a man or by his servants or his animals. Not content with that, the later Jews spent hour after hour and generation after generation defining what work is and listing the things that may and may not be done on the Sabbath day. The *Mishnah* is the codified scribal law. It was the scribes who spent their lives working out these rules and regulations. In the *Mishnah* the section on the Sabbath extends to no fewer than twenty-four chapters. The *Talmud* is the explanatory commentary on the *Mishnah*, and in the Jerusalem *Talmud* the section explaining the Sabbath law runs to sixty-four and a half columns; and in the

Babylonian *Talmud* it runs to one hundred and fifty-six double folio pages. And we are told about a rabbi who spent two and a half years in studying one of the twenty-four chapters of the *Mishnah*.

The kind of thing they did was this: to tie a knot on the Sabbath was to work. But a knot has to be defined. " The following are the knots the making of which renders a man guilty; the knot of camel drivers and that of sailors; and as one is guilty by reason of tying them, so also of untying them." On the other hand knots which could be tied or untied with one hand were quite legal. Further, " a woman may tie up a slit in her shift and the strings of her cap and those of her girdle, the straps of shoes or sandals, of skins of wine and oil." Now see what happens. Suppose a man wishes to let down a bucket into a well to draw water on the Sabbath day. He cannot tie a rope to it, for a knot on a rope was illegal on the Sabbath; but he could tie it to a woman's girdle and let it down, for a knot in a girdle was quite legal. That was the kind of thing which to the Scribes and Pharisees was a matter of life and death; that was religion; that to them was pleasing and serving God.

Take the case of journeying on the Sabbath. *Exodus* 16: 29 says: " Abide ye every man in his place; let no man go out of his place on the seventh day." A Sabbath day's journey was therefore limited to two thousand cubits, that is, one thousand yards. But, if a rope was tied across the end of a street, the whole street became one house and a man could go a thousand yards beyond the end of the street. Or, if a man deposited enough food for one meal on Friday evening at any given place, that place technically became his house and he could go a thousand yards beyond it on the Sabbath day. The rules and the regulations and evasions piled up by the hundred and the thousand.

Take the case of carrying a burden. *Jeremiah* 17: 21-24 said: " Take heed to yourselves and bear no burden on the Sabbath day." So a burden had to be defined. It was defined as " food equal in weight to a dried fig, enough wine for mixing in a goblet, milk enough for one swallow, honey enough to put upon a wound, oil enough to anoint a small member, water enough to moisten an eye-salve," and so on and on. It had then to be settled whether or not a woman could wear a brooch, a man could wear a wooden leg or dentures, on the Sabbath; or would it be carrying a burden to do so? Could a chair or even a child be lifted? And so on and on the discussions and the regulations went.

It was the *Scribes* who worked out these regulations; it was the *Pharisees* who dedicated their lives to keeping them. Obviously, however misguided a man might be, he must nonetheless be desperately in earnest if he proposed to undertake obedience to every one of the thousands of rules. That is precisely what the Pharisees did. The name *Pharisee* means *The Separated One*; and the Pharisees were those who had separated themselves from all ordinary life in order to keep every detail of the law of the scribes.

Nicodemus was a Pharisee, and it is plain how astonishing a thing it is that a man who regarded goodness in that light and who had given himself to that kind of life in the conviction that he was pleasing God should wish to talk to Jesus at all.

(iii) Nicodemus was a ruler of the Jews. The word is *archōn*. This is to say that Nicodemus was a member of the Sanhedrin. The Sanhedrin was a court of seventy members and it was the supreme court of the Jews. Of course under the Romans its powers were more limited than once they had been; but they were still extensive. In particular the Sanhedrin had religious jurisdiction over every Jew in the world; and one of its duties was to examine and deal with anyone suspected of being a false prophet. Again it is clear that it is an amazing thing that Nicodemus should come to Jesus at all.

(iv) It may well be that Nicodemus belonged to one of the most distinguished Jewish families. Away back in 63 B.C. when the Romans and the Jews had been at war, Aristobulus, the Jewish leader, sent a certain Nicodemus as his ambassador to Pompey, the Roman Emperor. Much later in the terrible last days of Jerusalem, the man who negotiated the surrender of the garrison was a certain Gorion, who was the son either of Nicomedes or Nicodemus. It may well be that both these men belonged to the same family as our Nicodemus, and that it was one of the most distinguished families in Jerusalem. If that is true it is amazing that this Jewish aristocrat should come to this homeless prophet who had been the carpenter of Nazareth that he might talk to Him about his soul.

It was by night that Nicodemus came to Jesus. There were probably two reasons for that.

(i) It may have been a sign of caution. Nicodemus quite frankly may not have wished to commit himself and his fellow-members of the Sanhedrin by coming to Jesus by day. We must not condemn Nicodemus. The wonder is that Nicodemus, with his background, came to Jesus at all; and it was infinitely better to come at night than not to come at all. It is a miracle of grace that Nicodemus overcame his prejudices and his upbringing and his whole view of life enough to come to Jesus at all.

(ii) But there may be another reason. The rabbis declared that the best time to study the law was at night when a man was undisturbed. Throughout the day Jesus was surrounded by crowds of people all the time. It may well be that Nicodemus came to Jesus by night because he wanted an absolutely private and completely undisturbed time with Jesus. He may have come at night because he wanted Jesus to himself in a way that would be impossible to get Him throughout the crowded hours of the day.

Nicodemus was a puzzled man, a man with all the honours and yet with something lacking in his life. He came to Jesus for a talk which would last all through the night hours that somehow in the darkness of the night he might find light.

THE MAN WHO CAME BY NIGHT

John 3: 1-6 (continued)

WHEN John relates conversations that Jesus had with enquirers, he has a way of following a certain scheme. We see that scheme very clearly here. The enquirer says something (verse 2). Jesus answers in a saying that is hard to understand (verse 3). That saying is misunderstood by the enquirer (verse 4). Jesus answers with a saying that is even more difficult to understand (verse 5). And then there follows a discourse and an explanation. John uses this method of telling us of the conversations that Jesus had with those who came to enquire, in order that we may see men thinking things out and discovering them for themselves and so that we may do the same.

When Nicodemus came to Jesus he said to Jesus that no one could help being impressed with the signs and the wonders that Jesus did. Jesus' answer was that it was not the signs and the wonders that were really important; the important thing was such a change in a man's inner life that it could only be described as a new birth.

When Jesus said that a man must be *born again* Nicodemus misunderstood Him, and the misunderstanding came from the fact that the word which the Authorised Version translates *again*, the Greek word *anōthen*, has three different meanings. (i) It can mean *from the beginning, completely, radically.* (ii) It can mean *again*, in the sense of *for the second time*. (iii) It can mean *from above*, and, therefore, *from God*. It is not possible for us to get all these meanings into any English word; and yet all three of them are in the phrase *born again*. To be born again is to undergo such a radical change that it is like a new birth; it is to have something happen to the soul which can only be described as being born all over again; and the whole process is not a human achievement, because it comes from the grace and the power of God. When we read the story and the words of Nicodemus, it looks at first sight as if Nicodemus took the word *again* in only the second sense, and as if he took it with a crude literalism. How can a man, he said, enter again into his mother's womb and be born a second time when he is already an old man? But there is more to Nicodemus' answer than that. In the heart of Nicodemus there was a great unsatisfied longing. It is as if Nicodemus said with infinite, wistful yearning: " You talk about being born again; you talk about this radical, fundamental change which is so necessary. I know that it is *necessary*; but in my experience it is so *impossible*. There is nothing I would like more; but you might as well tell me, a full grown man, to enter into my mother's womb and to be born all over again." It is not the *desirability* of this change that Nicodemus questioned; that he knew only too well; it is the *possibility*. Nicodemus is up against the eternal problem, the problem of the man who wants to be changed, and who cannot change himself.

This phrase *born again*, this idea of *rebirth*, runs all through the New Testament. Peter speaks of the God who has *begotten* us to a living hope (I *Peter* I: 3); he talks about being *born again* not of corruptible seed, but of incorruptible (I *Peter* I: 22, 23). James speaks of God *begetting* us with the word of truth (*James* I: 18). The Letter *to Titus* speaks of *the washing of regeneration* (*Titus* 3: 5). Sometimes this same idea is spoken of as a death, followed by a resurrection or a re-creation. Paul speaks of the Christian as dying with Christ and the rising to life anew (*Romans* 6: 1-11). He speaks of those who have lately come into the Christian faith as *babes in Christ* (1 *Corinthians* 3: 1, 2). If any man is in Christ it is as if he had been *created* all over again (2 *Corinthians* 5: 17). In Christ there is a new creation (*Galatians* 6: 15). The new man is *created* after God in righteousness (*Ephesians* 4: 22-24). The person who is at the first beginnings of the Christian faith is a babe (*Hebrews* 5: 12-14). All over the New Testament this idea of *rebirth, re-creation* occurs.

Now this was not an idea which was in the least strange to the people who heard it in New Testament times. The Jew knew all about rebirth. When a proselyte came into Judaism, when a man from another faith became a Jew, when he had been accepted into Judaism, by prayer and sacrifice and baptism, he was regarded as being *reborn*. "A proselyte who embraces Judaism," said the rabbis, "is like a new-born child." So radical was the change that the sins he had committed before his reception were all done away with, for now he was a different person. It was even theoretically argued that such a man could marry his own mother or his own sister, because he was a completely new man, and all the old connections were broken and destroyed. The Jew knew the idea of rebirth. The Greek knew the idea of rebirth and knew it well. By far the most real religion of the Greeks at this time was the faith of the Mystery Religions. The Mystery Religions were all founded on the story of some suffering and dying and rising god. This story was played out as a passion play. The initiate had a long course of preparation, instruction, asceticism and fasting. The drama was then played out with gorgeous music, marvellous ritual, incense and everything to play upon the emotions. As it was played out the worshipper's aim was to become one with the god, identified with the god, in such a way that he passed through the god's sufferings and shared the god's triumph and the god's divine life. The Mystery Religions offered mystic union with some god. When that union was achieved the initiate was, in the language of the Mysteries, *a twice-born*. The Hermetic Mysteries had as part of their basic belief: " There can be no salvation without regeneration." Apuleius, who went through initiation, said that he underwent " a voluntary death," and that thereby he attained " his spiritual birthday," and was " as it were reborn." Many of the Mystery initiations took place at midnight when the day dies and is reborn. In the Phrygian the initiate, after his initiation, was fed with milk as if he was a new-born babe. The ancient world knew all about rebirth and regeneration. It longed for it and searched for it everywhere. The most famous of all Mystery ceremonies was the *taurobolium*. The candidate was put into a pit. On the top of the pit there was a lattice-work cover. On the cover a bull was slain by having its throat cut. The blood poured down and the initiate lifted up his head and bathed himself in the blood; he was washed in blood; and when he came out of the pit he was *renatus in aeternum*, reborn for all eternity. When Christianity came to the world with a message of rebirth, it came with precisely that for which all the world was seeking.

What, then, does this rebirth mean for us? In the New Testament, and especially in the Fourth Gospel, there are four closely inter-related ideas. There is the idea of rebirth; there is the idea of the Kingdom of God, into which a man cannot enter unless he is reborn; there is the idea of sonship of God; and there is the idea of eternal life. This idea of being reborn is not something which is peculiar to the thought of the Fourth Gospel. In *Matthew* we have the same great truth put more simply and more vividly: " Except ye be converted and become as little children, ye shall not enter the Kingdom of Heaven " (*Matthew* 18: 3). All these three ideas have a common thought behind them.

BORN AGAIN

John 3: 1-6 (*continued*)

LET us start with the idea of the Kingdom of Heaven. What does the Kingdom of Heaven mean? We get our best definition of it from the Lord's Prayer. There are two petitions side by side:

> Thy Kingdom come:
> Thy will be done in earth as it is in heaven.

Now it is characteristic of Jewish style to say things twice, and the second way of saying a thing explains, amplifies, repeats in a different way the first way. Any verse of the Psalms will show us this Jewish habit of what is technically known as parallelism:

> The Lord of Hosts is with us:
> The God of Jacob is our refuge (*Psalm* 46: 7).
> I acknowledge my transgressions:
> And my sin is ever before me (*Psalm* 51: 3).
> He maketh me to lie down in green pastures:
> He leadeth me beside the still waters (*Psalm* 23: 2).

Now let us apply that principle to these two petitions in the Lord's Prayer; the second petition amplifies, explains, develops the first; we then arrive at the definition: *The Kingdom of Heaven is a society where God's will is as perfectly done on earth as it is in heaven.* To be in the Kingdom of Heaven is therefore to lead a life in which we have completely and willingly submitted everything to the will of God; it is to have arrived at a stage when we fully, perfectly and completely accept the will of God.

Now let us take the idea of *sonship*. In one sense sonship is a tremendous *privilege*. To those who believe there is given the power to become sons (*John* 1: 18). But the very essence of sonship is necessarily *obedience*. " He that hath my commandments, *and keepeth them*, he it is that loveth me " (*John* 14: 21). The essence of sonship is love; and the essence of love is obedience. We cannot with any reality say that we love a person and then do things which hurt and grieve that person's heart. Sonship

117

is a privilege, but a privilege which is only entered into when full obedience is given. So then we come to see that to be a son of God and to be in the Kingdom are one and the same thing. The son of God and the citizen of the Kingdom are both people who have totally and completely and willingly and finally accepted the will of God.

Now let us take the idea of *eternal life*. It is far better to speak of *eternal* life than to speak of *everlasting* life. The main idea behind eternal life is not simply that of duration. It is quite clear that a life which went on for ever could just as easily be hell as heaven. The idea behind eternal life is the idea of a certain quality, a certain kind of life. What kind of life? There is only one person who can properly be described by this adjective eternal (*aiōnios*) and that one person is God. Eternal life is the kind of life that God lives; it is God's life. To enter into eternal life is to enter into possession of that kind of life which is the life of God. It is to be lifted up above merely human, temporary, passing, transient things, into that joy and peace which belong only to God. And clearly a man can only enter into this close communion and fellowship with God when he renders to God that love, that reverence, that devotion, that obedience which truly bring him into fellowship with God.

Here then we have three great kindred conceptions, the conception of entry into the Kingdom of God, the conception of sonship of God and the conception of eternal life; and all are dependent on, all are the products of, perfect acceptance of and perfect obedience to the will of God. It is just here that the idea of being *reborn* comes in. It is the idea of being reborn that links all these three conceptions together. It is quite clear that, as we are and in our own strength, we are quite unable to render to God this perfect obedience; it is only when the grace of God enters into us and takes possession of us and changes us that we can give to God the reverence and the devotion we ought to give. It is Jesus Christ who can work the change in us; it is through Him that we are reborn; it is when He enters into possession of our hearts and lives that the change comes.

When that happens we are born of *water and the Spirit*. There are two thoughts there. *Water* is the symbol of cleansing. When Jesus takes possession of our lives, when we love Him with all our heart, the sins of the past are forgiven and forgotten. *The Spirit* is the symbol of *power*. When Jesus takes possession of our lives it is not only that the past is forgotten and forgiven; if that were all, we might well proceed to make the same mess of life all over again; but into life there enters this new power which enables us to be what by ourselves we could never be, and to do what by ourselves we could never do. Water and the Spirit stand for the cleansing and the strengthening power of Christ, which wipes out the past and which gives us victory in the future.

Finally in this passage John lays down a great law. That which is born of the flesh is flesh and that which is born of the Spirit is spirit. A man by himself is flesh, and his power is limited to what the flesh can do. By himself he cannot be other than defeated and frustrated; that we know only too well; that is the universal fact of human experience. But the very essence of the Spirit is the power and the life which are beyond human power and human life; and when the Spirit takes possession of us the Spirit does what only the Spirit can do and the defeated life of human nature becomes the victorious life of God.

To be born again is to be changed in such a way that it can only be described as rebirth and re-creation. The change comes when we love Jesus and allow Him into our hearts. Then we are forgiven for the past and armed by the Spirit for the future. Then we can truly accept the will of God. And then we become citizens of the Kingdom; then we become sons of God; then we enter into eternal life, which is the very life of God.

THE DUTY TO KNOW AND THE RIGHT TO SPEAK

John 3: 7-13

> Do not be surprised that I said to you: "You must be reborn from above. The wind blows where it will, and you hear the sound of it, but you do not know whence it comes and whither it goes. So is every one that is born of the Spirit." Nicodemus answered: "How can these things happen?" Jesus answered: "Are you the man whom everyone regards as the teacher of Israel, and you do not understand these things? This is the truth I tell you—we speak what we know, and we bear witness to what we have seen; but you do not receive our witness. If I have spoken to you of earthly things and you do not believe me, how will you believe me if I speak to you about heavenly things." No one has gone up to heaven, except He who came down from heaven, I mean, the Son of Man, who is in heaven.

THERE are two kinds of misunderstanding. There is the misunderstanding of the man who misunderstands because he has not yet reached a stage of knowledge and of experience at which he is able to grasp the truth. There is a genuine inability to understand, an inability which is the inevitable result of lack of knowledge. When a man is in that state our duty is to do all that we can to explain things to him so that he will be able to grasp the knowledge which is being offered to him. But there is a failure to understand which comes from unwillingness to understand; there is a failure to see which comes from the refusal to see. A man can deliberately shut his mind to truth which he does not wish to see; he can be deliberately dense towards teaching which he does not wish to accept. Nicodemus was like that. The teaching about a new birth from God should not have been strange to him. Ezekiel, for instance, had spoken repeatedly about the new heart that must be created in a man. "Cast away from you all your transgressions, whereby ye have transgressed; and make you a new heart and a new spirit; for why will ye die, O house of Israel? " (*Ezekiel* 18: 31). " A new heart will I give you, and a new spirit will I put within you " (*Ezekiel* 36: 26). Nicodemus was an expert in scripture and again and again the prophets had spoken of that very experience of which Jesus was speaking. If a man does not wish to be reborn, he will deliberately misunderstand what rebirth means. If a man does not wish to be changed, he will deliberately shut his eyes and his mind and his heart to the power which can change him. In the last analysis what is the matter with so many of us is simply the fact that, when Jesus Christ comes with His offer to change us and re-create us, if we were honest, we would answer: " No thank you: I am quite satisfied with myself as I am, and I don't want to be changed."

But Nicodemus was driven back on another defence. In effect he said: " This rebirth about which you talk may be possible; but I can't understand how it happens, and how it works." The answer of Jesus depends for its point on the fact that the Greek word for *spirit* which is *pneuma* has two meanings. *Pneuma* is the word for *spirit*, but it is also the regular word for *wind*. The same is true of the Hebrew word *ruach*; it too means *spirit* and *wind*. So Jesus said to Nicodemus: " You can hear and see and feel the *wind* (*pneuma*); but you do not know where the wind comes from and where it is going to; you may not understand how and why the wind blows; but you can see what the wind does. You may not understand where a gale came from and where a gale is going to, but you can see the trail of flattened fields and uprooted trees which that gale leaves behind it. There are many things about the wind you may not understand; but the effect of the wind is plain for all to see." " So," Jesus went on, " the *Spirit* (*pneuma*) is exactly the same. You may not know how the Spirit works; but you can see the effect of the Spirit in human lives." Jesus said: " This is no theoretical, academic thing of which we are speaking.

We are talking of things which we know and which we have actually seen. We can point to man after man who has been re-made, re-created, re-born by the power and the effect and the work of the Spirit." Dr. John Hutton used to tell of a workman, who had been a drunken reprobate and who was converted. His work-mates did their best to make him feel a fool. " Surely," they said to him, " you can't believe in miracles and things like that. Surely, for instance, you don't believe that Jesus turned water into wine." " I don't know," the man answered, " whether He turned water into wine when He was in Palestine, but I do know that in my own house and home He has turned beer into furniture! " There are any number of things in this world which we use every day without knowing how they work. Comparatively few of us know how electricity or wireless or television works; but we do not deny that they exist because of that. Many of us drive a motor car with only the haziest notion of what goes on below the bonnet of it; but our lack of understanding does not prevent us from using and enjoying the benefits which a motor car confers upon us. We may not under-stand how the Spirit works; but the effect of the Spirit on the lives of men is there for all to see; and the only unanswerable argument for Christianity is a Christian life. No man can disregard a religion and a faith and a power which is able to make bad men good.

So Jesus said to Nicodemus: " I have tried to make things simple for you; I have used simple human pictures taken from everyday life; and you have not understood. How can you ever expect to understand the deep things, if even the simple things are beyond you? " There is a warning here for every one of us. It is easy to sit in discus-sion groups, to sit in a study and to read books, it is easy to discuss the intellectual truth of Christianity; but the essential thing is to experience the power of Chris-tianity. And it is fatally easy to start at the wrong end.

It is fatally easy to think of Christianity as something to be discussed and not as something to be experienced. It is certainly important to have an intellectual grasp of the orb of Christian truth; but it is still more important to have a vital, living experience of the power of Jesus Christ. When a man undergoes treatment from a doctor, when he has to have an operation, when he is given some medicine to take, he does not need to know the anatomy of the human body, the scientific effect of the anæsthetic, the way in which the drug works on his body in order to be cured. Ninety-nine men out of every hundred accept the cure without being able to say how it was brought about. There is a sense in which Christianity is like that. At the heart of Christianity there is a mystery, but it is not the mystery of intellectual appreciation; it is the mystery of redemption.

There is one difficulty in reading the Fourth Gospel. It is the difficulty of knowing when the words of Jesus stop and when the words of the writer of the Gospel begin. John has thought so long about the words of Jesus that insensibly he glides from them to his own thoughts about them. Almost certainly the last words of this passage are the words of John. It is as if someone asked: " All this that Jesus is saying may or may not be true; but what right has He to say it? What guarantee have we got that this is true? " John's answer is simple and profound. " Jesus," he says, " came down from heaven to tell us the truth of God. And, when He had companied with men and died for men, He returned to His glory." It was John's contention that Jesus' right to speak came from the fact that Jesus knew God personally, that Jesus had come direct from the secrets of heaven to earth, that what Jesus said to men was most literally God's own truth. The right of Jesus to speak comes directly from that which Jesus was and is—the embodied mind of God.

THE UPLIFTED CHRIST

John 3: 14, 15

> And as Moses lifted up the serpent in the wilderness,
> so the Son of Man must be lifted up, that every one
> who believes in Him may have eternal life.

HERE John goes back to a strange Old Testament story
which is told in *Numbers* 21. 4-9. On their journey through
the wilderness the people of Israel murmured and complained and regretted that they had ever left Egypt.
To punish them God sent a plague of deadly, fiery serpents.
The people repented and cried for mercy, and God instructed
Moses to make an image of a serpent and to hold it up
in the midst of the camp; and he who looked upon the
serpent was healed and saved. That story much impressed
the Israelites. They told how in later times that brazen
serpent became an image and an idol and how
in the days of Hezekiah it had to be destroyed because
people were worshipping it (2 *Kings* 18: 4). The
Jews themselves were always a little puzzled and perplexed
by this incident, especially in view of the fact that they
were absolutely forbidden to make graven images. The
rabbis explained it this way: " It was not the serpent that
killed and gave life. Israel looked, and, so long as Moses
lifted up the serpent, they believed on Him who had
commanded Moses to act thus. It was God who healed
them." The healing power lay not in the brazen serpent
itself. The serpent was only a sign and a symbol and a
pointer to turn their thoughts to God; and when they
turned their thoughts to God they were healed.

So John took that old story and he used it as a type and
a forecast and a kind of parable of Jesus. He says: " The
serpent was lifted up; men looked at it; and their thoughts
were turned to God; and by the power of that God in
whom they trusted they were healed. Even so Jesus must
be lifted up; and when men turn their thoughts to Him,

and believe in Him, they too will find eternal life and salvation."

There is a wonderfully suggestive thing here. The verb *to lift up* is *hupsoun*. The strange thing about this word is that it is used of Jesus in two senses. It is used of His being *lifted up upon the Cross*. And it is used of His being *lifted up into glory* at the time of His Ascension into heaven. It is used of the Cross in *John* 8: 28; 12: 32. It is used of Jesus' Ascension into glory in *Acts* 2: 33; 5: 31; *Philippians* 2: 9. There was a double lifting up in Jesus' life—the lifting on the Cross, and the lifting into glory. And the two are inextricably connected. The one could not have happened without the other. For Jesus the Cross was the way to glory; had He refused the Cross, had He evaded it, had He taken steps to escape it, as He might so easily have done, there would have been no glory for Him. It is the same for us. We can, if we like, choose the easy way; we can, if we like, refuse the cross that every Christian has to bear; but if we do, we lose the glory. It is one of the unalterable laws of life that if there is no cross, there is no crown.

In this passage we have two expressions the meaning of which we must face. It will not be possible for us to extract all the meaning from them, because they both mean more than ever we can discover; but we must try to grasp at least something of their meaning.

(i) There is the phrase which speaks of *believing in Jesus*. What does that phrase mean? It means at least three things. (*a*) It means believing with all our hearts that God is as Jesus declared Him to be. It means believing that God loves us, believing that God cares for us, believing that God wants nothing more than to forgive us, believing that God is love. It was not easy for a Jew to believe that. The Jew looked on God as essentially a God of law who imposed His laws upon His people and who punished them if they broke them. The Jew looked on God as the judge and on man as the criminal at the judgment seat of God. The Jew looked on God as a demanding God. God was a God who demanded sacrifices and offerings. To get into God's presence man had to pay the price that God laid down. It was hard to think of God, not as a judge waiting to exact penalty, not as a task-master waiting to pounce, but as a Father who longed for nothing so much as to have His erring children come back home. It cost the life and the death of Jesus to tell men that. And we cannot begin to be Christian at all until with all our hearts we believe that. (b) Jesus said that, but what right had Jesus to say it? How can we be sure that Jesus knew what He was talking about? What guarantee is there that that wonderful good news is true? It sounds far too good to be true. What proof is there that it is true? Here we come upon the second article in belief. We must believe that Jesus is the Son of God. We must believe that in Jesus there is the mind of God. We must believe that Jesus knew God so well, that Jesus was so close to God, that Jesus was so one with God, that He could tell us the absolute truth about God. We have to be sure that Jesus knew what He was talking about, and that He told us the truth about God, because the mind of God was in Him. (c) But belief has a third element. We believe that God is a loving Father. We believe that that is true because we believe that Jesus is none other than one who can only be called the Son of God, and that therefore what He says about God is true. Then there comes this third element. We must stake everything on the fact that what Jesus says is true. Whatever He says we must do; whenever He commands we must obey. When He tells us to cast ourselves unreservedly on the mercy of God we must do so. In action we must take Jesus at His word. Every smallest action in life must be done in unquestioning obedience to Him. So then belief has these three elements—belief that God is the loving

Father, belief that Jesus is the Son of God and therefore tells us the truth about God and life, unswerving and unquestioning obedience to Jesus, life lived in the certainty that what Jesus says is true.

(ii) The second great phrase is the phrase *eternal life*. We have already seen that eternal life is the very life of God Himself. But let us ask this: if we possess eternal life, what do we possess? If we enter into eternal life, what is life like? To have eternal life changes every relationship in life. It envelops every relationship in life with peace. (*a*) It gives us peace with God. We are no longer cringing before a tyrannical king or seeking to hide from an austere judge. We are at home with our Father. (*b*) It gives us peace with men. If we have been forgiven we must be forgiving. It enables us to see men as God sees them. It makes us and all men into one great family joined in love. (*c*) It gives us peace with life. If God is Father, God is working all things together for good. Lessing used to say that if he had one question to ask the Sphinx, who knew everything, it would be: " Is this a friendly universe? " When we believe that God is Father, we also believe that a father's hand will never cause his child a needless tear. We may not understand life any better, but we will not resent life any longer. (*d*) It gives us peace with ourselves. In the last analysis a man is more afraid of himself than of anything else. He knows his own weakness; he knows the force of his own temptations; he knows his own tasks and the demands of life. But now he knows that he is facing it all with God. It is not he who lives but Christ who liveth in him. There is a peace founded on strength in his life. (*e*) It makes him certain that the dearest joy on earth is only a foretaste of the greater joy that will be; that the deepest peace on earth is only a shadow of the ultimate peace which is to come. It gives him a hope, a goal, an end to which he travels. It gives him a life of glorious wonder here, and yet, at the same time, a life in which the best is yet to be.

THE LOVE OF GOD

John 3: 16

> For God so loved the world that He gave His **only** Son so that every one who believes in Him should not perish but have everlasting life.

ALL great men have had their favourite texts; but this text has been called " Everybody's Text." Herein for every simple heart is the very essence of the gospel. This text tells us certain very great things.

(i) It tells us that the origin and initiative in all salvation lies with God. Sometimes Christianity is presented in such a way that it sounds as if God had to be pacified, as if God had to be persuaded to forgive. Sometimes men speak as if they would draw a picture of a stern, angry, unforgiving, legal God, and a gentle, loving, forgiving Jesus. Sometimes men present the Christian message in such a way that it sounds as if Jesus did something which changed the attitude of God to men from condemnation to forgiveness. But this text tells us that it was with God that it all started It was God who sent His Son, and He sent His Son because He loved men. At the back of everything there is the love of God.

(ii) It tells us that the mainspring of the being of God is love. It is easy to think of God as looking at men in their heedlessness and their disobedience and their rebellion and saying: " I'll break them: I'll humble them and lash them and discipline them and punish them and scourge them until they come back." It is easy to think of God as seeking the allegiance of men in order to satisfy His own desire for power, and His own desire for what we might call a completely subject universe. But the tremendous thing about this text is that it shows us God acting, not for His own sake, but for ours. It was not to satisfy His desire for power that God acted. It was not to bring into being a universe brought tᴏ heel. It was to satisfy His love. God is not like an absolute monarch who treats each man

THE GOSPEL OF JOHN

as a subject to be reduced to an abject obedience. God is the Father who cannot be happy until His wandering children have come home. God does not smash men into submission; He yearns over them and woos them into love.

(iii) It tells us of the width of the love of God. It was *the world* that God so loved. It was not a nation; it was not the good people; it was not only the people who loved Him; it was the world. The unlovable and the unlovely, the lonely who have no one else to love them, the man who loves God and the man who never thinks of God, the man who rests in the love of God and the man who spurns the love of God—all are included in this vast inclusive love, the love of God. As Augustine had it: " God loves each one of us as if there was only one of us to love."

LOVE AND JUDGMENT
John 3: 17-21

> For God did not send His Son into the world to condemn the world, but that the world might be saved through Him. He who believes in Him is not condemned; but he who does not believe already stands condemned. And this is the reason of this condemnation—the light came into the world and men loved the darkness rather than the light, for their deeds were evil. Every one whose deeds are depraved hates the light, and does not come to the light, but his deeds stand convicted. But he who puts the truth into action comes to the light, that his deeds may be made plain for all to see, because they are done in God.

HERE we are faced with one of the apparent paradoxes of the Fourth Gospel—the paradox of love and judgment. We have just been thinking of the love of God, and now suddenly we are confronted with judgment and condemnation and conviction. John has just said that it was because God so loved the world that He sent His Son into the world. Later he will go on to show us Jesus saying: " For judgment came I into the world " (*John* 9: 39). How can both things be true?

It is quite possible to offer a man an experience in nothing but love, and for that experience to turn out a judgment. It is quite possible to offer a man an experience which is meant to do nothing but to bring joy and bliss to a man, and yet for that experience to turn out a judgment and a condemnation. Suppose we love great music; suppose we get nearer to God in the midst of the surge and thunder of a great symphony than anywhere else. Suppose we have a friend who does not know anything about such music. Suppose we wish to introduce this friend of ours to this great experience; we wish to share it with him; we wish to give him this contact with the invisible beauty which we ourselves enjoy. We have no aim other than to give this friend the happiness of a great new experience. We take him to a symphony concert; in a very short time he is fidgetting and gazing around the hall, obviously completely uninterested and clearly bored. That friend has passed a judgment on himself; he has no music in his soul. The experience which was designed to bring him a new happiness has become a judgment. This always happens when we confront a man with greatness. We may take a man to see some great masterpiece of art; we may take him to listen to someone who is a prince of preachers; we may give him some soul-nourishing book to read; we may take him to gaze upon some beauty. His reaction is a judgment. If he finds no beauty and no thrill we know that he has a blind spot in his soul. It is told that a visitor was being shown round an art gallery by one of the attendants. In that gallery there were certain masterpieces beyond all price, possessions of eternal beauty and unquestioned genius. At the end of the tour the visitor said: " Well, I don't think much of your old pictures." The attendant answered quietly: " Sir, I would remind you that these pictures are no longer on trial, but those who look at them are." All that the man's reaction had done was to show his own pitiable blindness.

This is so with Jesus. If, when a man is confronted

with Jesus, his soul goes out in a thrill to that wonder and beauty, that man is on the way to salvation. But if, when he is confronted with Jesus, a man sees nothing lovely then he stands condemned. His reaction has condemned him. God sent Jesus in love. He sent Him for that man's salvation. But that which was sent in love has become a condemnation. But it is not God who has condemned the man; God only loved him; the man has condemned himself.

The man who reacts in hostility to Jesus has loved the darkness rather than the light. The terrible thing about a really good person is that he always has a certain unconscious element of condemnation in him. It is when we compare ourselves with him that we see ourselves as we are. Alcibiades, the spoilt young man of genius of Athens, was a companion of Socrates, but every now and again he used to break out: " Socrates, I hate you, for every time I meet you, you let me see what I am." The man who is engaged on an evil task does not want a flood of light shed on it and him. But the man who is engaged on an honourable task does not fear the light. It is told that once an architect came to Plato and offered for a certain sum of money to build him a house into none of the rooms of which it would be possible to see. Plato said: " I will give you double the money to build a house into every room of which everyone can see." It is only the evil-doer who does not wish to see himself, and who does not wish anyone else to see him. Such a man will inevitably hate Jesus Christ, for Christ will show him what he is, and that is the last thing that he wants to see. It is the concealing darkness that he loves, and not the revealing light.

By a man's reaction to Jesus Christ, that man stands revealed. By his reaction to Jesus Christ his soul is laid bare. If he regards Christ with love, even with wistful yearning, for him there is hope; but if in Christ he sees nothing lovely he has condemned himself. He who was sent in love has become to him for judgment.

A MAN WITHOUT ENVY

John 3: 22-30

> After these things Jesus and His disciples went to
> the district of Judaea. He spent some time there
> with them, and He was baptizing; and John was
> baptizing at Ainon, near Salem, because there was
> much water there. The people kept coming to him
> and being baptized, for John had not yet been thrown
> into prison. A discussion arose between some of
> John's disciples and a Jew about the matter of
> cleansing. So they came to John and said to him:
> " Rabbi, look now! The man who was with you
> on the other side of Jordan, the man to whom you
> bore your witness, is baptizing and they are all going
> to Him." John answered: " A man can only receive
> what is given to him from heaven. You yourselves
> can testify that I said, ' I am not the Anointed One
> of God,' but, ' I have been sent before Him.' He who
> has the bride is the bridegroom. But the friend of
> the bridegroom who stands and listens for him, rejoices
> at the sound of the voice of the bridegroom. So, then,
> my joy is complete. He must increase, but I must
> decrease."

WE have already seen that part of the aim of the writer
of the Fourth Gospel was to ensure that John the Baptist
received his proper place as the forerunner of Jesus, but
no higher place than that. There were those who were
still ready to call John master and lord; the writer of the
Fourth Gospel wishes to show that John had a high place,
but that the highest place was reserved for Jesus alone;
and he also wishes to show that John himself had never
had any other idea than that Jesus was supreme. To that
end the writer of the Fourth Gospel shows us the ministry
of John and the ministry of Jesus overlapping. The
synoptic gospels are different: *Mark* 1: 14 tells us that
it was *after* John was put into prison that Jesus began
His ministry. We need not argue which account is histor-
ically correct. The likelihood is that the Fourth Gospel
makes the two ministries overlap so that by the contrast
the supremacy of Jesus may be clearly shown.

One thing is certain—this passage shows us the loveliness of the humility of John the Baptist. It was clear that men were leaving John for Jesus. John's disciples were worried about it. They did not like to see their master take a back seat and a second place. They did not like to see him abandoned while the crowds flocked out to hear and see this new teacher.

In answer to their complaints, it would have been very easy for John to feel injured, neglected and unjustifiably forgotten. Sometimes a friend's sympathy can be the worst possible thing for us. It can make us feel sorry for ourselves and encourage us to think that we have not had a fair deal. But John had a mind above that. He told his disciples three things.

(i) He told them that he had never expected anything else. He told them that in point of fact he had assured them that his was not the leading place, but that he was merely sent as the herald, the announcer, the forerunner and the preparer for the greater one who was to come. It would ease life a great deal if more people were prepared to play the second part and the subordinate role. So many people look for great things to do. John was not like that. He knew well that God had given him a second place and a subordinate task. It would save us a lot of resentment and heartbreak if we realised that there are certain things which are not for us, and if we accepted with all our hearts, and did with all our might, the work that God has given us to do. To do a secondary task *for God* makes that task a great task. As Mrs. Browning had it: " All service ranks the same with God." Any task done for God is necessarily a great work.

(ii) He told them that no man could receive more than God gave him. If the new teacher was winning more followers and more converts it was not because he was stealing them from John, but because God was giving them to him. There was a certain American minister called Dr. Spence; once he was popular and his church was full; but as the years passed his people drifted away. To the church across the road there came a new young minister who was attracting the crowds. One evening in Dr. Spence's church there was a very small gathering. The doctor looked at the little flock. " Where have all the people gone? " he asked. There was an embarrassed silence; then one of his office-bearers said: " I think they have gone to the church across the street to hear the new minister." Dr. Spence was silent for a moment; then he smiled. " Well, then," he said, " I think we ought to follow them." And he descended from his pulpit and led his people across the road. What jealousies, what heartburnings, what resentfulness we might escape, if we would only remember that someone else's success is given to him by God, and if we accepted God's verdict and God's choice.

(iii) Finally, John uses a very vivid picture which every Jew would recognize, for it was part of the heritage of Jewish thought. He called Jesus the bridegroom and himself the friend of the bridegroom. One of the great pictures of the Old Testament is the picture of Israel as the bride of God, and God as the bridegroom of Israel. The union between God and Israel was so close that it could only be likened to a wedding. When Israel went after strange gods it was as if she had been guilty of infidelity to the marriage bond (*Exodus* 34: 15 cp. *Deuteronomy* 31:16; *Psalm* 73: 27; *Isaiah* 54: 5). The New Testament took this picture over and spoke of the Church as the bride of Christ (2 *Corinthians* 11: 2; *Ephesians* 5: 22-32). It was this picture that was in John's mind. Jesus had come from God; Jesus was the Son of God; Israel was His rightful bride, and He was Israel's bridegroom. But one place John did claim for himself, that of the friend of the bridegroom. The friend of the bridegroom, the *shoshben*, had a unique place at a Jewish wedding. He acted as the liaison between the bride and the bridegroom; he arranged the wedding; he took out the invitations; he presided at the wedding feast. He brought the bride and the bridegroom together. And he had one special duty. It was his duty to guard the bridal chamber and to let no false lover in. He would only open the door when in the dark he heard the bridegroom's voice and recognized it. When he heard the bridegroom's voice he was glad and he let him in, and he went away rejoicing, for his task was completed and the lovers were together. He did not grudge the bridegroom the bride. He knew that his only task had been to bring bride and bridegroom together. And when that task was done he willingly and gladly faded out of the centre of the picture. John's task had been to bring Israel and Jesus together; to arrange the marriage between Christ, the bridegroom, and Israel the bride. That task completed he was happy to fade into obscurity for his work was done. It was not with envy that he said that Jesus must increase and he must decrease; it was with joy. It may be that sometimes we would do well to remember that it is not to ourselves that we must try to attach people; it is to Jesus Christ. It is not for ourselves we seek the loyalty of men; it is for Him.

THE ONE FROM HEAVEN

John 3: 31-36

> He who comes from above is above all. He who is from the earth is from the earth and speaks from the earth. He who comes from heaven is above all. It is to what He has seen and heard that He bears witness; and no one receives His witness. He who has received His witness sets his seal on the fact that God is true. He whom God sent speaks the words of God, for He does not partially measure out the Spirit upon Him. The Father loves the Son and has given all things into His hand. He who believes in the Son has eternal life. He who does not believe in the Son will not see life, but the wrath of God rests upon him.

As we have seen before, one of the difficulties in the Fourth Gospel is to know when the characters are speaking, and when John is adding his own commentary. These verses may be the words of John the Baptist; but more likely they are the witness and the comment of John, the writer of the Gospel.

John begins by asserting the supremacy of Jesus. If we want information, we have to go to the person who possesses that information. If we want information about a family, we will only get it at first hand from a member of that family. If we want information about a town we will only get it at first hand from someone who comes from that town. So, then, if we want information about God, we will get it only from the Son of God; and if we want information about heaven and heaven's life, we will only get it from Him who comes from heaven. When Jesus speaks about God and about the heavenly things, says John, it is no carried story, no second-hand tale, no information from a secondary source. He tells us that which He Himself has seen and heard. To put it very simply, because Jesus alone knows God, He alone can give us the facts about God, and these facts are the gospel.

It is John's grief that so few accept the message that Jesus brought; but when a man does accept it he attests the fact that in his belief the word of God is true. In the ancient world, if a man wished to give his full approval to a document, such as a will or an agreement or a constitution, he affixed his seal to the foot of it. The seal was the sign that he agreed with this and regarded it as legal and binding and true. So when a man accepts the message of Jesus, he affirms and agrees and attests that he believes that what God says is true.

John goes on: we can believe what Jesus says, because on Jesus God poured out the Spirit in full measure, keeping nothing back. Even the Jews themselves said that the prophets received from God *a certain measure of the Spirit*. The full measure of the Spirit was reserved for God's own chosen one. Now, in Hebrew thought, the Spirit of God had two functions—first, the Spirit revealed God's truth to men; and, second, the Spirit enabled men to recognize and understand that truth when it came to them. So to say that the Spirit was on Jesus in the completest possible way is to say that He perfectly knows and perfectly understands the truth of God. To put that in another way—to listen to Jesus is to listen to the very voice of God.

Finally, John again sets before men the eternal choice. That choice is life or death. All through history this choice had been set before Israel. *Deuteronomy* records the words of Moses: " See, I have set before thee this day life and good, death and evil. . . . I call heaven and earth to record this day against you, that I have set before you life and death, blessing and cursing; therefore choose life, that both thou and thy seed may live " (*Deuteronomy* 30: 15-20). The challenge was reiterated by Joshua: " Choose you this day whom you will serve " (*Joshua* 24: 15). It has been said that all life concentrates upon a man at the crossroads. Once again John returns to his favourite thought. What matters is a man's reaction to Christ. If that reaction be love and longing, that man will know life. If it be indifference or hostility, that man will know death. God offered him love; by his rejection of it he has condemned himself. It is not that God sent His wrath upon him; it is that he has brought that wrath upon himself.

BREAKING DOWN THE BARRIERS

John 4: 1-9

So when the Lord learned that the Pharisees had heard that Jesus was making and baptizing more disciples than John (although it was not Jesus Himself who was in the habit of baptizing but His disciples), He quitted Judaea and went away again to Galilee. Now he had to pass through Samaria. He came to a town of Samaria, called Sychar, which is near the piece of ground which Jacob gave to Joseph, his son,

And Jacob's well was there. So Jesus, tired from the journey, was sitting by the well just as He was. It was about midday. There came a woman of Samaria to draw water. Jesus said to her: " Give me to drink." For His disciples had gone away into the town to buy provisions. So the Samaritan woman said to Him: " How is it that you who are a Jew ask a drink from me, a Samaritan woman? " (For there is no familiarity between Jews and Samaritans).

FIRST of all, let us set the scene of this incident. The land of Palestine is only 120 miles long from north to south. But within that 120 miles there were in the time of Jesus three definite divisions of territory. In the extreme north there lay Galilee; in the extreme south there lay Judaea; and in between them there lay Samaria. Jesus did not wish at this stage in His ministry to be drawn into and involved in a controversy about baptism; so he decided to quit Judaea for the time being and to transfer His operations to Galilee. There was a centuries-old feud between the Jews and the Samaritans, the cause of which we will shortly see. But nonetheless the quickest way from Judaea to Galilee lay through Samaria. The journey from Judaea to Galilee could be done in three days going *via* Samaria. The alternative route was to cross the Jordan, to go up the eastern side of the river, to avoid Samaria, to recross the Jordan north of Samaria and then to enter Galilee. Obviously this was a route which would take twice as long. So then Jesus had to pass through Samaria if He wished to take the shortest route to Galilee.

On the way they came to the town of Sychar. Just short of Sychar the road to Samaria forks. The one branch goes north-east to Scythopolis; the other goes, first, west to Nablus and then north to Engannim. Just at the fork of the road there stands to this day the well which is known as Jacob's well. This was an area which had many Jewish memories attached to it. There was a piece of ground there which had been bought by Jacob (*Genesis* 33: 18, 19). Jacob, on his deathbed, had bequeathed that ground to

Joseph (*Genesis* 48: 52). And, on Joseph's death in Egypt, his body had been taken back to Palestine and had been buried there (*Joshua* 24: 32). So around this area there gathered many Jewish memories. The well itself was more than 100 feet deep. It is not a springing well of water; it is a well into which the water percolates and in which it gathers. But clearly it was a well so deep that no one could gain water from it unless he had something with which to draw the water.

When Jesus and His little band came to the fork in the road Jesus sat down to rest, for He was tired with the journey. It was midday. The Jewish day runs from 6 a.m. to 6 p.m. and the sixth hour is twelve o'clock midday. So the heat was at its greatest, and Jesus was weary and thirsty from the way. His disciples went on ahead to buy some food in the Samaritan town. Something must have been beginning to happen to them. Before they had met Him it is entirely unlikely that they would have even thought of buying food in any Samaritan town. Little by little, perhaps even unconsciously, the barriers were going down. So as Jesus sat there, there came to the well a Samaritan woman. Why she should come to that well is something of a mystery, for it was more than half-a-mile from Sychar where she must have stayed and there was water there. May it be that she was so much of a moral outcast that even the village women drove her away from the village well, and she had to come here to draw water? Jesus asked her to give Him a drink. She turned in astonishment. " I am a Samaritan," she said. " You are a Jew. How is it that you ask a drink from me? " And then John explains to the Greeks for whom he was writing that there was no kind of come and go at all between the Jews and the Samaritans. Now it is certain that all we have got here is the briefest possible report of what must have been a long conversation. Clearly there was much more to this meeting than is recorded here. If we may use an analogy, this is like the minutes of a committee meeting where we have only the salient points of the discussion recorded. I think that the Samaritan woman must have unburdened her soul to this stranger. How else could Jesus have known of her tangled domestic affairs? For one of the very few times in her life she had found one with kindness in His eyes instead of critical superiority; and she opened her heart.

There are few stories in the Gospel record which show us so much about the character of Jesus as this story does.

(i) It shows us the reality of His humanity. Jesus was weary with the road, and He sat there by the side of the well tired and exhausted. It is very significant that John who stresses the sheer deity of Jesus Christ more than any other of the gospel writers also stresses His humanity to the full. John does not show us a figure freed from the tiredness and the exhaustion and the effort and the struggle of our humanity. He shows us one for whom life was an effort as it is for us; he shows us one who also was tired and who also had to go on.

(ii) It shows us the warmth of His sympathy. From an ordinary religious leader, from one of the orthodox church leaders of the day the Samaritan woman would have fled in embarrassment. She would have avoided such a one. If by any unlikely chance such a one had spoken to her she would have met him with an ashamed and even a hostile silence. But to Jesus it seemed the most natural thing in the world to talk to her. She had at last met someone who was not a critic but a friend, one who did not condemn but who understood.

(iii) It shows us Jesus as the breaker down of barriers. The quarrel between the Jews and the Samaritans was an old, old story. Away back about 720 B.C. the Assyrians had invaded the northern kingdom of Samaria and had captured and subjugated it. They did what conquerors often did in those days—they transported practically the whole population to Media (2 Kings 17: 6). Into the district the Assyrians brought other people—from Babylon, from

Cuthah, from Ava, from Hamath and from Sepharvaim
(2 *Kings* 17: 24). Now it is not possible to transport
a whole people. Some of the people of the northern kingdom
were left. Almost inevitably they began to inter-marry
with the incoming foreigners; and thereby they committed
what to the Jew was an unforgivable crime. They lost
their racial purity. In a strict Jewish household even to
this day if a son or a daughter marries a Gentile, his or
her funeral service is carried out. Such a person is dead
in the eyes of orthodox Judaism. So then the great majority
of the inhabitants of Samaria and the Northern Kingdom
were carried away to Media. They never came back;
they were assimilated into the country into which they
were taken and they are the lost ten tribes. Those who
remained in the country inter-married with the incoming
strangers and lost their right to be called Jews at all.

In course of time a like invasion and a like defeat
happened to the Southern Kingdom, whose capital was
Jerusalem. Its inhabitants also were carried off to Babylon;
but they did not lose their identity; they remained
stubbornly and unalterably Jewish. In time there came
the days of Ezra and Nehemiah and the exiles returned to
Jerusalem by the grace of the Persian king. Their immediate
task was to repair and rebuild the shattered Temple. The
Samaritans came and offered their help in this sacred task.
They were contemptuously told that their help was not
wanted. They had lost their Jewish heritage and they had
no right to share in the rebuilding of the house of God.
Smarting under this repulse, they turned bitterly against
the Jews of Jerusalem. It was about 450 B.C. when that
quarrel took place, and it was as bitter as ever in the days
of Jesus.

It had further been embittered when the renegade
Jew Manasseh married a daughter of the Samaritan
Sanballat (*Nehemiah* 13: 28) and proceeded to found a
rival temple on Mount Gerizim which was in the
centre of the Samaritan territory and to which the Samaritan

woman refers. Still later in the Maccabean days, in 129 B.C., John Hyrcanus, the Jewish general and leader, led an attack against Samaria and sacked and destroyed the temple on Mount Gerizim. Between Jews and Samaritans there was an embittered hatred. The Jews contemptuously called them Chuthites or Cuthaeans after one of the peoples whom the Assyrians had settled there. The Jewish Rabbis said: " Let no man eat of the bread of the Cuthaeans, for he who eats their bread is as he who eats swine's flesh." *Ecclesiasticus* depicts God as saying: " With two nations is my soul vexed, and the third is no nation: they that sit upon the mountain of Samaria, and the Philistines, and that foolish people that dwell in Sichem " (*Ecclesiasticus* 50: 25, 26). Sichem or Shechem was one of the most famous of Samaritan cities. The hatred was returned with interest. It is told that Rabbi Jochanan was passing through Samaria on his way to Jerusalem to pray. He passed by Mount Gerizim. A Samaritan saw him, and asked him: " Where are you going? " " I am going to Jerusalem," he said, " to pray." The Samaritan answered: " Would it not be better for you to pray in this holy mountain (Mount Gerizim) than in that accursed house? " Pilgrims from Galilee to Jerusalem had to pass through Samaria, if, as we have seen, they travelled by the quickest way; and the Samaritans delighted to hinder them.

The Jewish-Samaritan quarrel was more than 400 years old. But it smouldered as resentfully and bitterly as ever. It was small wonder that the Samaritan woman was astonished that Jesus, a Jew, should speak to her, a Samaritan.

(iv) But there was still another way in which Jesus was taking down the barriers. The Samaritan was a woman. Now the strict Rabbis forbade a Rabbi to greet a woman in public. A Rabbi might not even speak to his own wife or daughter or sister in public. There were even Pharisees who were called " The bruised and bleeding Pharisees " because they shut their eyes when they saw a woman on the street and so walked into walls and houses! For a Rabbi to be seen speaking to a woman in public was the end of his reputation—and yet Jesus spoke to this woman. Not only was she a woman; she was also a woman of a character which was notorious. No decent man, let alone a Rabbi, would have been seen in her company, or even exchanging a word with her—and yet Jesus spoke to her.

To a Jew this was an amazing story. Here was the Son of God tired and weary and thirsty. Here was the holiest of men listening with understanding to a sorry story. Here was Jesus breaking through the barriers of nationality and orthodox Jewish custom. Here is the beginning of the universality of the gospel; here is God so loving the world, not in theory, but in action.

THE LIVING WATER

John 4: 10-15

> Jesus answered her: " If you knew the free gift that God is offering you, and if you knew who is speaking to you, and if you knew who was saying to you: ' Give me to drink,' you would have asked Him, and He would have given you living water." The woman said to Him: " Sir, you have no bucket to draw with and the well is deep. Where does this living water that you have come from? Are you greater than our father Jacob who gave us the well, and who himself drank from it with his children and his cattle?" Jesus answered her: " Everyone who drinks of this water will thirst again; but whoever drinks of the water that I will give him will never thirst again for ever. But the water that I will give him will become a well of water within him, springing up to give him life eternal." The woman said to Him: " Sir, give me this water, so that I will not thirst, and so that I will not have to come here to draw water."

WE have to note that this conversation with the Samaritan woman follows exactly the same pattern as the conversation with Nicodemus. Jesus makes a statement. The statement

143

is misunderstood and taken in the wrong sense. Jesus remakes the statement in an even more vivid way. It is still misunderstood; and then Jesus compels the person with whom He is speaking to discover and to face the truth for himself or herself. That was Jesus' usual way of teaching; and it was a most effective way, for, as someone has said: " There are certain truths which a man cannot *accept*; he must *discover* them for himself."

Just as Nicodemus did, the woman took the words of Jesus quite literally, when she was meant to understand them spiritually. It was *living* water of which Jesus spoke. Now in ordinary language to the Jew *living* water was *running* water. It was the water of the running stream in contradistinction to the water of the stagnant cistern or pool. This well, as we have seen, was not a springing well, but a well into which the water percolated from the subsoil. To the Jew, *running, living* water from the stream was always better. So the woman is saying: " You are offering me pure stream water. Where are you going to get it? " She goes on to speak of " our father Jacob." The Jews would of course have strenuously denied that Jacob was the father of the Samaritans, but it was part of the Samaritan claim that they were descended from Joseph, the son of Jacob, by way of Ephraim and Manasseh. The woman is in effect saying to Jesus: " This is blasphemous talk. Jacob, our great ancestor, when he came here, had to dig this well to gain water for his family and his cattle. Are you claiming to be able to get fresh, running stream water? If you are, you are claiming to be wiser and more powerful than Jacob. That is a claim that no one has any right to make." When people were on a journey they usually carried with them a bucket made from the skin of some beast so that they could draw water from any well at which they halted. No doubt Jesus' band had such a bucket; and no doubt the disciples had taken it into the town with them. The woman saw that Jesus did not possess such a traveller's leathern bucket, and so again she says in effect: " You need not talk about drawing water and giving it to me. I can see for myself that you have not got a bucket with which to draw water." H. B. Tristram begins his book entitled *Eastern Customs in Bible Lands* with this personal experience. He was sitting beside a well in Palestine beside the scene of the inn which figures in the story of the Good Samaritan. " An Arab woman came down from the hills above to draw water; she unfolded and opened her goat-skin bottle, and then untwined a cord, and attached it to a very small leathern bucket which she carried, by means of which she slowly filled her skin, fastened its mouth, placed it on her shoulder, and, bucket in hand, climbed the mountain. I thought of the woman of Samaria at Jacob's well, when an Arab footman, toiling up the steep path from Jericho, heated and wearied with his journey, turned aside to the well, knelt and peered wistfully down. But he had ' nothing to draw with and the well was deep.' He lapped a little moisture from the water spilt by the woman who had preceded him, and, disappointed, passed on." It was just that that the woman was thinking of when she said that Jesus had nothing wherewith to draw water from the depths of the well.

But the Jews had another way of using the word *water*. The Jews often spoke of the *thirst* of the soul for God; and they often spoke of quenching that thirst with *living water*. Jesus was not using terms that were bound to be misunderstood; He was using terms that anyone with spiritual insight should have understood. In the *Revelation* the promise is: " I will give unto him who is athirst of the fountain of the water of life freely " (*Revelation* 21: 6). The Lamb is to lead them to fountains of living waters (*Revelation* 7: 17). The promise was that the Chosen People would draw water with joy from the wells of salvation (*Isaiah* 12: 3). The Psalmist spoke of his soul being thirsty for the living God (*Psalm* 42: 1). God's promise was: " I will pour water on him who is thirsty " (*Isaiah* 44: 3).

The summons was that every one who was thirsty should come to the waters and freely drink (*Isaiah* 55: 1). Jeremiah's complaint was that the people had forsaken God who was the fountain of living waters and had hewed themselves out broken cisterns which could hold no water (*Jeremiah* 2: 13). Ezekiel had had his vision of the river of life (*Ezekiel* 47: 1-12). In the new world there would be a cleansing fountain opened (*Zechariah* 13: 1). The waters would go forth from Jerusalem (*Zechariah* 14: 8). Sometimes the Rabbis identified this living water with the wisdom of the Law; sometimes they identified it with nothing less than the Holy Spirit of God. All Jewish pictorial religious language was full of this idea of the thirst of the soul which could only be quenched with the living water which was the gift of God. But the woman chose to understand this with an almost crude literalism. She was blind because she would not see.

But Jesus went on to make a still more startling statement. He went on to say that He could give her living water which would banish thirst for ever. Now the point of this is that again the woman took this literally; but in point of fact it was nothing less than a Messianic claim. In the prophetic vision of the age to come, the age of God, the promise was: " They shall not hunger or thirst " (*Isaiah* 49: 10). It was with God and none other that the living fountain of the all-quenching water existed. " With Thee is the fountain of life," the Psalmist had cried (*Psalm* 36: 9). It is from the very throne of God that the river of life is to flow (*Revelation* 22: 1). It is the Lord who is the founatin of living waters (*Jeremiah* 17: 13). It is in the Messianic age that the parched ground is to become a pool and the thirsty land springs of waters (*Isaiah* 35: 7). When Jesus spoke about bringing to men the water which quenches thirst for ever, He was doing no less than stating that He was the Anointed One of God who was to bring the new age in.

But again the woman did not see it. And, I think, that this time she spoke with a jest, as if humouring one who was a little mad. " Give me this water," she said, " so that I will never be thirsty again and so that I will not have to walk to the well day after day." She was jesting with a kind of humouring contempt about eternal things.

At the heart of all this there is the fundamental truth that in the human heart there is a thirst for something that only Jesus Christ can satisfy. Sinclair Lewis in one of his books draws a picture of a respectable little business man who kicked over the traces. He is talking to the girl he loves. She says to him: " On the surface we seem quite different; but deep down we are fundamentally the same. We are both desperately unhappy about something— and we don't know what it is." In every man there is this nameless unsatisfied longing; this vague discontent; this something lacking; this frustration; this longing which sometimes makes a man squirm his shoulders, he does not know why. In *Sorrel and Son* Warwick Deeping tells of a conversation between Sorrel and his son. The boy is talking about life. He says that it is like groping in an enchanted fog. The fog breaks for a moment; you see the moon or a girl's face; you think you want the moon or the face; and then the fog comes down again; and leaves you groping in that enchanted fog for something, you don't quite know what. Wordsworth, in the *Ode on the Intimations of Immortality*, speaks of,

> " Those obstinate questionings
> Of sense and outward things,
> Fallings from us, vanishings;
> Blank misgivings of a creature
> Moving about in worlds not realised."

Augustine talks about " our hearts being restless till they rest in Thee." Part of the human situation is the fact that we cannot find happiness out of the things that the human situation has to offer. As Browning had it:

" Just when we're safest, there's a sunset touch,
  A fancy from a flower-bell, someone's death,
  A chorus ending from Euripides—
  And that's enough for fifty hopes and fears
  As old and new at once as Nature's self,
  To rap and knock and enter in our soul."

We are never safe from the longing for eternity which God
has put in man's soul. There is the thirst, which only the
waters of eternity can quench, and which only Jesus Christ
can satisfy.

FACING THE TRUTH

John 4: 15-19

The woman said to Him: " Sir, give me this water,
so that I will not thirst, and so that I will not have
to come here to draw water." Jesus said to her:
" Go, call your husband, and come back here." The
woman answered: " I have not got a husband."
Jesus said to her: " You spoke well when you said,
' I have not got a husband.' For you have had five
husbands, and the one you now have is not your
husband. This is the truth that you have told."
The woman said to Him: " Sir, I see that you are a
prophet. Our fathers worshipped in this mountain
and you say Jerusalem is the place where we ought to
worship." Jesus said: " Woman, believe me, the
hour is coming when you will worship the Father
neither in this mountain nor in Jerusalem."

WE have seen how the woman light-heartedly and jestingly
asked Jesus to give her the living water, in order that she
should not thirst again and in order that she might be
spared the tiring journey to the well. And then suddenly
and stabbingly Jesus brought her to her senses. The time
for verbal by-play was past; the time for jesting was over.
" Go," said Jesus, " and fetch your husband and come
back with him." The woman stiffened as if a sudden pain
had caught her; she recoiled as if hit by a sudden shock;
she grew white as one who had seen a sudden apparition;
and so indeed she had, for *she had suddenly caught sight of*

herself. She was suddenly compelled to face herself and the looseness and the immorality and the total inadequacy of her life. There are two revelations in Christianity; there is the revelation of God and the revelation of ourselves. No man ever really sees himself until he sees himself in the presence of Christ; and then he is appalled at the sight of himself. There is another way of putting it—Christianity begins with a sense of sin. It begins with the sudden realization that life as we are living it will not do. We awake to ourselves and we awake to our need of God.

Some people have held, because of this mention of the five husbands, that this whole story is not the story of an incident in actual fact, but an allegory. We have seen that when the original people of Samaria were exiled and transported to Media, people from five other places were brought in. In that story we read how each of these five different people brought in their own gods (2 *Kings* 17: 29); and it has been held that the woman stands for Samaria; the five husbands stand for the five false gods to whom the Samaritans, as it were, married themselves. The sixth husband would stand for the true God; but, as Jesus said, they worship Him, not truly, but in ignorance; and therefore they are not married to him at all. It may be that there is a reminder of this Samaritan infidelity to God in this story; but the story is far too vivid to be a manufactured allegory. It reads too much like life.

Someone has said that prophecy is criticism based on hope. A prophet points out to a man or a nation what is wrong; but he does so, not to push the man or the nation into despair; he does so to point the way to cure and to amendment and to rightness of life. So Jesus began by revealing to this woman her own sinful state; but He goes on to tell her of the true worship in which our souls can meet God.

The woman's question comes in strangely to us. She says, and she is obviously troubled when she says it:

" Our fathers say that we ought to worship here on Mount Gerizim; you say that we ought to worship in Jerusalem; what am I to do?" The Samaritans adjusted history to suit themselves. They taught that it was on Mount Gerizim that Abraham had been willing to sacrifice Isaac; they taught that it was there that Melchizedek had appeared to Abraham; they declared that it was on Mount Gerizim that Moses had first erected an altar and sacrificed to God when the people entered the promised land, when in fact it was on Mount Ebal that that was done (*Deuteronomy* 27: 4). They tampered with the text of scripture and with history to glorify Mount Gerizim. The woman had been brought up to regard Mount Gerizim as the most sacred spot in the world and to despise Jerusalem. Now what was in her mind was this. She was saying to herself: " I am a sinner before God; I must offer to God an offering for my sin; I must take that offering to the house of God to put myself right with Him; where am I going to take it?" To her, as to all her contemporaries, the only cure for sin was sacrifice. Her great problem was, where was that sacrifice to be made? By this time she is not arguing about the respective merits of the Temple on Mount Gerizim and the Temple on Mount Zion; all that she wants to know is: Where can I find God?

Jesus' answer was that the day of the old man-made rivalries was coming to an end; and the time was on the way when men would find God everywhere. It had been Zephaniah's vision that men shall worship God " everyone from his own place " (*Zephaniah* 2: 11). It was Malachi's dream that in every place incense would be offered as a pure offering to the name of God (*Malachi* 1: 11). Jesus' answer to the woman was that she did not need to go anywhere special to find God, neither to Mount Gerizim or to Mount Zion; that she did not need to offer sacrifice in some special place. Jesus' answer was that the true worship finds God in every place.

THE TRUE WORSHIP

John 4: 22-26

" You do not know what you are worshipping. We do know what we worship, because the world's salvation has its origin among the Jews. But the hour is coming —the hour is now here—when the real worshippers will worship the Father in spirit and in truth; for it is worshippers like that that the Father is looking for. God is Spirit; and those who worship Him must worship Him in spirit and in truth." The woman said to Him: " I know that the Messiah, He who is called Christ, is coming. When He has come He will announce all things to us." Jesus said to her: " I who am speaking to you am He."

JESUS had told the Samaritan woman that the old rivalries were on the way out, that the day was coming when controversy about the respective merits of Mount Gerizim and Mount Zion would be an irrelevancy, that he who truly sought God would find God anywhere. But for all that Jesus still stressed the fact that the Jewish nation had a unique place in God's plan and revelation.

The Samaritans worship in ignorance, He says. There was one sense in which that was factually true. The Samaritans only accepted the Pentateuch, the first five books of the Old Testament. They rejected all the rest of the Old Testament. They had therefore rejected all the great messages of the prophets and all the supreme devotion of the Psalms. They had in fact a truncated religion because they had a truncated Bible; they had in fact rejected the knowledge that was open to them and that they might have had. Further, the Jewish Rabbis had always charged the Samaritans with a merely superstitious worship of the true God. They always said that the Samaritan worship was founded not on love and knowledge, but on ignorance and fear. As we have seen, when these foreign peoples were brought in to dwell in Samaria, they brought their own gods with them (2 *Kings* 17: 29). We are told that a priest from Bethel came and

told them how they should fear the Lord (2 *Kings* 17: 28).
But in point of fact all the probability is that they merely
added Jehovah to their list of gods because they were
superstitiously afraid to leave Him out. After all He was
the God of the land in which they were living and it might
be dangerous not to include Him in their worship.

So then in a false worship we may detect three faults.

(i) A false worship selects what it wishes to know and
understand about God, and omits what it does not wish.
The Samaritans took as much of scripture as they wished
and paid no attention to the rest. One of the most dangerous
things in the world is a one-sided religion. It is very easy
for a man to accept and hold such parts of God's truth as
suit him and to disregard the rest. We have seen, for
instance, how there are thinkers and churchmen and
politicians who will justify *apartheid* and racial segregation
by appeal to certain parts of scripture, while they con-
veniently forget the far greater parts which forbid it.
There was a minister in a great city who organised a
petition to help a man who had been condemned for a
certain crime. It seemed to him that this was a case where
Christian mercy ought to operate. His telephone bell
rang, and a woman's voice said to him: " I am astonished
that you, a minister, should be lending your weight to
this petition for mercy." " Why should you be surprised? "
he asked. The voice said: " I suppose you know your
Bible." " I hope so," he said. " Then," said the voice,
" are you not aware that the Bible says, ' An eye for an
eye and a tooth for a tooth '? " Here was a woman who
took the part of the Bible which suited her argument and
forgot the great merciful teaching of Jesus in the Sermon
on the Mount. We would do well to remember that,
although no man will ever grasp the whole orb of truth,
it is total truth that we should aim at, not the snatching at
fragments which happen to suit ourselves and our own
position.

(ii) A false worship is an ignorant worship. Worship ought to be the approach to God of the whole man. A man has a mind and he has a duty to exercise that mind. Religion may begin with an emotional response; but the time comes when that emotional response has to be thought out. E. F. Scott has said that religion is far more than merely the strenuous exercise of the intellect, but that nonetheless a very great part of religious failure is due to nothing other than intellectual sloth. To fail to think things out is in itself a sin. In the last analysis religion is never safe until a man can tell, not only what he believes, but why he believes it. Religion is hope, but it is hope with reason behind it (I *Peter* 3: 15).

(iii) A false worship is a superstitious worship. It is a worship given, not out of a sense of need nor out of any real desire, but basically because a man feels that it might be dangerous not to give it. Many a person will refuse to walk beneath a ladder; many a person will have a pleased feeling when a black cat crosses his path; many a person will pick up a pin with the idea that good luck will follow; many a person will have an uncomfortable feeling when he is one of thirteen people sitting at a table. He does not believe in these superstitions, but he has the feeling that there might be something in them, and he had better be safe. There are many people whose religion is founded on a kind of vague fear of what might happen if they leave God out of the reckoning. But real religion is not founded on fear, but on the love of God in gratitude for what God has done, and the desire for God in order to find life. There is too much religion which is a kind of superstitious ritual to avert the possible wrath of the unpredictable gods.

So Jesus pointed to the true worship. God, He said, is Spirit. Immediately a man grasps that, a new flood-light breaks in on him. If God is Spirit, God is not confined to *things*; and therefore idol worship is not only an irrelevancy, it is an insult to the very nature of God. If God is Spirit, God is not confined to *places*; and therefore to limit the worship of God to Jerusalem or to any other place is to set a limit to that which by its nature overpasses all limits. If God is Spirit, a man's gifts to God must be gifts of the spirit. Animal sacrifices, man-made things become insufficient and inadequate. The only gifts that befit the nature of God are the gifts of the spirit—love, loyalty, obedience, devotion. A man's spirit is the highest part of a man. That is the part of him which lasts when the physical part of him has vanished. That is the part of him which dreams the dreams and sees the visions, which, because of the weakness and faultiness of the body and the physical part of man, may never be carried out. It is the spirit of a man which is the source and origin of his highest dreams and thoughts and ideals and desires. The true, the genuine worship is when man, through his spirit, attains to friendship and intimacy with God. True and genuine worship is not to come to a certain place; it is not to go through a certain ritual or liturgy; it is not even to bring certain gifts. True worship is when the spirit, the immortal and invisible part of man, speaks to and meets with God, who is immortal and invisible.

So this passage closes with the great declaration. There had opened before this Samaritan woman a vista which bewildered and staggered her. Here were things which were beyond her understanding, things full of wonder. All that she could say was: " When the Messiah, the Christ, the Anointed One of God comes, then we will know all about it." Jesus said to her: " I who am speaking to you am he." It is as if Jesus said this is not a dream of the truth; this *is* the truth itself.

SHARING THE WONDER

John 4: 27-30

> Upon this His disciples came up; and they were in a state of amazement that He was talking to a woman; but no one said: " What are you looking for? " or, " Why are you talking to her? " So the woman left

her water-pot, and went away to the town and said to the people: " Come and see a man who told me all things that I have done! Can this be the Anointed One of God? " They came out of the town and were coming to Him.

THERE is little wonder that the disciples were in a state of bewildered amazement when they returned from their errand to the town of Sychar and found Jesus talking to the Samaritan woman. We have already seen the Jewish idea of women. The Rabbinic precept ran: " Let no one talk with a woman in the street, no, not with his own wife." The Rabbis so despised women and so thought them incapable of receiving any real teaching that they said: " Better that the words of the law should be burned than delivered to women." They had a saying: " Each time that a man prolongs converse with a woman he causes evil to himself, and desists from the law, and in the end inherits Gehinnom." By Rabbinic standards Jesus could hardly have done a more shatteringly unconventional thing than to talk to this woman. Here is Jesus taking the barriers down.

Then there follows a curiously revealing touch. It is the kind which could hardly have come from anyone except from one who had actually shared in this scene. However staggered the disciples might be, it did not occur to them to ask the woman what she was looking for, or to ask Jesus why He was talking to her. They were beginning to know Jesus; and they had already arrived at the conclusion that however surprising Jesus' actions were, if He did them, they were not to be questioned. A man has taken a great step to real discipleship when he learns to say: " It is not for me to question the actions and the demands of Jesus. My prejudices and my conventions must go down before His actions and commands."

By this time the woman was on her way back to the village without her water-pot. The fact that she had left her water-pot showed two things. It showed that she was in a hurry to share this extraordinary experience, and it showed that she never dreamed of doing anything else but coming back. The whole action of this Samaritan woman has much to tell us of real Christian experience.

(i) Her experience began with being compelled to face herself and to see herself as she was. The same thing happened to Peter. After the draft of fishes, when Peter suddenly discovered something of the majesty of Jesus, all that Peter could say was: " Depart from me; for I am a sinful man, O Lord " (*Luke* 5: 8). Our Christian experience will often begin with a humiliating wave of self-disgust. It usually happens that the last thing that a man sees is himself. And it often happens that the first thing that Christ does for a man is to compel him to do what he has spent his life refusing to do—to look at himself.

(ii) The Samaritan woman was staggered by Christ's ability to see into her heart. She was amazed at His intimate knowledge of the human heart, and of her heart in particular. The Psalmist was awed by that same thought. " Thou understandest my thoughts, afar off. . . . There is not a word in my tongue, but, lo, O Lord, Thou knowest it altogether " (*Psalm* 139: 1-4). It is told that once a small girl heard a sermon by C. H. Spurgeon, and whispered to her mother at the end of it: " Mother, how does he know what goes on in our house? " There are no wrappings and disguises which are proof against the gaze of Christ. It is His power to see into the depths of the human heart. It is not that He sees only the evil of it; He sees also the sleeping hero in the soul of every man. He is like the surgeon who sees the evil and the diseased thing, but who also sees the health which will follow when the evil thing is taken away.

(iii) The first instinct of the Samaritan woman was to share her discovery. Having discovered this amazing person, she was compelled to share her discovery with others. The Christian life is based on the twin pillars of discovery and communication. No discovery is complete until the desire to share it fills our hearts; and we cannot communicate Christ to others until we have discovered Him for ourselves. First to find, then to tell are the two great steps of the Christian life.

(iv) This very desire to tell others of her discovery, killed in this woman the feeling of human shame. She was no doubt an outcast; she was no doubt a byword; the very fact that she was drawing water from this distant well shows how she avoided her neighbours and how they avoided her. But now she ran to tell them of her discovery. A person may have some trouble which he is embarrassed to mention and which he keeps secret, but once he is cured he is often so filled with wonder and gratitude and amazement at the cure that he tells everyone about it. A man may hide his sin; but once he discovers Jesus Christ as Saviour, his first instinct is to say to men: " Look at what I was; and look at what I am; this is what Christ has done for me."

THE MOST SATISFYING FOOD

John 4: 31-34

> Meanwhile His disciples asked Him: " Rabbi! Eat something! " " I have food," He said to them, " of which you do not know." " Surely," His disciples kept saying to each other, " someone can't have given Him something to eat? " " My food," said Jesus to them, " is to do the will of Him who sent me and to complete His work."

ONCE again this passage follows the normal pattern of the conversations of the Fourth Gospel. Jesus says something which is misunderstood. He says something which has an inner and a spiritual meaning. It is at first taken with an uncomprehending literalism and then slowly He unfolds the meaning and the meaning is grasped and realised. This is exactly the same as Jesus did when He talked to Nicodemus about being born again, and when He talked to the woman about the water which quenched the thirst of the heart for ever.

By this time the disciples had come back with food, and they asked Jesus to eat. They had left Him so tired and exhausted that they were worried that He did not seem to want to eat any of the provisions which they had brought back. It is always a strange thing how a great task can lift a man above and beyond bodily needs. All his life Wilberforce, who freed the slaves, was a little, insignificant, ailing creature. When he rose to address the House of Commons the members at first used to smile at this queer little figure; but as the fire and the power came from the man they used to crowd the benches whenever he rose to speak. As it was put: " The little minnow became a whale." His message, his task, the flame of truth, and the dynamic of power conquered his physical weakness. There is a picture of John Knox preaching in his old age. He was a done old man; he was so weak that he had to be half lifted up the pulpit steps and left supporting himself on the book-board; but before he had long begun his sermon the voice had regained its old trumpet-call, and he was like " to ding the pulpit into blads (to knock the pulpit into splinters) and leap out of it." The message filled the man with a kind of divine and supernatural strength.

Jesus' answer to His disciples was He had food of which they knew nothing. In their simplicity they wondered if someone had brought Him food to eat. Then He told them: " My food is to do the will of Him who sent me."

The great keynote of Jesus' life is submission to the will of God. The uniqueness of Jesus lies in the very fact that He was the only person who ever was or who ever will be perfectly obedient to the will of God. It can be truly said that Jesus is the only person in all the world who never did what He liked, and who always did what God liked. He was God-sent. Again and again the Fourth Gospel speaks of Jesus being *sent* by God. There are two Greek words used in the Fourth Gospel for this sending. There is *apostellein* which is used seventeen times and *pempein* which is used twenty-seven times. That is to say, no fewer than forty-four times the Fourth Gospel speaks, or shows us Jesus speaking, about His being sent by God. Jesus was one who was under orders. He was God's man. Then once Jesus had come, again and again He spoke of the work that was given Him to do. In *John* 5: 36 He speaks of the works which His Father has given Him to do. In 17: 4 His only claim is that He has finished the work His Father gave Him to do. When He speaks of taking up and laying down His life, of living and of dying, He says: " This commandment have I received of my Father " (10: 18). He speaks continually, as He speaks here, of *the will of God.* " I came down from heaven," He says, " not to do my own will, but the will of Him that sent me " (6: 38). " I do always those things," He says, " that please Him " (8: 29). In 14: 23 He lays it down, out of His personal experience and on His personal example, that the only proof of love lies in the keeping of the commandments of the one a man claims to love. This obedience of Jesus was not a thing which at one moment flickered and flamed and at another died. It was not, as it is with us, a spasmodic obedience. It was the very essence and being, the mainspring and the core, the dynamic and the moving power of His life.

It is His great desire that we should be as He is.

(i) To do the will of God is the only way to peace. There can be no peace when we are at variance with the King of the universe.

(ii) To do the will of God is the only way to happiness. There can be no happiness when we set out human ignorance against the divine wisdom of God.

(iii) To do the will of God is the only way to power. When we go our own way we have nothing to call on but our own power, and therefore collapse is inevitable. When we go God's way we go in God's power, and therefore victory is secure.

THE SOWER, THE HARVEST AND THE REAPERS

John 4: 35-38

> " Are you not in the habit of saying: ' Four months, and the harvest will come '? Look you! I say to you, lift up your eyes and look at the fields, because they are already white for the harvesting. The harvester receives his reward and stores up fruit which makes for eternal life, so that he who sows and he who harvests may rejoice together. In this the saying is true—one sows and another harvests. I have sent you to harvest a crop which your labour did not produce. Others have laboured, and you have entered into their labours."

ALL this that was happening in Samaria had given Jesus a vision of a world to be harvested for God. When Jesus said: " Four months, and the harvest will come," we are not to think that He was speaking of the actual time of year that it was in Samaria at that time. If that were so, it would have been somewhere round about January. There would have been no exhausting heat; and there would have been no scarcity of water; one would not have needed a well to find water; it would have been the rainy season, and there would have been water everywhere. What Jesus is doing is that He is quoting a proverb. The Jews had a sixfold division of the agricultural year. Each division was held to last two months—seedtime, winter, spring, harvest, summer and the season of extreme heat. Jesus is saying: " You have got a proverb; if you sow the seed, you must wait for at least four months before you can hope to begin to reap the harvest." And then Jesus looked up. Sychar is in the midst of a region that is still famous for its corn. Agricultural land is very limited in stony, rocky Palestine. Practically nowhere else in the country could a man look up and see the waving fields of golden corn. So Jesus swept His gaze and His hand round. " Look," He said, " the fields are white and ready for the harvest. They took four months to grow; but in Samaria there is a harvest for the reaping *now*." For once, it is the *contrast* between nature and grace of which Jesus is thinking. In the ordinary harvest men sowed and waited; in Samaria things had happened with such divine suddenness that the word was sown and on the spot the harvest waited. H. V. Morton has a specially interesting suggestion about this passage about the fields white for the harvest. He himself was sitting on this very spot where the well was. As he sat he saw the people come out from the village and start to climb the hill. They came in little batches; and they were all wearing white robes and the white robes stood out against the ground and the sky. It may well be that just at this moment in the story the people started to flock out to Jesus in response to the woman's story. As they streamed out in their white robes across the fields perhaps Jesus said: " Look at the fields! See them now! They are white to the harvest! " The white-robed crowd was the harvest which He was eager to reap for God.

So Jesus went on to show that the incredible had happened. The sower and the harvester could rejoice at the same time. Here was something that no man might expect. To the Jew sowing time was a sad and a laborious time; it was harvesting time which was the time of joy. " They that sow in tears shall reap in joy. He that goeth forth and weepeth bearing precious seed shall doubtless come again with rejoicing, bringing his sheaves with him " (*Psalm* 136: 5, 6). But there is something else hidden below the surface here. The Jews had their dreams of the golden age, the age to come, the age of God, when the world would be God's world, when sin and sorrow would be done away with, and God would reign supreme. Amos paints his picture of it: " Behold the days come, saith the Lord, that the plowman shall overtake the reaper, and the treader of grapes him that soweth seed " (*Amos* 9: 13). " Your threshing shall reach unto the vintage, and the vintage shall reach unto the sowing time " (*Leviticus* 26: 5). It was the dream of that golden age that sowing and reaping, planting and harvesting, would follow hard upon the heels of each other. There would be such fertility that the old days of waiting would be at an end. So we see what Jesus is gently doing here. His words are nothing less than a claim that with Him the golden age has dawned; God's time is here; the time when the waiting is ended and the word is spoken and the seed is sown and the harvest waits.

But there was another side to that—and Jesus knew it. "There is another proverb," He said, "and it too is true—one sows and another harvests." Then Jesus went on to make two applications of that. (*a*) He told His disciples that they would reap a crop which had been produced not by their labour. He meant that *He* was sowing the seed, that in His Cross above all the seed of the love and the power of God was sown, and that the day would come when the disciples would go out into the world, and reap the harvest that His life and His death and His Cross had sown. (*b*) He told His disciples that the day would come when *they* would sow and others would reap. There would be a time when the Christian Church sent out its evangelists; they would never see the harvest; some of them would die as martyrs, but the blood of the martyrs would be the seed of the Church. It is as if He said: "Some day you will labour and you will see nothing for it. Some day you will sow and you will pass from the scene before the harvest is reaped. Never fear! Never be discouraged! The sowing is not in vain; the seed is not wasted! Others will see the harvest which it was not given to you to see."

So in this passage there are two things.

(i) There is *the reminder of an opportunity*. The harvest waits to be reaped for God. There come times in history when men are curiously and strangely sensitive to God. What a tragedy it is that Christ's Church at such a time fails to reap Christ's harvest!

(ii) There is *the reminder of a challenge*. It is given to many a man to sow but not to reap. Many a ministry succeeds, not by its own force and merits, but because of some saintly man who lived and preached and died and left an influence which was greater in his absence than in his presence. Many a man has to work and never sees the results of his labours. I was once taken round an estate which was famous for its rhododendrons. Its owner loved the acres of them and knew them all by name. He showed me certain seedlings which would take twenty-five years to flower. He was nearly seventy-five. He would never see their beauty—*but someone would.* No word for Christ and no great undertaking ever fail. If we do not see the result of our labours others will. There is no room for despair in the Christian life.

THE SAVIOUR OF THE WORLD

John 4: 39-42

> Many of the Samaritans from that city believed on Him, because of the woman's story, for she testified: " He told me all things that I have done." So when the Samaritans came to Him, they asked Him to stay amongst them, and He stayed there two days. And many more believed when they heard His word, and they said to the woman: " No longer do we believe because of your talk. We ourselves have listened to Him, and we know that this is really the Saviour of the World."

IN the events which happened at Samaria we have the pattern by which the gospel so often spreads. In the rise of belief among the Samaritans there were three stages.

(i) There was introduction. The Samaritans were, as it were, introduced to Christ by the woman. It is here that we see full-displayed God's need of us. As Paul had said: " How shall they hear without a preacher? " (*Romans* 10: 14). The word of God must be transmitted by man to man. God cannot deliver His message to those who have never heard it unless there is someone to deliver it.

" He has no hands but our hands
　　To do His work to-day:
He has no feet but our feet
　　To lead men in His way:
He has no voice but our voice
　　To tell men how He died:
He has no help but our help
　　To lead them to His side."

It is at once our precious privilege and our terrible responsibility that it is our task to bring men to Christ. The
introduction cannot be made unless there is a man to
make it. Further, that introduction is made on the strength
of personal witness. The cry of the Samaritan woman was:
" Look what He has done for me and to me." It was not
to a theology and a theory that she called her neighbours;
it was to a dynamic and changing and recreating power.
The Church can only expand until the kingdoms of the
world become the kingdoms of the Lord when men and
women themselves experience the power of Christ, and
then transmit that experience to others.

(ii) There was nearer intimacy and growing knowledge.
Once the Samaritans had been introduced to Christ, they
sought His company. They asked Him to stay with them
that they might learn of Him and come to know Him
better. It is true that a man must be introduced to Christ,
but it is equally true that once he has been introduced
he must himself go on to live in the presence of Christ.
It is possible to bring a man into the presence of Christ,
but after that the man must himself go on to discover
Christ for himself. No man can go through an experience
for another man. Others can put us into the position
when the experience is open to us, but they cannot go
through the experience for us. Others may lead us to the
friendship of Christ, but we must claim and enjoy that
friendship ourselves.

(iii) There comes discovery and surrender. And here we
see what that discovery is. The Samaritans discovered

in Christ the Saviour of the World. It is not likely that they themselves put it in exactly that way. We must remember that John was writing years afterwards, and he is putting the discovery of the Samaritans into his own words, words which enshrine the discovery of a lifetime's living with and thinking about Jesus Christ. It is only in John that we find this tremendous title. We find it here and in I *John* 4: 14. To him it was the title *par excellence* by which Christ must be known. John did not invent the title. In the Old Testament God had often been called the God of Salvation, the Saviour, the saving God. Many of the Greek gods had acquired this title Saviour. At the time John was writing it was actually a title of the Roman Emperor. The Emperors were invested with the title Saviour of the World. It is as if John said: " All that you have dreamed of and longed for and waited for, has at last in Jesus come true." We do well to remember this title. Jesus was not simply a *prophet*, who came with a message in words from God. He did not come only with a prophet's fiery rebuke and a prophet's flame of truth. Jesus was not simply an *expert psychologist* with an amazing insight and knowledge of human nature, and with an uncanny faculty for seeing into the human mind. True, He showed that very skill in the case of the Samaritan woman, but He showed more than that. Jesus was not simply a *pattern and an example.* He did not come simply to show men the way in which life ought to be lived and to leave them a demonstration of life. A great example can be merely a heart-breaking and frustrating thing when we find ourselves powerless to follow it. Jesus was *Saviour.* That is to say, He rescued men from the evil and hopeless situation in which they found themselves; He broke the chains that bound them to the past and gave them a power and a presence which enabled them to meet the future. The Samaritan woman is in fact the great example of His saving power. The town where she stayed would no doubt have labelled her a character beyond reformation;

and she herself would no doubt have agreed that a respectable life was beyond her. But Jesus came and He doubly rescued her; He enabled her to break away from the past and He opened a new future to her. There is no title adequate to describe Jesus except the title the Saviour of the World.

THE UNANSWERABLE ARGUMENT

John 4: 43-45

> Two days after Jesus left there and went to Galilee. Jesus Himself declared that a prophet has no honour in his own country. But when He came into Galilee, the Galilaeans welcomed Him, because they had seen all that He had done at Jerusalem at the Feast, for they too had gone to the Feast.

ALL the three synoptic gospels tell of the saying of Jesus that a prophet has no honour in his own country (*Mark* 6: 4; *Matthew* 13: 57; *Luke* 4: 24). It was indeed an ancient proverb with something the same meaning as our own proverb which says that " familiarity breeds contempt." But John here introduces it in a very strange place. The other gospels introduce it on occasions when it did happen that Jesus was rejected by His own countrymen; John introduces it on an occasion when He was actually accepted. It may be that on this occasion John is reading the mind of Jesus. We have already seen that Jesus had left Judaea and had set out for Galilee to avoid the controversy that an increasing publicity was bringing to Him. The hour of conflict had not yet come (*John* 4: 1-4). It may be that Jesus' astonishing success in Samaria had actually surprised Himself; His words about the astonishing harvest have the ring of glad surprise about them. And it may well be that Jesus set out for Galilee, hoping to find rest and retirement there, because He did not expect those of His native country to respond to Him. And it may be that exactly the same happened in Galilee as happened in

THE GOSPEL OF JOHN

Samaria, that against all expectations and beyond all hopes there was a surge of response to His teaching. We must either explain this saying in this way, or we must assume that somehow it has crept into the wrong place here.

However that may be, this passage and the passage before give us the unanswerable argument for Christ. The Samaritans believed in Jesus, not because of someone else's story, but because they themselves had heard Him speak and they had never in their lives listened to anything like the things He had to say. The Galilaeans believed in Jesus, not because someone had told them about Him, but because they had seen Him do in Jerusalem things the like of which they had never hoped to see any man do. The Samaritans had themselves heard Jesus speaking; the Galilaeans had themselves seen Jesus acting; and the words He spoke and the deeds He did were arguments to which there was no answer.

Here we have one of the great truths of the Christian life. *The only real argument for Christianity is a Christian experience.* It may be that sometimes we have to argue with people until the intellectual barriers which they have erected are battered down and the citadel of their mind capitulates. It may be that we have to present Christianity to people in some cases in such a way that intellectual conviction follows upon the presentation. But in the great majority of cases the only persuasion that we can use is to say to people: " I know what Jesus is like, and I know what Jesus can do. All that I can ask you to do is to try Him yourself and to see what happens." In the last analysis no one can convince a man of what an experience is like; all that can be done is to invite him to undertake the steps which will enable him to undergo the same experience. It is true that the intellectual understanding must some time follow. But effective Christian evangelism really begins when we can say: " I know what Christ has done for me," and when we go on to say: " Try Him, and see what He can do for you." Here again the tremendous personal responsibility is laid upon us. No one is likely to attempt the experience unless our own lives show the value of the experience. There is little use in telling people that Christ will bring them joy and peace and power, if our own lives are grumbingly and discontendedly gloomy, anxiously worried and harassed, obviously frustrated and defeated. To win men for Christ our lives must be such that it obviously means something when we say: " Look at what Jesus Christ has done for me." Men will only be persuaded to try the experiment when they see that for us the experiment has ended in an experience which is beyond argument to be desired.

A COURTIER'S FAITH

John 4: 46-54

So again He came to Cana in Galilee, where He had made the water into wine. Now there was a certain courtier whose son was ill in Capernaum. When this man heard that Jesus had come from Judaea into Galilee, he went to Him and asked Him to come down and heal his son, for he was going to die. Jesus said to him: " Unless you see signs and wonders you will never believe." The courtier said to Him: " Sir, come down before my little lad dies." Jesus said to him: " Go your way! Your son lives! " The man believed the word which Jesus spoke to him, and started on his way home. While he was still on the way down, his slaves met him and said: " Your son lives! " So he asked them at what hour his condition had improved. They told him: " Yesterday, at one o'clock in the afternoon, the fever left him." The father knew that that was the hour at which Jesus said to him: " Your son lives! " And he and his whole household believed.

This is the second sign which Jesus did after He had come from Judaea into Galilee.

Most of the commentators think that this is another version of the story of the healing of the centurion's

servant which is told in *Matthew* 8: 5-13 and *Luke* 7: 1-10.
It may be so, but there are differences which justify us in
treating it as a quite independent story. There are certain
things about the conduct of this courtier which are an
example to all men.

(i) *Here is a courtier who came to a carpenter.* In Greek
the man is called a *basilikos*. The word could even mean
that he was a petty king. But it is used for a royal official,
and this man was a man of high standing at the court of
Herod. Jesus on the other hand had no greater status
than that of the village carpenter of Nazareth. Further,
Jesus was in Cana and this man lived in Capernaum, and
Cana is almost twenty miles away from Capernaum. That is
what explains why he took so long to get back home.
Here then is a courtier coming twenty miles to ask the
help of a carpenter. There could be no more improbable
scene in the world than an important court official hastening
twenty miles to beg a favour from a village carpenter.
First and foremost, this courtier swallowed his pride.
He was in need, and neither convention nor custom stopped
him bringing his need to Christ. Beyond a doubt his
action would cause a sensation but he did not care what
people said so long as he obtained the help he so much
wanted. If we want the help which Christ can give we must
be humble enough to swallow our pride and not to care
what any man may say. The first essential is such a sense
of need that pride and convention have no place in life at all.

(ii) *Here is a courtier who refused to be discouraged.* Jesus
met him with the at first sight bleak statement that people
would not believe unless they were supplied with signs
and wonders. It may well be that Jesus aimed that saying,
not so much at the courtier himself, as at the crowd that
must have gathered to see the outcome of this sensational
happening. They would be there all agape and all agog
to see what would happen. It was perhaps to these sensation-
mongers that Jesus was speaking. But Jesus had a way

of making sure that a person was in earnest. He did that to the Syro-Phoenician woman (*Matthew* 15: 21-28). If the man had turned irritably and petulantly away; if he had been too proud to accept a rebuke; if he had given up despairingly on the spot—Jesus would have known that his faith was not real. A man must be in earnest before the help of Christ comes to him.

(iii) *Here was a courtier who had faith.* It must have been hard for him to turn away and go home with Jesus' assurance that his little lad would live. Nowadays men are beginning to realize the power of thought and the power of telepathy in such a way that no one would reject this miracle simply because it was wrought at a distance. But it must have been difficult for the courtier. Yet he had faith enough to turn and walk back on that twenty mile road with nothing but Jesus' assurance to comfort his heart. It is of the very essence of faith that we should believe that what Jesus says is true. So often we have a kind of vague, nebulous, wistful longing that the promises of Jesus are true. The only way really to enter into them is to believe in them with the clutching intensity of a drowning man. If Jesus says a thing, it is not a case of " It *may* be true "; it is a case of " It *must* be true."

(iv) *Here was a courtier who surrendered.* He was not a man who got out of Christ what he wanted and then went away to forget. He and all his household believed. That would not be easy for him, for the idea of Jesus as the Anointed One of God must have cut across all his pre-conceived notions. To him it must have been a staggering fact that the carpenter from Nazareth was the Messiah. It would not be easy at the court of Herod to profess faith in Jesus. He would have mockery and laughter to endure; and no doubt there would be those who thought that he had gone slightly mad. But this courtier was a man who faced and accepted the facts. He had seen what Jesus could do; he had experienced it; and there was nothing left for it but surrender. He had begun with a sense of desperate need; that need had been supplied; and his sense of need had turned into an overwhelming and an overmastering love—and that must always be the story of the progress of the Christian life.

Most New Testament scholars think that at this point in the Fourth Gospel the chapters are in the wrong order and have somehow or other become misplaced. They hold that chapter 6 should come *before* chapter 5. The reason for this view is this. Chapter 4 finishes with Jesus in Galilee (*John* 4: 54). Chapter 5 begins with Jesus in Jerusalem. Chapter 6 again shows us Jesus in Galilee. Chapter 7 begins with the implication that Jesus had just come into Galilee because of the opposition which He met in Jerusalem. The changes between Jerusalem and Galilee become very difficult to follow. On the other hand chapter 4 (4: 54) ends: " This is the second miracle that Jesus did, when He was come out of Judaea into Galilee." Chapter 6 begins (6: 1): " After these things Jesus went over the Sea of Galilee," which is an entirely natural sequence. Chapter 5 then shows us Jesus going up to Jerusalem for a Feast and meeting with very serious trouble with the Jewish authorities. We are in fact told that from that time they began to persecute Him (5: 10). Then chapter 7 begins by saying that Jesus went to Galilee and " would not walk in Jewry, because the Jews sought to kill Him" (7: 1). It is certainly true that the sequence of the events is much clearer if chapter 6 be read before chapter 5. In our own studies we have not altered the order; but we must note that many New Testament scholars think that the chapters should come in the order chapter 4, chapter 6, chapter 5, and that that order does give an easier and more natural order of events.

MAN'S HELPLESSNESS AND CHRIST'S POWER

John 5: 1-9

> After this there was a Feast of the Jews, and Jesus
> went up to Jerusalem. In Jerusalem, near the sheep-
> gate, there is a bathing-pool with five porches, which
> is called in Hebrew Bethzatha. In these porches
> there lay a crowd of people who were ill and blind
> and lame and whose limbs were withered (waiting
> expectantly for the moving of the water. For an
> angel of the Lord came down into the pool every now
> and then and disturbed the water; so the first person
> to go in after the disturbing of the water regained
> his health from any illness which had him in its grip).
> There was a man there who had been ill for thirty-
> eight years. When Jesus saw him lying there, and
> since He knew that he had already been there for a
> long time, He said to him: " Do you want to be
> made well? " The sick man answered: " Sir, I have no
> one to hurry me into the pool when the water is
> disturbed; so, while I am on the way, someone gets
> down before me." Jesus said to him: " Get up!
> Lift your bed! and walk! " And the man was made
> well, and he lifted up his bed and walked.

THERE were three Jewish Feasts which were feasts of
obligation. Every adult male Jew who lived within twenty
miles of Jerusalem was legally bound to attend them.
These Feasts were three in number—Passover, Pentecost
and the Feast of Tabernacles. If we assume that chapter 6
should come before chapter 5 we may think of this Feast
as Pentecost, because the events of chapter 6 happened
when the Passover was near (*John* 6: 4). The Passover
was in mid-April, and Pentecost was seven weeks later;
and Pentecost would be the next official Feast in the Jewish
calendar. John always shows us Jesus attending the great
Feasts, for Jesus did not disregard the obligations which
Jewish worship laid upon the people. To Jesus it was not
a duty but a delight to worship with His own people.

When Jesus arrived in Jerusalem He was apparently
alone. In this section there is no mention of His disciples.
He found His way to a famous pool. The name of the pool

was either *Bethesda*, which means House of Mercy, or more likely, *Bethzatha* which means House of the Olive. The better manuscripts all have the second name, and we know from Josephus that there was a quarter of Jerusalem which was actually known as Bethzatha. The word for *pool* is *kolumbēthron*, which comes from the verb *kolumban*, which means *to dive*. The pool was such that it was deep enough to swim in. The passage which we have put in brackets is not in any of the greatest and the best manuscripts, and it was probably added later as an explanation of what people were doing at that pool. Beneath the pool there was a subterranean stream, and every now and again the stream bubbled up and disturbed the waters of the pool; and the belief was that the disturbance was caused by an angel, and that the first person to get into the pool after the angel had troubled it would be healed from any illness from which he might be suffering.

To us this sounds like a mere superstition, as indeed it is. But it was the kind of belief which was spread all over the world in ancient days and which still exists in certain places. In the ancient days people believed in all kinds of spirits and demons. The air, as they thought, was thick with them. These spirits and demons had their homes and abodes in certain places. Every tree, every river, every stream, every hill, every pool had its resident spirit. Further, ancient peoples were specially impressed with the sacredness and the holiness of water and especially of rivers and springs. Water was so precious, rivers in spate could be so powerful, water could be so dangerous that it is not surprising that they were so impressed. In the west it may be that we know water only as something which comes out of a tap; but in the ancient world, and in many places still to-day, water is the most precious of all things, and water can be the most dangerous of all things. Sir J. G. Frazer in *Folk-lore in the Old Testament* (ii, 412-423) quotes many instances of this reverence for water. Hesiod, the Greek poet, said that when a man was about to ford a river, he should pray and wash his hands, for he who wades through a stream with unwashed hands incurs the wrath of the gods. When the Persian king Xerxes came to the Strymon in Thrace his magicians offered white horses and went through other ceremonies before the army ventured to cross. Lucullus, the Roman general, offered a bull to the River Euphrates before he crossed it. To this day, in south-east Africa some of the Bantu tribes believe that rivers are inhabited by demons or malignant spirits and that they must be propitiated by flinging a handful of corn or some other offering into the river before it is crossed. When anyone is drowned in a river he is said to be " called by the spirits." The Baganda in Central Africa would not try to rescue a man carried away by a river because they thought that the spirits had taken him. This belief in the sacredness of rivers and streams and springs was once universal and still exists. The people who waited for the pool in Jerusalem to be disturbed were children of their age believing the things of their age.

It may be that as Jesus walked around, the man of this story was pointed out to him as a chronic and a most pitiable case, because his disability made it very unlikely, even impossible, that he would ever be the first to get into the pool after it had been troubled. He had no one to help him in, and Jesus was always the friend of the friendless, and the helper of the man who has no earthly help. Jesus did not trouble to read the man a lecture on the useless superstition of waiting for the water to be troubled. Jesus' one desire was to help, and with His word of power He healed the man who had waited so long.

In this story we can see very clearly the conditions under which the power of Jesus operated. It is to be noted that Jesus speaks in imperatives. He gave His orders, His commandments to men, and it was in proportion as they tried to obey that power came to them.

(i) Jesus began by asking the man if he wanted to be cured. It is not so foolish a question as it may sound. The man had waited for thirty-eight years and it might well have been that hope had died, and left behind it a passive and dull despair. It might well be that in his heart of hearts the man might be well content to remain an invalid, for, if he was cured, he would have to shoulder all the burden of making a living and accepting his own responsibilities again. There are invalids for whom invalidism is a not unpleasant thing, because someone else does all the working and all the worrying. But this man's response was immediate. He wanted to be healed, though he did not see that he ever could be healed, for he had no one to help him. The first essential towards receiving the power of Jesus is the intense desire for it. Jesus comes to us and says: " Do you really want to be changed? " If in our inmost hearts we are well content to stay as we are there can be no change for us. The desire for the better things must be surging in our hearts.

(ii) So Jesus went on to tell the man to get up. It is as if Jesus said to the man: " Man, bend your will to it! Make a supreme effort and you and I will do this thing together! " The power of God never dispenses with the effort of man. No man can sit back and relax and expect a miracle. Nothing is truer than that we must realize our own helplessness; but in a very real sense it is true that a miracle happens when our will and God's power co-operate to make it possible.

(iii) In effect Jesus was commanding the man to attempt the impossible. " Get up! " said Jesus. The man might well have said with a kind of injured resentment that that was the one thing he could not do. His bed would simply be a light stretcher-like frame—the Greek word is *krabbatos*, which is a colloquial word and really means a pallet— and Jesus told him to pick it up and carry it away. The man might well have said that for thirty-eight years his bed had been carrying him and that there was not much sense in telling him to carry the bed. But again the man made the effort along with Christ—and the thing was done.

(iv) Here is the road to achievement. There are so many things in this world which beat us and defeat us and conquer us. When there is in us intensity of desire, when there is in us the determination to make the effort, although it may seem hopeless, then the power of Christ gets its opportunity, and with Christ we conquer that which for so long has conquered us.

THE INNER MEANING

John 5: 1-9 (continued)

BEFORE we leave this passage we must note that there are certain scholars who think that it is an allegory. They think that the man and the scene have an inner meaning. In the allegory the inner truth is said to be this.

The *man* stands for the people of Israel. The *five porches* stand for the five books of the law. In the porches the people lay ill, and yet uncured. The law was that which could show a man his sin, but which could never mend it; the law was that which could uncover a man's weakness, but which could never cure it. The law, like the porches, sheltered the sick soul but could never heal it. The *thirty-eight years* stand for the thirty-eight years in which the Jews wandered in the desert before they entered the promised land; or they stand for the number of the centuries for which men had been waiting for the Messiah. All this long time men had been waiting—and now the power of God had come. The *stirring of the waters* stands for baptism. In point of fact in early Christian art a man is often depicted as rising from the baptismal waters carrying a bed upon his back.

It may well be that it is now possible to read all these meanings into this story; but it is highly unlikely that John wrote it as an allegory. The whole story has the vivid stamp of truth and of fact. But we would do well to remember this—that any Bible story has in it far more than fact. There are deeper truths below the surface and even the simple stories are meant to leave us face to face with eternal things.

HEALING AND HATRED

John 5: 10-18

> It was Sabbath on that day. So the Jews said to the man who had been cured: " It is Sabbath and you have no right to lift your bed." He answered them: " He who made me well, it was He who said to me: ' Lift your bed and walk! ' " They asked him: " Who is the fellow who said to you: ' Lift your bed and walk '? " The man who had been cured did not know who He was, for Jesus had slipped away, for there was a crowd in the place. Afterwards Jesus found him in the Temple and said to him: " Look now! You have been made well. Sin no more in case something worse happens to you! " The man went away and told the Jews that it was Jesus who had made him well. Because of this the Jews were out to persecute Jesus, because He had done these things on the Sabbath. But Jesus answered them: " My Father continues His work until now, and so do I continue mine." Because of this the Jews tried all the harder to find a way to kill Him, because not only was He habitually breaking the Sabbath, but He also kept on saying that God was His own Father, thereby making Himself equal with God.

A MAN had been healed from a disease which, humanly speaking, was incurable. Anyone would have thought that this was a matter of joy and thanksgiving and rejoicing. But there were those who met the whole business with bleak and black looks. The man who had been healed was walking through the streets carrying his bed; the orthodox Jews stopped him, and reminded him that he was breaking the law by lifting and carrying a burden on the Sabbath day. We have already seen what the Jews did with the law of God. The law had been a series of great wide principles which a man had been left to apply and to carry out for himself. They, throughout the years, had become a mass of thousands of little rules and regulations. The law had simply said that the Sabbath day must be different from other days, and that on it neither a man nor his servants nor his animals must work. The Jews had set to to define what work was. They had set out thirty-nine different classifications of work. One of these classifications was that work consisted in carrying a burden. They founded particularly on two passages. Jeremiah had said: " Thus saith the Lord: take heed to yourselves and bear no burden on the Sabbath day, nor bring it in by the gates of Jerusalem; neither carry forth a burden out of your houses on the Sabbath day, neither do ye any work, but hallow the Sabbath day as I commanded your fathers " (*Jeremiah* 17: 19-27). Nehemiah had been worried at the work and the trading that went on on the Sabbath day, and he had stationed servants at the gates of Jerusalem to see that no burdens were carried in or out on the Sabbath (*Nehemiah* 13: 15-19). Now the Nehemiah passage (*Nehemiah* 13: 15) makes it perfectly clear that what was in question was trading on the Sabbath day as if it had been an ordinary day. But the Rabbis of Jesus' day solemnly argued that a man was sinning if he carried a needle in his robe on the Sabbath. They even argued as to whether he could wear his artificial teeth or his wooden leg. They were quite clear that any kind of brooch could not be worn on the Sabbath. To them all this petty detail was a matter of life and death—and certainly the man was breaking the rabbinic law by carrying his bed on the Sabbath day.

The man's defence was that the man who had healed him had told him to do it, and he did not know who the man was. Later Jesus met him in the Temple. As soon as the man discovered who Jesus was he hastened back to the authorities to tell them who had told him to carry his bed. He did not mean to get Jesus into trouble, but the actual words of the law were: "If anyone carries anything from a public place to a private house on the Sabbath intentionally he is punishable by death by stoning." The man was simply trying to extricate himself from the situation in which he found himself. He was simply trying to explain that it was not his fault that he had broken the law.

So the authorities levelled their accusations against Jesus. He habitually broke the Sabbath law. The verbs in verse 18 are *imperfect tense*, which describes not merely one single action in past time, but repeated action in past time. Clearly this story is only a sample of what Jesus habitually did.

Jesus' defence was wholly shattering. His defence was that God did not stop working on the Sabbath day, and that neither did He. Here was an argument of which any scholarly Jew would see the full force. Philo had said: "God never ceases doing, but as it is the property of fire to burn and snow to chill, so it is the property of God to do." God was for ever doing. As another writer said: "The sun shines; the rivers flow; the processes of birth and death go on on the Sabbath as on any other day; and that is the work of God." True, according to the creation story, God rested on the seventh day; but He rested from *creation*; His higher works of judgment and mercy and compassion and love still went on. It was *only* from creation He rested. So Jesus said: "Even on the Sabbath God's love and mercy and compassion act; *and so do mine.*" It was this last passage which shattered the Jews, for it meant nothing less than that the work of Jesus and the work of God were the same. To them it seemed that Jesus was putting Himself on an equality with God. What Jesus really was saying we shall see in our next section; but at the moment we must note this—it is the teaching of Jesus that human need must always be helped; that there is no greater task than to relieve someone's pain

179

and distress; that no day can be made a reason for with-holding help that might be given; that the compassion of the Christian must be like the compassion of God—unending and unceasing. Other work may be laid aside, but the work of compassion can never be laid aside.

There is one other Jewish belief which enters into this passage. When Jesus met the man in the Temple He told him to sin no more in case something worse yet might happen to him. To the Jew sin and suffering were inextri-cably and inevitably connected. If a man suffered, neces-sarily he had sinned. Nor could he ever be cured until his sin was forgiven. The Rabbis said: " The sick arises not from his sickness, until his sins be forgiven." Now the man might argue that he had sinned and had been forgiven and had, so to speak, got away with it; and he might go on to argue that, since he had found someone who could release him from the consequences of sin, he could very well go on sinning and escaping. There were those in the Church who used their liberty as an excuse for the flesh (*Galatians* 5: 13). There were those who sinned in the confidence that grace would abound (*Romans* 6: 1-18). There have always been those who have used the love and the forgiveness and the grace of God as an excuse to sin. We have only to think what God's forgiveness cost, we have only to look at the Cross of Calvary, to know that we must for ever hate sin with a perfect hatred, because every sin breaks again the heart of God.

THE TREMENDOUS CLAIMS

John 5: 19-29

> This is the truth I tell you—the Son cannot do any-thing which proceeds from Himself. He can only do what He sees the Father doing. In whatever way the Father acts, the Son likewise acts in the same way; for the Father loves the Son and has shown Him everything that He does. And He will

show Him greater works than these, so that you will be moved to wondering amazement. For, as the Father raises the dead and makes them alive, so also the Son makes alive those whom He wishes. Neither does the Father judge anyone, but He has given the whole process of judging to the Son, that all may honour the Son, as they honour the Father. He who does not honour the Son does not honour the Father who sent Him.

This is the truth I tell you—he who listens to my word and believes on Him who sent me has eternal life, and is not on the way to judgment, but he has crossed from death to life.

This is the truth I tell you—the hour is coming and now is when the dead will hear the voice of the Son of God, and, when they have heard, they will live. For, as the Father has life in Himself, so He has given to the Son to have life in Himself; and He has given Him authority to exercise the process of judgment, because He is the Son of Man. Do not be astonished at this, for the hour is coming when everyone in the tombs will hear His voice, and will come forth; those who have done good will come out to a resurrection which will give them life, but those whose actions were base will come out to a resurrection which will issue in judgment.

HERE we come to the first of the long discourses of the Fourth Gospel. When we read passages like this we must remember that John is not seeking so much to give us the words that Jesus spoke as the things which Jesus meant. He was writing somewhere round about A.D. 100. For seventy years he had thought about Jesus and about the wonderful things which Jesus had said. Many of these things he had not fully understood when he had heard them from the lips of Jesus. But more than half a century of thinking under the guidance of the Holy Spirit had shown John deeper and deeper meaning in the words of Jesus. And so he sets down for us, not only what Jesus said, but also what Jesus meant. In the light of the thought of his mind, and in the light of the guidance of the Holy Spirit, he unfolds and expands the words of Jesus.

This passage is so important that we must first study it as a whole and then we must divide it up into shorter sections and think about each one of them in turn.

First, then, let us look at this passage as a whole. When we turn to a passage like this, we must try to think, not only about how it sounds to us, but we must also try to think how it sounded to the Jews who heard it for the first time. They had a background of thoughts and of ideas; they had a background of theology and of belief; they had a background of literature and of religion which is not our background, and which is very far from our background; and, to understand a passage like this, we must try to think ourselves back into the mind of a Jew who listened to it for the first time.

When we do that, this is an amazing passage, because it is woven together of thoughts and claims and expressions every one of which is a claim by Jesus to be the promised Messiah, the Anointed One of God. Many of these claims we do not now readily see, because we do not live in the same atmosphere and background as the Jews did; but these claims would be crystal clear to a Jew, and would leave him standing aghast as he listened to such things.

(i) The clearest claim is the plain statement that Jesus is the Son of Man. We know how common that strange title is in the gospels and in the speech of Jesus. It has a long history. It was born in the *Book of Daniel* in *Daniel* 7: 1-14. In that passage the Authorised Version mistranslates it. The Authorised Version has it that the seer sees one coming who is like unto *the Son of Man* (*Daniel* 7: 13). There should be no capital letter at *Son*, and it should not be *the* Son of Man, but *a* son of man. The point of the passage is this. *Daniel* was written in days of terror and of persecution, and it is a vision of the glory which will some day take the place of the suffering in the midst of which the people are. In *Daniel* 7: 1-7 the seer described the great heathen empires which have held sway under the guise and the symbolism of beasts. There is the lion with eagle's wings (7: 4), which stands for the Babylonian Empire. There is the bear with the three ribs in his mouth, as one devouring the carcase (7: 5), which stands for the Median Empire. There is the leopard with four wings and four heads (7: 6), which stands for the Persian Empire. There is the beast, great and terrible, with iron teeth and with ten horns (7: 7), which stands for the Macedonian Empire. All these terrible powers will pass away and the power and the dominion will be given to one *like a son of man*. The meaning is that the Empires which have held sway have been so savage and so cruel and so sadistic and so destructive and so terrible that they could only be described in terms of wild beasts; but into the world there is going to come a power, so gentle, so kind, so generous, so humane, that it will be a power which is human and not bestial. The new power will be humane and gentle, not savage and bestial any more. In *Daniel* the phrase describes the kind of power which is going to rule the world.

But very naturally, someone has to introduce that power; someone has to exercise that power; and the Jews took this title, this description, and gave it to the chosen one of God who some day would bring in the new age of gentleness and love and peace; and so they came to call the Messiah *Son of Man*. Between the Old and the New Testaments there arose a whole literature which dealt with the golden age which was to come. One of the books which was specially influential was the *Book of Enoch* and in it there appears again and again a great figure called *That Son of Man*, who is waiting in heaven until God sends Him to earth to bring in His kingdom and to rule over it. So when Jesus called Himself the Son of Man, He was doing nothing less than call Himself the Messiah, the Chosen One, The Anointed One of God. Here was a claim so clear that it could not be misunderstood.

(ii) But not only is this claim to be God's Messiah made in so many words; in phrase after phrase it is implicitly there. The very miracle which had happened to the paralysed man was a sign that Jesus was Messiah. It was Isaiah's picture of the new age of God that " then shall the lame man leap as an hart " (*Isaiah* 35: 6). It was Jeremiah's vision that the blind and the lame would be gathered in (*Jeremiah* 31: 8, 9). The miracle itself, wherein the lame walked, was nothing less than a Messianic claim and sign.

(iii) There is Jesus' repeated claim to raise the dead and to be their judge when they are raised. Now in the Old Testament God alone can raise the dead and God alone has the right to judge. " I, even I, am he and there is no god with me: I kill and I make alive " (*Deuteronomy* 32: 39). " The Lord killeth and maketh alive " (I *Samuel* 2: 6). When Naaman, the Syrian, came seeking to be cured from leprosy, the king of Israel said in bewildered despair: " Am I God to kill and to make alive? " (2 *Kings* 5: 6). The function of killing and making alive belonged inalienably to God. It is the same with judgment. " The judgment is God's " (*Deuteronomy* I: 17). In later thought this function of resurrecting the dead and then acting as judge became part of the duty of God's Chosen One when He brought in the new age of God. *Enoch* says of the Son of Man: " The sum of judgment was committed to him " (*Enoch* 69: 26, 27). Jesus in our passage speaks of those who have done good things being resurrected to life and of those who have done evil things being resurrected to death. *The Apocalypse of Baruch* lays it down that when God's age comes: " The aspect of those who now act wickedly shall become worse than it is, as they shall suffer torment," whereas those who have trusted in the law and acted upon it shall be clothed in beauty and in splendour (*Baruch* 51: 1-4). *Enoch* has it that in that day: " The earth shall be wholly rent asunder, and all that is on earth shall perish, and there shall be judgment on all men " (*Enoch* I: 5-7). *The Testament of Benjamin* has it: " All men shall rise, some to be exalted, and some to be humbled and put to shame."

The significance of this passage is hidden to us until we read it against its Jewish background, and until we ask ourselves how it would sound to the Jews who heard it for the first time. To them it would be at once clear that Jesus was claiming rights which belonged to God alone; that He was declaring that the things which marked the dawn of the age of God had begun to happen; that He was claiming functions and privileges and powers which belonged to the Messiah and to no one else. When we really understand the meaning of this passage we see that it is nothing else than a series of deliberate claims to be the Chosen One of God.

And when we understand that, this passage becomes not simply a discourse of Jesus. It becomes an act of the most extraordinary and unique courage. Jesus must have known well that to speak like this would sound the sheerest blasphemy to the orthodox Jewish leaders of His day. He must have known that to speak like this was to court death. It is His claim to be King; and He knew well that the man who listened to words like this had only two alternatives—the listener must either accept Jesus as the Son of God, or he must hate Him as a blasphemer and seek to destroy Him. There is hardly any passage where Jesus appeals for men's love and defies men's hatred as He does here.

We must now go on to take this passage section by section.

THE FATHER AND THE SON

John 5: 19, 20

> This is the truth I tell you—the Son cannot do anything which proceeds from Himself. He can only do what He sees the Father doing. In whatever way

the Father acts, the Son likewise acts in the same way; for the Father loves the Son, and has shown Him everything that He does. And He will show Him greater works than these, so that you will be moved to wondering amazement.

THIS is the beginning of Jesus' answer to the Jews to the charge that He was making Himself equal to God. In this passage Jesus lays down three things about His relationship with God.

(i) He lays down His *identity* with God. To see Jesus in action is to see God in action. The things that God does are the things that Jesus does; and the things that Jesus does are the things that God does. The great, salient truth about Jesus is that in Jesus we see God. If we wish to see how God feels to men, if we wish to see how God reacts to sin, if we wish to see how God regards the human situation, we must look at Jesus. The mind of Jesus is the mind of God; the words of Jesus are the words of God; the actions of Jesus are the actions of God.

(ii) But this identity is not so much based on equality as it is based on complete *obedience*. Jesus does not do anything which proceeds from Himself. Jesus never did what He wanted to do; He always did what God wanted Him to do. It is because the will of Jesus was completely submitted to the will of God that we do see God in Him. Jesus' identity with God is not based on independence of God, but on complete dependence on God. His identity is not based on independence but on submission. Jesus is to God as we must be to Jesus.

(iii) But this obedience is not based on the submission to power; it is based on *love*. The unity between Jesus and God is a unity of love. We speak of two minds having only a single thought, and two hearts beating as one. In human terms that is a perfect description of the relationship between Jesus and God. The love between Father and Son is so intimate, so close that Father and Son are one.

There is such complete understanding, such complete identity of mind and will and heart, that Father and Son are one.

But this passage has something still more to tell us about Jesus.

(i) It tells us of His complete *confidence*. He is quite sure that what men were seeing then was only a beginning; He was quite certain that they would see even greater things than they had seen. On purely human grounds the one thing that Jesus might reasonably expect was death. The forces of Jewish orthodoxy were gathering against Him and the end was already certain. But Jesus was quite certain that the future was in the hands of God and not of men. He did not fear anything that men could do to Him, and He never dreamed that men could stop what God had sent Him to do.

(ii) It tells of His complete *fearlessness*. That He would be misunderstood was quite certain. That His words would simply inflame the minds of His hearers and endanger His own life was beyond argument. There was no human situation in which Jesus would lower His claims or adulterate the truth. He would make His claim and speak His truth no matter what men might threaten to do. To Him it was much more important to be true to God than to respect or to fear men.

LIFE, JUDGMENT AND HONOUR

John 5: 21-23

> For as the Father raises the dead and makes them alive, so the Son also makes alive those whom He wishes. Neither does the Father judge anyone, but He has given the whole process of judging to the Son, that all may honour the Son, as they honour the Father. He who does not honour the Son does not honour the Father who sent Him.

HEREIN we see three great functions which belong to Jesus Christ, as the Son of God.

(i) He is *the giver of life*. John meant this in a double sense. He meant it *in time*. No man is fully alive until Jesus Christ enters into him and he enters into Jesus Christ. When we make the discovery of the realm of music or of literature or of art or of travel, we sometimes speak of a new world opening out to us. That man into whose life Jesus Christ has entered finds life made new. He himself is changed; his personal relationships are changed; his conception of work and duty and pleasure are changed; his relationship to God is changed. Life is redirected, recreated, remade. He meant it in *eternity*. John meant that, after this life is ended, for the man who has accepted Jesus Christ there opens life still more full and still more wonderful; while for the man who has refused Jesus Christ, after life has ended, there comes that death which is separation from God. For John—as for us—Jesus Christ is the one who gives us life in this world and life in the world to come.

(ii) He is *the bringer of judgment*. John says that God committed the whole process of judgment to Jesus Christ. What he means is this—a man's judgment depends on his reaction to Jesus. If the man finds in Jesus the altogether lovely, if, in spite of failures, he finds in Jesus the one person to be loved, obeyed, adored and followed, then that man is on the way to life. But if he sees in Jesus nothing but an enemy, if in Jesus for him there is nothing lovely and nothing to be desired, that man has condemned himself. Jesus is the touchstone by which all men are tested; reaction to Him is the test by which all men are divided. Simply by being Himself and confronting men with Himself, He brings judgment to men.

(iii) Jesus is *the receiver of honour*. The most uplifting thing about the New Testament is its unquenchable hope and its unconquerable certainty. It tells the story of a crucified Christ and yet it never has any doubt that at the end of all the days all men will be drawn to that crucified figure and that all men will know Him and acknowledge Him and love Him. Amid persecution and disregard, in spite of smallness of numbers and poverty of influence, in the face of failure and disloyalty, the New Testament and the early Church never doubted the ultimate triumph of Christ. Even when Jesus was hated, He never doubted the ultimate victory of love. Even when He was faced with the Cross, He never doubted the ultimate conquest. When we are tempted to despair we would do well to remember that the salvation of men is the plan and the purpose of God, and that nothing, in the end, can frustrate the will of God. The evil will of man can delay God's purpose; it cannot defeat it.

ACCEPTANCE MEANS LIFE

John 5: 24

> This is the truth I tell you—he who listens to my word and believes on Him who sent me has eternal life, and is not on the way to judgment, but he has crossed from death to life.

HERE Jesus says quite simply that to accept Him is life; and to reject Him is death. What does it mean to listen to Jesus' word and to believe in the Father who sent Him? To put it at its briefest it means three things. (i) It means to believe that God is as Jesus says He is; it means to believe that God is love and so to enter into a new and intimate relationship with Him, in which fear is banished and we rest in Him. (ii) It means to accept the way of life that Jesus offers us, however hard and difficult it may be, and whatever sacrifices it may involve, certain that to accept it is the ultimate way to peace and to happiness, and to refuse it is the ultimate way to death and judgment. (iii) It means to accept the help that the Risen Christ gives to us and the guidance that the Holy Spirit offers us, and so to find strength for all that the way of Christ involves. When we do that we enter into three new relation ships. (i) We enter into a new relationship with God. The judge becomes the father; the distant becomes the near; strangeness becomes intimacy and fear becomes love. (ii) We enter into a new relationship with our fellow men. Hatred becomes love; selfishness becomes service; and bitterness becomes forgiveness. (iii) We enter into a new relationship with ourselves. Weakness becomes strength; frustration becomes achievement; and tension becomes peace.

To accept the offer of Jesus Christ is to find life. Everyone in one sense may be said to be alive; but there are few people who can be said to know life in the real sense of the term. Most people exist, but they do not live. When Grenfell was writing to a nursing sister about her decision to come out to Labrador to help in his work there, he told her that he could not offer her much money, but that if she came she would discover that in the work of serving Christ and the people of the country she would have the time of her life. Browning describes the meeting of two people into whose hearts love had entered. She looked at him; he looked at her as a lover can, and " suddenly life awoke." A modern novelist makes one character say to another: " I never knew what life was till I saw it in your eyes." The person who accepts the offer and the way of Christ has passed from death to life. In this world life becomes a new and a thrilling thing; in the world to come eternal life with God becomes a certainty.

DEATH AND LIFE

John 5: 25-29

This is the truth I tell you—the hour is coming and now is when the dead will hear the voice of the Son of God, and, when they have heard, they will live. For, as the Father has life in Himself, so He has given to the Son to have life in Himself. And He has given Him authority to exercise the process of judgment, because He is the Son of Man. Do not be astonished at this, for the hour is coming when everyone in the tombs will hear His voice and will come forth; those who have done good will come out to a resurrection which will give them life, but those whose actions were base will come out to a resurrection which will issue in judgment.

HERE of all sections in this passage the Messianic claims of Jesus stand out most clearly and unmistakable. He is the Son of Man. He is the life-giver and the life-bringer. He will raise the dead to life, and, when they are raised, He will be the judge who will assign their destiny to them. It is Jesus' direct claim to exercise all the functions of the Messiah, of the Chosen One of God, and to be the Anointed One who will introduce the new age, the age of God.

In this passage John seems to use the word *dead* in two senses.

(i) He uses it of those who are spiritually dead. To the spiritually dead Jesus will bring new life. What does it mean to be spiritually dead? (*a*) To be spiritually dead is *to have stopped trying*. It is to have accepted oneself as one is. It is to have come to look on all faults as ineradicable and all virtues as unattainable. It is to have given up all hope of progress. The Christian life cannot stand still. It must either go on or slip back. And to stop trying is to abandon even the attempt at progress and therefore to slip back to death. (*b*) To be spiritually dead is to *have stopped feeling*. There are many people who at one time felt intensely in face of the sin and the sorrow and the suffering of the world. But slowly they have become used to it; they have become insensitive. They can look at evils and feel no indignation; they can look at sorrows and feel no answering sword of grief and pity pierce their heart. When compassion dies the heart is dead. (*c*) To be spiritually dead is *to have stopped thinking*. J. Alexander Findlay tells of a saying of a friend of his—" When you reach a conclusion you're dead." He meant that when a man's mind becomes so shut that it can accept no new truth, then that man may be physically alive, but he is mentally and spiritually dead. The day when the desire to learn leaves us, the day when new truth, new methods, new thought become simply a disturbance with which we cannot be bothered, is the day of our spiritual death. To the Christian, life and the discovery of new truth are synonymous terms. (d) To be spiritually dead is *to have stopped repenting*. The day when a man can sin in peace is the day of his spiritual death. The day when a man does not care whether he sins or not, when sin loses its horror, when he does a wrong thing without a regret and without a struggle, is the day when his soul is dead. On that day the heart is petrified. It is easy to slip into that frame of mind. The first time we do a wrong thing we do it with fear and regret. If we do it a second time it is easier to do it. If we do it a third time it is easier yet. If we go on doing it the time comes when we do it almost without a thought. To avoid spiritual death a man must keep himself sensitive to sin by keeping himself sensitive to the presence of Jesus Christ.

(ii) But John, in this passage, also uses the word *dead* literally. It is Jesus' teaching that the resurrection will come, and that what happens to a man in the after-life is inextricably bound up with what he has done in this life. There is a popular advertisement which says: " How you feel to-morrow depends on what you do to-day." The terrible importance of this life is that it determines eternity. All through life we are fitting or unfitting ourselves for the life which is to come; we are making ourselves fit or unfit for the presence of God. In this life we can choose the way which leads to life or the way which leads to death. It is the tremendous truth that every deed we do in this life is either making or marring a destiny, winning or losing a crown. In this life a man can either make himself fit to win life, or he can commit that most terrible and tragic of all things—spiritual suicide.

THE ONLY TRUE JUDGMENT

John 5: 30

> I cannot do anything which originates in myself. As I hear, so I judge. But the judgment which I exercise is just, because I do not seek to do what I wish to do, but I seek to do what He who sent me wishes me to do.

IN the preceding passage Jesus has claimed the right of judgment. It was not unnatural that men should ask Him by what right He proposed to judge others. Jesus' answer was that His judgment was true and final because He had no desire to do anything other than the will of God, and to speak the words that God gave Him to speak, and to think the thoughts that God gave Him to think. It was Jesus' claim that, when He judged, His judgment was the judgment of God. It was the basis on which He judged people which gave Him the right to judge; for that basis was nothing else than the mind of God.

It is very difficult for any man to judge another man fairly. If we will honestly and frankly examine ourselves we will see that many motives affect our judgment, and that our judgment is based on many things. Our judgment may be rendered unfair by *injured pride*. It may be rendered blind and unjust by our *prejudices*. It may be made bitter by *jealousy*. It may be made arrogant by *contempt*. It may be made harsh by *intolerance*. It may be made condemnatory by *self-righteousness*. It may be affected by our own *self-conceit*, and may be based on *envy* and not on justice. It may be quite invalid because we do not know, and have never tried to know, anything about the circumstances of the person whom we judge. That is to say, it may be vitiated by a blind or insensitive or deliberate *ignorance*. It is only a man whose heart is pure and whose motives are completely unmixed who can judge another man—and that is to say that no man can judge any other man.

On the other hand the judgment of God is based on the character of God and must be perfect.

God alone is *holy* and therefore God alone knows the standards by which all men and all things must be judged. God alone is perfectly *loving* and God's judgment alone is delivered in the charity in which all true judgment must be given. God alone has full *knowledge*, the knowledge of a man's mind, his trials, his troubles, his temptations. Judgment is only perfect when it takes into account *all* the circumstances and only God can do that.

The claim of Jesus to judge is based on the claim that in Him there is the perfect mind of God. He does not judge with the inevitable mixture of human motives; He judges with the perfect holiness, the perfect love and the perfect sympathy of God.

WITNESS TO CHRIST

John 5: 31-36

> If I bear witness about myself, my witness need not be accepted as true; but it is Another who is bearing witness about me, and I know that the witness which He bears about me is true. You sent your envoys to John, and he bore witness to the truth; but the testimony which I receive is not from any man, but I say these things that you may be saved. He was the lamp which burns and shines. For a time you were pleased to take pleasure in his light. But I have a greater testimony than John's. The works which the Father granted to me to accomplish, the very works which I do, are evidence about me to prove that my Father has sent me.

ONCE again Jesus is answering the charges of His opponents. His opponents are demanding, " What evidence can you adduce that your claims are true? " They are saying in effect, " You are making the most startling and the most far-reaching claims. What evidence do you bring to support them? " In this whole passage Jesus is arguing in a way

that the Rabbis would understand. He is using their own
methods, and following their own rules of argument.

(i) Jesus begins by admitting the universal principle
that the unsupported evidence of one person cannot be
taken as proof. Before a thing could be taken as proved
there must be at least two witnesses. " At the mouth of
two witnesses, or three witnesses, shall he that is worthy
of death be put to death; but at the mouth of one witness
he shall not be put to death " (*Deuteronomy* 17: 6). " One
witness shall not rise up against a man for any iniquity,
or for any sin, in any sin that he sinneth; at the mouth
of two witnesses, or at the mouth of three witnesses shall
the matter be established " (*Deuteronomy* 19: 15). When
Paul threatens to come to the Corinthians with rebuke
and discipline he says that all his charges will be confirmed
by two or three witnesses (2 *Corinthians* 13: 1). It is
Jesus' instruction that when a Christian has a legitimate
complaint against a brother he must take with him some
others to confirm the charge (*Matthew* 18: 16). In the
early Church it was the rule that no charge against an
elder would be entertained unless it was supported by
two or three witnesses (1 *Timothy* 5: 19). Jesus began by
fully admitting the normal Jewish law of evidence. Further,
it was universally held that a man's evidence about himself
could not be accepted. The *Mishnah* said: " A man is
not worthy of belief when he is speaking about himself."
Demosthenes, the great Greek orator, lays it down as a
principle of justice: " The laws do not allow a man to give
evidence on his own behalf." Ancient law well knew that
self-interest and self-protection had an effect on any man's
statements about himself. So Jesus accepts the normal
Jewish standards and regulations of justice, and agrees
that His own unsupported testimony to Himself need
not be true.

(ii) But there are other witnesses to Him. He says that
Another is His witness, and by Another He means God.
He will return to that, but for the moment He cites the

witness of John the Baptist. Repeatedly John had borne witness to Him (*John* 1: 19, 20, 26; 1: 29; 1: 35, 36). Then Jesus pays a tribute to John and issues a rebuke to the Jewish authorities. He says that John was the lamp which burns and shines. That was the perfect tribute to John. (*a*) A lamp bears a borrowed light. It does not light itself; it is lit. (*b*) John had warmth, for his message was not the cold message of the intellect but the burning message of the kindled heart. (*c*) John had light. The function of light is to guide, and John pointed men on the way to repentance and to God. (*d*) In the nature of things a lamp burns itself out. In giving light it consumes itself. John was to decrease while Jesus increased. The true witness burns himself out for God. But, in paying tribute to John, Jesus rebukes the Jews. They were pleased to take pleasure in John for a time. They never really took John seriously. They were, as one has put it, like " gnats dancing in the sunlight," or like children playing while the sun shone. John was a pleasant sensation, to be listened to as long as he said the things they liked, and to be abandoned whenever he became awkward. There are many people who still listen to God's truth like that. They enjoy a sermon as a performance. A famous preacher tells how after he had preached a sombre sermon on judgment, he was greeted with the comment of thanks: " That sermon was sure cute! " God's truth is not a thing by which to be pleasantly titillated; it is not something to be enjoyed; it is often something to be received in the dust and ashes of humiliation and repentance. But Jesus did not even plead John's evidence. He said that it was not the human evidence of any fallible man which He was going to adduce to support His claims.

(iii) So Jesus adduces the witness of His works. He had done that when John had sent from prison to ask if Jesus was the Messiah, or if they must look for another. He had told John's enquiring envoys to go back and tell John what they saw happening (*Matthew* 11: 4; *Luke* 7: 22).

But Jesus adduced the witness of His works, not to point to Himself, but to point to the power of God which was working in Him and through Him. He cites His works, not to glorify Himself, but to point to the God beyond, whose works they are. So then Jesus cites His supreme witness—and that witness is God.

THE WITNESS OF GOD

John 5: 37-43

> And the Father who sent me has borne witness about me. You have never heard His voice, nor have you ever seen His form. You do not have His word dwelling in you, because you do not believe in the One whom He sent. You search the scriptures, because you think that in them you have eternal life. It is they which bear witness about me, yet you refuse to come to me that you may have life. I receive no glory from men; but I know you and I know that you do not have the love of God in you. I came in the name of my Father and yet you do not receive me. If another comes in his own name, you will receive him.

THE early part of this section may be taken in two ways.

(i) It may be that it refers to the unseen witness of God in a man's heart. In his first letter John wrote: " He who believes in the Son of God, has the witness (of God) within " (I *John* 5: 9, 10). The Jew would have insisted that no man has ever seen God, or can ever see God. Even in the giving of the Ten Commandments " ye heard the voice of the words but saw no similitude; only ye heard a voice " (*Deuteronomy* 4: 12). So this may mean: " It is true that you have never seen God; it is true that you have never directly heard His voice; it is true that God is invisible; and so is His witness; for His witness is the response which rises in the human heart when a man is confronted with Christ." When we are confronted with Christ we see in Him the altogether lovely and the altogether wise; that conviction is the witness of God in our

197

hearts. The Stoics held that the highest kind of knowledge comes not by thought; it comes by what they called "arresting impressions." A conviction comes to a man and seizes him like someone laying an arresting hand on his shoulder. With all his heart he believes, although he cannot tell how or why. It may be that Jesus here means that the conviction in our hearts of the supremacy of Christ is the witness of God to Christ within.

(ii) It may be that John is really meaning that God's witness to Christ is to be found in the scriptures. To the Jew the scriptures were all in all. " He who has acquired the words of the Law has acquired eternal life." " He who has the Law has a cord of grace drawn around him in this world and in the world to come." " He who says that Moses wrote even one verse of the Law in his own knowledge is a despiser of God." " This is the book of the commandments of God and the Law that endureth for ever. All they that hold it fast are appointed to life, but such as leave it shall die " (I *Baruch* 4: 1, 2). " If food which is your life but for an hour, requires a blessing before and after it be eaten, how much more does the Law in which lies the world that is to be, require a blessing? " The Jew had the Law; he searched the Law; and yet he failed to recognize Christ when He came. What was wrong? We have here the astonishing fact that the best Bible students in the world, the people with the greatest reverence for scripture, the people who meticulously and consistently and continuously read scripture, rejected Jesus Christ. How could that happen?

One thing is clear—they read scripture in the wrong way.

(i) They read scripture with a shut mind. They read scripture, not to search for God and to listen to God, but to find arguments to support their own positions, and to find defences for their own beliefs. They did not really love God; they loved their own ideas about God. Because of that the word did not abide in them. Water had as much chance of getting into concrete as the word of God had of getting into their minds. They did not take themselves to scripture; they brought scripture to themselves. They did not humbly learn a theology from scripture; they used scripture to defend a theology which they themselves had produced. It is still the supreme danger in Bible reading that we should use the Bible to prove our beliefs and not to test our beliefs.

(ii) But they made a still bigger mistake than that. They regarded God as having given men a written revelation. Now the revelation of God is a revelation in history. Revelation is not God speaking, but God acting. And the Bible itself is not God's revelation; it is *the record* of God's revelation. They worshipped the words. They completely forgot that God's revelation shows itself in events. There is only one way to read the Bible—to read it as all pointing to Jesus Christ, and to read it in the light of Jesus Christ. Then many of the things which puzzle us, and sometimes distress us, are clearly seen as stages on the way; then we see event after event as a climbing up, a pointing forward to Jesus Christ, who *is* the supreme revelation, and by whose light all other revelation is to be tested. The Jews worshipped a God who wrote and not a God who acted and therefore when Christ came they did not recognize Him. The great function of the scriptures is not to give life, but to point to Him who alone can give life to men.

There are two most revealing things here.

(i) Back in verse 34 Jesus had said that He was saying all that He was saying " that you may be saved." Here He says: " I am not looking for any glory from man." What Jesus is saying is this: " I am not arguing like this because I want to win an argument. I am not talking sternly like this because I wish to silence you, and to prove how clever I am and to bring you to heel. I am not talking like this because I want to score off you and win the applause of men. I am talking like this because I love you and I want to save you." There is something tremendous here. When people get up against us, when they oppose us, when they argue with us, when we argue back, what is our main feeling? Is it wounded pride? Is it the conceit that hates any kind of failure? Is it anger? Is it annoyance? Is it a desire to cram our opinions down other people's throats because we think them fools? Jesus only talked as He did because He loved men. His voice never rose to stridency; He never tried to bludgeon men into silence; His voice might be stern, but in the sternness there was still the accent of yearning love. His eyes might flash fire, but the flame was the flame of love.

(ii) Jesus said: " If another comes in his own name, you will receive him." The Jews had their succession of impostors claiming to be the Messiah and every one of them had his following (cp. *Mark* 13: 6, 22; *Matthew* 24: 5, 24). Why do men follow the impostor? They do so because, as someone has said, the impostors are " men whose claims correspond with men's own desires." The impostors came promising empires and victory and the blaze of glory and material prosperity; Jesus came offering a Cross. The characteristic of the impostor is the offer of the easy way. The impostor offers men the easy way to satisfy their own desires; Jesus offered men the hard way of the way of God. But the impostors perished and the Christ lives on.

THE ULTIMATE CONDEMNATION

John 5: 44-47

How can you believe when you are out for the glory that you get from each other, and when you do not search for the glory which comes from the only God? Do not think that it is I who will accuse you to the Father. You have an accuser—it is Moses I mean—on whom you set your hopes. If you had believed in Moses, you would have believed in me, for he wrote about me. If you do not believe in his writings, how will you believe in my words?

It was characteristic of the scribes and Pharisees that they desired the praise of men. They dressed in such a way that everyone would recognize them. They prayed in such a way that everyone would see. They loved the front seats in the Synagogue. They loved the deferential greetings of men on the street. And just because of that they could not hear the voice of God. Why? So long as a man measures himself against his fellow men he will be well content. So long as a man makes it his aim to receive human respect and praise, he can achieve his aim. But the point is not: "Am I as good as my neighbour?" The point is: "Am I as good as God?" The point is not: "Is my scholarship and is my piety greater than that of other people whom I could name?" The point is: "What do I look like to God?" So long as we judge ourselves by human comparisons there is plenty of room for self-satisfaction, and self-satisfaction kills faith, for faith is born of the sense of need. But when we compare ourselves with Jesus Christ, and through Him, with God, we are humbled to the dust, and then faith is born, for there is nothing left to do but to trust to the mercy of God.

So Jesus finishes with a charge that would strike home. We have seen what the Jews thought of the books which they believed that Moses had given them; they believed them to be the very word of God. Jesus said: "If you had read these books aright, you would have seen that they all pointed to me." He went on: "You think that because you have Moses to be your mediator you are safe; but Moses is the very one who will condemn you. Maybe you could not be expected to listen to me, but you are bound to listen to the words of Moses to which you attach such value—and they all spoke of me."

Here there is the great and threatening truth. That which had been the greatest privilege of the Jews had become their greatest condemnation. No one could condemn a man who had never had a chance; no one could condemn a man who had been left in ignorance. But knowledge had been given to the Jews; and the knowledge they had failed to use had become their condemnation. Let us ever remember that the greater our privilege the greater our condemnation. The more chances we have to know the more we are condemned if we fail to know. Responsibility is always the other side of privilege.

THE LOAVES AND FISHES

John 6: 1-13

After these things Jesus went away across the Sea of Galilee, that is, the Sea of Tiberias. A great crowd was following Him, because they were watching the signs which He did on those who were ill. Jesus went up into the hill and He was sitting there with His disciples. The Passover, the Feast of the Jews, was near. When Jesus lifted up His eyes and saw that a great crowd was coming to Him, He said to Philip: "Where are we to buy bread for these to eat?" He was testing Philip when He said this, for He Himself knew what He was going to do. Philip answered Him: " Seven pounds worth of bread is not enough to give each of them a little to eat." One of the disciples said to Him—it was Andrew, Simon Peter's brother—" There is a lad here who has five barley loaves and two little fishes. But what use are they among so many? " Jesus said: " Make the men sit down." There was much grass in the place. So the men sat down to the number of about five thousand. So Jesus took the loaves and gave thanks for them, and divided them up among those who were reclining there. So too He gave them of the fishes, as much as they wished. When they were satisfied, He said to the disciples: " Collect the broken pieces that are left over, so that nothing may be wasted." So they collected them, and they filled twelve baskets with the broken pieces of the loaves which remained over after the people had eaten.

THERE were times when Jesus desired to withdraw from the crowds of men. He was under a continuous strain and He needed rest. It was always necessary that sometimes He should get His disciples alone that He might lead them more deeply into the understanding of Himself. He needed time for prayer and for contact with the power and the presence of God. And on this particular occasion it was wise to withdraw before a head-on collision with the authorities took place, for the time of the final conflict had not yet come.

From Capernaum to the other side of the Sea of Galilee was a distance of about four miles. So Jesus set sail. But the people had been watching with astonishment the amazing things that He did. It was easy to see the direction in which the boat was going; and they hastened round the top of the lake by land. The River Jordan flowed into the Sea of Galilee at the north end. Two miles up the river there were the fords of Jordan. Near the fords there was a village called Bethsaida Julias, to distinguish it from the other Bethsaida in Galilee, and it was for that place that Jesus was making (*Luke* 9: 10). Near Bethsaida Julias, almost on the lakeside, there is a little plain where the grass always grows. Its name is El-Batiyah and it was to be the scene of this wondrous happening. At first Jesus went up into the hill behind the plain and He was sitting there with His disciples. And then the crowd began to appear in droves. It was nine miles round the top of the lake and across the ford, and they had made the journey with all the speed of which they were capable. We are told that the Feast of the Passover was near. There would be even bigger crowds on the roads at that time. Quite possibly many were on the way to Jerusalem by that route. Many Galilaean pilgrims travelled north and crossed the ford and went through Peraca, and then re-crossed the Jordan near Jericho. The way was longer but it avoided the territory of the hated and dangerous Samaritans. It is very likely that the great crowd was swelled by detachments of the pilgrims who were on their way to the Passover Feast and who were already on the road.

At the sight of the crowd Jesus' sympathy was kindled. They were hungry and they were tired, and they must be fed. Philip was the natural man to whom to turn, for he came from Bethsaida (*John* 1: 44) and he would have local knowledge. Jesus asked him where food could be got. Philip's answer was despairing. He said that even if food could be got it would cost more than two hundred *denarii* to give this vast crowd even a little food each. A *denarius* was worth between 8d. and 9d. and it was the standard day's wage for a working man. It was Philip's calculation that it would take more than six months' wages to begin to feed a crowd like this. Then Andrew appeared on the scene. He had discovered a lad with five barley loaves and two little fishes. Quite likely the boy had brought them as a picnic lunch. Maybe he had been out for the day, and as a boy would, had got accidently attached to the crowd. Andrew, as usual, was bringing people to Jesus. The boy had not much to bring. Barley bread was the cheapest of all bread, and was held in contempt. There is a regulation in the *Mishnah* about the offering that a woman who has committed adultery must bring. She must of course bring a trespass offering. With all offerings a meat-offering was made, and the meat offering consisted of flour and wine and oil intermixed. Ordinarily the flour used was made of wheat; but it was laid down that, in the case of an offering for adultery, the flour should be barley flour, for barley is the food of beasts and the woman's sin was the sin of a beast. Barley bread was the bread of the very poor. The fishes would be no bigger than sardines. Pickled fish from Galilee were known all over the Roman Empire. In those days fresh fish was an unheard-of luxury, for there was no means of transporting it any distance and of keeping it in an eatable condition. Small sardine-like fish swarmed in the waters of the Sea of Galilee. They were caught and pickled and made into a kind of savoury. The boy had his little pickled fish to help to make the dry barley bread go down.

So Jesus told the disciples to make the people sit down. He took the loaves and the fishes and He blessed them.

When He did that He was acting as the father of the family. The Jewish grace He used would be the one that was used in every home: " Blessed art Thou, O Lord, our God, who causest to come forth bread from the earth." So the people ate and were filled. Even the word that is used for *filled* (*chortazesthai*) is suggestive. Originally, in classical Greek, it was a word which was used for feeding animals with fodder, and when used of people it meant that they were glutted, sated, fed to repletion.

When the people had eaten their fill, Jesus bade His disciples to gather up the fragments that were left. Why the fragments? At Jewish feasts the regular practice and custom was to leave something for the servants. That which was left was called the *Peah*; and no doubt the people left their usual part for those who had served them with the meal.

Of the fragments twelve baskets were taken up. No doubt each of the disciples had his basket (*kophinos*). The baskets were bottle-shaped. No Jew ever travelled without his *kophinos*. Twice Juvenal (3: 14; 6: 542) talks of " the Jew with his basket and his truss of hay." (The truss of hay was to use as a bed, for many of the Jews lived a gipsy life.) The Jew with his inseparable basket was a notorious figure. He carried the basket partly because he was characteristically acquisitive, and partly because he needed to carry his own food if he was going to observe the Jewish rules of cleanness and uncleanness. So from the fragments the disciples filled, each man, his basket. And so the hungry crowd were fed and more than fed.

THE MEANING OF A MIRACLE

John 6: 1-13 (continued)

WE will never know exactly what happened on that grassy plain near Bethsaida Julias. We may look at it in three ways. (*a*) We may regard it simply as a miracle in which

Jesus literally multiplied loaves and fishes. There may be some who find that very hard to conceive of. And there may be some who find that hard to reconcile with the fact that that is just what Jesus refused to do at his temptations when He refused to turn the stones into bread (*Matthew* 4: 3, 4). If we can believe in the sheerly miraculous character of this miracle, then let us continue to do so. But if we are puzzled, there are two explanations. (*b*) It may be that this was really a sacramental meal. In the rest of the chapter the language of Jesus is exactly the language of the Last Supper, when He speaks about eating His flesh and drinking His blood. It could be that at this meal at El-Batiyah it was but a morsel, like the sacrament, that each person received; and that the thrill and wonder of the presence of Jesus and the reality of God turned the sacramental crumb into something which richly nourished men's hearts and souls. That is something which happens at every Communion Table to this day. (*c*) There may be another and very lovely explanation. It is not really to be thought that the crowd left on a nine-mile expedition without making any preparations at all. If there were pilgrims with them they would certainly possess supplies for the way. But it may be that none of them would produce what they had, for they selfishly—and very humanly—wished to keep it all for themselves. It may then be that Jesus, with that rare smile of His, produced the little store that He and His disciples had; with sunny faith He thanked God for it and shared it out. Moved by His example, everyone who had anything did the same; and in the end there was enough, and more than enough, for all. It may be that this is a miracle in which the presence of Jesus and His loveliness turned a crowd of selfish men and women into a fellowship of sharers. It may be that in the presence of Jesus those whose one thought was to keep were miraculously turned into people whose one thought was to give. It may be that this story represents the biggest miracle of all—a miracle which changed human nature, and altered, not loaves and fishes, but men and women.

However that may be, there were certain people there without whom the miracle would not have been possible.

(i) There was Andrew. There is a contrast between Andrew and Philip. Philip was the man who said: " The situation is hopeless; there is nothing to be done." Andrew was the man who said: " I'll see what I can do; and I'll trust Jesus to do the rest." It was Andrew who brought that lad to Jesus, and by bringing him made the miracle possible. No one ever knows what will happen and what will come out of it when we bring someone to Jesus. If a parent trains up his or her child in the knowledge and the love and the fear of God, no man can say what mighty things that child may some day do for God and for men. If a Sunday School teacher slowly brings a child to Christ, no man knows what that child may some day do for Christ and His Church. There is a tale of an old German school-master who, when he entered his class of boys in the morning, used to remove his cap and bow ceremoniously to them. One asked him why he did this. His answer was: " You never know what one of these boys may some day become." He was right—because one of the boys was named Martin Luther. Andrew did not know what he was doing when he brought that lad to Jesus that day, but he was providing material for a miracle. We never know what possibilities we are releasing when we bring someone to Jesus Christ.

(ii) There was the boy. He had not much to offer but out of what he had Jesus found the materials of a miracle. There would have been one great and shining deed fewer in history if that boy had refused to come or if he had withheld his loaves and fishes. The fact of life is that Jesus Christ needs what we can bring Him. We may not have much to bring but He needs what we have. It may well be that the world is denied miracle after miracle and triumph after triumph because we will not bring to

Christ what we have and what we are. If, just as we are, we would lay ourselves on the altar of the service of Jesus Christ, there is no saying what Christ could do with us and through us. We may be sorry and embarrassed that we have not more to bring—and rightly so; but that is no reason for failing or refusing to bring what we have and what we are. Little is always much in the hands of Christ.

THE RESPONSE OF THE MOB

John 6: 14, 15

> So when the men had seen the sign which He had done, they said: " Truly, this is the prophet who is to come into the world." So Jesus, aware that they were going to come and seize Him to make Him king, withdrew again to the mountain alone.

HERE we have the reaction of the mob. The Jews were waiting for the Prophet whom they believed Moses had promised to them. " The Lord thy God will raise up unto thee a Prophet from the midst of thee, of thy brethren, like unto me; unto him shalt thou hearken " (*Deteronomy* 18: 15). The Jews were waiting for the Messiah, the Chosen One of God. All through their history they had been waiting, and they were waiting then. In that moment at Bethsaida Julias they were willing to accept Jesus as that Prophet and that King. They were willing to carry Him, to sweep Him to power on a wave of popular acclaim and mob support. But it was not so very long before another mob was clamouring: " Crucify Him! Crucify Him! " Why was it at that moment that the mob acclaimed Jesus?

For one thing, the mob was eager to support Jesus when He gave them what they wanted. He had healed them and fed them; and they would thereupon have made Him their leader. There is such a thing as a bought loyalty, a loyalty that depends on favours, on gifts, to put it crudely, on bribes. There is such a thing as cupboard love, a love that is based on what we can get out of people, and on what they can do for us. Dr. Johnson, in one of his more cynical moments, defined gratitude as " a lively sense of favours still to come." The very thought of the attitude of that mob disgusts us. But are we so very different? When we want comfort in sorrow, when we want strength in difficulty, when we want peace in turmoil, when we want help when life has got us down, there is no one so wonderful as Jesus. Then we talk to Him and walk with Him and open our hearts to Him. But when He comes to us with some stern demand for sacrifice, with some challenge to effort, with the offer of some cross, then we will have nothing to do with Him. When we examine our hearts, it may be that we will find that we too love Jesus for what we can get out of Him, and when He comes to us with His great challenges and demands we too grow lukewarm, and even resentful and hostile to this disturbing and demanding Christ.

For another thing, they wished to use Him for their own purposes and to mould Him to their own dreams. They were waiting for the Messiah. But they visualised the Messiah in their own way. They looked for a Messiah who would be King and Conqueror, who would set his foot upon the eagle's neck and drive the Romans from Palestine, who would change the status of Israel from that of a subject nation to that of a world power, who would liberate her from the fate of being an occupied country and exalt her to being the occupier of other nations' countries. They had seen what Jesus could do; and the thought in their minds was: " This man has power, miraculous and marvellous power. If we can harness Him and His power to our dreams and our plans and our desires, things will begin to happen." If they had been honest, they would have had to admit that they wished to make use of Christ. Again, are we so very different? When we appeal to Christ, is it for strength to go on with our own schemes and plans and ideas, or, is it for humility and obedience to accept His plans and wishes? Is our prayer: " Lord, give me strength to do what you want me to do " or, is it in reality: " Lord, give me strength to do what I want to do " ?

That crowd of Jews would have followed Christ at that moment because He was giving them what they wanted, and they wished to use Him for their plans and dreams and purposes. That attitude to Christ still lingers in men's minds. We would like Christ's gifts without Christ's Cross; we would like to use Christ instead of allowing Him to use us.

A VERY PRESENT HELP IN TIME OF TROUBLE

John 6: 16-21

> When evening came, His disciples went down to the sea, and, when they had embarked upon a boat, they started across the sea to Capernaum. By this time darkness had come on, and Jesus had not yet come to them; and the sea was roused because a great wind was blowing. So, when they had rowed between three and four miles, they saw Jesus walking on the sea, and coming near the boat, and they were afraid. But He said to them: " It is I; don't be afraid." So they wished to take Him on board the boat; and immediately the boat reached the land for which they were making.

THIS is one of the most wonderful stories in the Fourth Gospel, and it is all the more wonderful when we press behind it to the original meaning of the Greek and the original incident, and when we find that it really describes, not some extraordinary miracle, but a simple incident in which John found, in a way that he never forgot, what Jesus was like.

First, let us reconstruct the story. After the feeding of the five thousand, and after the attempt to make Him king, Jesus had slipped away to the hills alone. The day wore on. It came to the time which the Jews described as " the second evening," the time between the twilight and the dark. Jesus had still not arrived. We must not think that the disciples were forgetful or discourteous in leaving Jesus behind, for, as Mark tells the story, Jesus sent them on ahead (*Mark* 6: 45), while He persuaded the crowds to go home. Doubtless it was His intention to walk round the head of the lake while they rowed across and to rejoin them in Capernaum. Now John was actually there, and, if ever there was an eye-witness account this is one. This is clearly an incident in which John took part, and about which he had thought for seventy years; and as he thought about it, it became simplicity clad with wonder.

So the disciples set sail. The wind got up, as it can in the narrow, land-locked lake; and the waters were whipped to foam. We must remember that this was Passover time, and Passover time was the time of the full moon (*John* 6: 4). Up on the hillside Jesus had prayed and communed with God; and as He set out the silver moon made the scene almost like daylight; and down on the lake below He could see the boat and the rowers toiling at the oars and He knew that they were making heavy weather of it. So He came down. Now here we must remember two facts. At the north end, as we have seen, the lake was no more than four miles across; and John tells us that the disciples had rowed between three and four miles; that is to say, they were very nearly at their journey's end. It is the natural and inevitable thing to suppose that in the wind they had hugged the shore of the lake, seeking what shelter they might find. That is the first fact, and now we come to the second. They saw Jesus, as the Authorised Version has it, *walking on the sea*. The Greek has it that He was walking *epi tēs thalassēs*. Now that is exactly and precisely, word for word, the same phrase which is used in *John* 21: 1, where it is said that Jesus showed Himself again to His disciples *at the sea* of Tiberias. In *John* 21: 1 this very phrase means beyond argument—it has never been questioned—that Jesus was walking on the seashore. And that is what the phrase means in our passage too. Jesus was walking *epi tēs thalassēs*, by the seashore. The toiling disciples looked up; and suddenly they saw Him; it was all so unexpected, they had been bent so long over their oars, that they were alarmed because they thought that it was a spirit that they were seeing. Then across the waters came that well-loved voice—" It is I; don't be afraid." They wanted Him to come on board; the Greek by far most naturally means that their wish was not fulfilled. Why? Remember the breadth of the northern end of the lake; and remember how far they had rowed. The breadth was four miles; they had rowed between three and four miles. The simple reason was that before they could take Him on board the boat grounded on the shingle, and they were there.

Here is just the kind of story that a fisherman like John would have loved and cherished and remembered. Every time he thought of it he could feel that night again, the grey silver of the moonlight, the rough oar against his hand, the flapping sail, the shriek of the wind, and the sound of the surging water, the astonishingly unexpected appearance of Jesus, the sound of His voice across the waves, and the crunch of the boat as it reached the Galilaean side.

And as he remembered John saw wonders there, wonders which are still there for us.

(i) He saw that Jesus *watches*. Up on the hill Jesus had been watching them. He had not forgotten. He was not too busy with God to think of them. Even in the quiet time they were written on His heart. John suddenly realised that all the time they had pulled at the oars Jesus' loving look was on them. When we are up against it Jesus watches. He does not make things too easy for us. He lets us fight our own battles and win our own victory. He is like a parent watching a son or daughter put up a splendid effort in some athletic contest, and He is proud of us; or, He is like someone watching someone tragically let the side down and He is sad. Life is lived with the loving eye of Jesus upon us.

(ii) He saw that Jesus *comes.* Down from the hillside Jesus came to enable the disciples to make the last pull that would reach safety and dry land. He does not watch us with serene unmoved detachment; He does not watch us, as it were, from the grandstand and from outside. Just when strength is failing and life is too much for us He comes, and with Him there comes the strength for the last spurt and the last effort which lead to victory and to achievement.

(iii) He saw that Jesus *helps.* He watches, He comes and He helps. It is the wonder of the Christian life that there is nothing that we are left to do alone. Margaret Avery tells how there was a teacher in a little country school who had told this story to her children, and she must have told it well. Some short time afterwards there was a blizzard of wind and snow. When school finished the teacher was helping the children home. Sometimes she had practically to drag them through the drifts. When they were all very nearly exhausted with the struggle, she overheard a little boy say, half to himself: " We could be doing with that chap Jesus here now." We could always be doing with Jesus and we never have to do without Him.

(iv) He saw that *Jesus brings us to the haven.* It seemed to John, as he remembered it, that as soon as Jesus arrived the keel of the boat grated on the shingle—and they were there. As the Psalmist had it: " Then are they glad because they be quiet; so he bringeth them unto their desired haven " (*Psalm* 107: 30). Somehow in the presence of Jesus the longest journey is short and the hardest battle easier.

It is one of the loveliest things in the Fourth Gospel, that John, the old fisherman turned evangelist, found all the wealth of Christ in the memory of a fisherman's story.

THE MISTAKEN SEARCH

John 6: 22-27

On the next day, the crowd which was still standing on the far side of the sea, saw that there had only been one boat, and that Jesus had not gone into the boat with His disciples, but that the disciples had gone away alone. But some boats from Tiberias put in near the place where they had eaten the bread, after the Lord had given thanks. So when they saw that Jesus was not there, nor His disciples either, they embarked on the boats, and came to Capernaum, looking for Jesus. When they had found Him on the other side of the sea, they said to Him: " Rabbi, when did you get here? " Jesus answered: " This is the truth I tell you—you are looking for me, not because you saw signs, but because you ate of the loaves until your stomachs were filled. Do not work for the food which perishes, but work for the food which lasts, and which gives eternal life, that food which the Son of Man will give you; for the Father—God— has set His seal upon Him."

THE crowd had lingered on the far side of the lake. In the time of Jesus people did not need to keep office- and working-hours. They had time to wait until He came back to them. They waited because they had seen that there was only one boat, and that the disciples had gone off in that boat without Jesus; and therefore they deduced that Jesus must still be somewhere near at hand. After they had waited for some time, they began to realize that He was not coming back. Into the bay there had come some little boats from Tiberias. No doubt they had been blown there and had taken shelter from the storm of the night. So the people who had waited embarked on them and made the crossing of the lake, back to Capernaum. When they got there they discovered to their surprise that Jesus was already there. They asked Him when He had got there, and how He had succeeded in getting back so soon since His disciples had gone off alone in the boat Now we must notice that to that question Jesus simply did not reply. This was no time to talk of things like that; life was too short for pleasant gossip about journeys. He went straight to the heart of the matter. " You have seen," He said, " wonderful things. You have seen how God's grace enabled a crowd to be fed. Your thoughts ought to have been turned to the God who did these things; but instead all that you are thinking about is bread. In your dull blindness it is bread, and not God, that you are thinking about." It is as if Jesus said: " You cannot think about your souls for thinking of your stomachs." He is rebuking them for an earthbound point of view. They had received bread as bread and not as a gift of God. " Men," as Chrysostom said, " are nailed to the things of this life." Here were people whose eyes never lifted beyond the ramparts of the world to the horizons and the eternities beyond. There is a story of Napoleon. Once he and an acquaintance were talking of life. It was late at night and dark. Napoleon and his friend walked to the window and looked out. There in the sky there were distant stars, little more than pin-points of light. Napoleon had sharp eyes and the friend was dim-sighted. Napoleon pointed to the sky: " Do you see these stars? " he asked the friend. " No," the friend answered. " I can't see them." " That," said Napoleon, " is the difference between you and me." The man who is earthbound is living half a life. It is the man with vision, who looks at the horizon and sees the stars, who is the great man.

So Jesus put His command in one sentence. " Don't work," He said, " for the food which perishes. Work for the food which lasts for ever and which gives eternal life." Long ago a prophet called Isaiah had asked the same question: " Wherefore do ye spend money for that which is not bread? and your labour for that which satisfieth not? " (*Isaiah* 55: 2). There are two kinds of hunger. There is physical hunger which physical food can satisfy; but there is a spiritual hunger which physical food can never satisfy. A man may be as rich as Croesus and may yet have this haunting dissatisfaction, this unsatisfied longing within his heart, this incompleteness in his life. It has been pointed out that in the years just after A.D. 60 the luxury of Roman society was unparalleled. It was at this time that the Romans served feasts of peacocks' brains and nightingales' tongues; that they discovered the odd habit of taking emetics between courses that the next might taste better; that meals costing thousands of pounds were a commonplace. It was at this time that Pliny tells us of a Roman lady who was married in a robe so richly jewelled and gilded that it cost the equivalent of £432,000. There was a reason for all this, and the reason was a deep dissatisfaction, a hunger that nothing could satisfy. They sought for anything for a new thrill and a new taste in life, because they were appallingly rich and appallingly hungry. As Matthew Arnold wrote:

" In his cool hall with haggard eyes,
    The Roman noble lay;
He drove abroad in furious guise
    Along the Appian Way;
He made a feast, drank fierce and fast;
    He crowned his hair with flowers;
No easier nor no quicker passed
    The impracticable hours."

The unsatisfied hunger was there.

It was Jesus' whole point that all that these Jews were interested in was physical satisfaction. They had received an unexpectedly free and lavish meal; and they wanted more. But there are other hungers—and these other hungers can only be satisfied by Jesus Christ. There is the hunger for truth—and He alone can give men truth. There is the hunger for life—and He alone can give men life and give it to them more abundantly. There is the hunger for love—and He alone can give men the love that outlasts sin and death. It is Christ alone who can satisfy the immortal longings and the insatiable hunger of the human heart and soul.

Why can He do that? There is a wealth of meaning wrapped in the phrase: " God has set His seal upon Him." H. B. Tristram in *Eastern Customs in Bible Lands* has a most interesting section on seals in the ancient world. In the east it is not the *signature*, but the *seal* that authenticates. In commercial and political documents it is the seal, imprinted with the signet ring, which really makes the document valid. In the Hellenistic world it was the seal which authenticated a will, the seal on the mouth of a sack or a crate that guaranteed the contents. Tristram tells how in the east even the humblest people use the authenticating seal. On his own eastern journeys when he made an agreement with his muleteers and his porters they set the impression of their seal upon it, to show that it was binding and that they agreed to it. Seals were made of pottery or metal or of jewels. In the British Museum there are the seals of most of the Assyrian kings. The seal was fixed on clay and the clay attached to the document. The document has long since perished but the seal is still there, and without it the document was not valid. Now the Rabbis had a saying: " The seal of God is truth." " One day," says the *Talmud*, " the great synagogue (the assembly of the Jewish experts in the law) were weeping, praying and fasting together, when a little scroll fell from the firmament among them. They opened it and on it was only one word, *Ameth*, which means *truth*. ' That,' said the Rabbi, ' is the seal of God.' " *Ameth* is spelt with three Hebrew letters—*aleph*, which is the first letter of the alphabet, *min* which is the middle letter, and *tau* which is the last. The truth of God is the beginning, the middle and the end of life.

That is why Jesus can satisfy the eternal hunger—He is sealed by God, He is God's truth incarnate. To see Him is to see God; to obey Him is to obey God; to receive Him is to receive God; and God alone can truly satisfy the hunger of the soul which He Himself created, and into which He put the hunger for Himself.

THE ONLY TRUE WORK

John 6: 28, 29

> They said to Him: "What are we to do to work the works of God?" Jesus answered: "This is the work of God, to believe in Him whom He has sent."

WHEN Jesus spoke about working the works of God the Jews immediately thought in terms of doing good works. It was always a Jewish conviction that a man by living a good and moral life could win and earn the favour of God. They held that men could be divided into three classes—those who were good, those who were bad, those who were in between and who, by doing one more good work, could be transferred to the category of the good. So when the Jews asked Jesus what the work of God was they expected Him to lay down rules and regulations and lists of things which they must do. But that is not what Jesus says at all.

The answer of Jesus is extremely compressed and we must expand it and work it out and see what lies behind it. Jesus said that God's work, the work which God wanted a man to do, was to believe in Him whom God had sent. We can put that in another way; we can put it in the way in which Paul would have put it. The one work that God desires from man is *faith*. Now what does faith mean? Faith means a certain *relationship with God*. Faith means being in such a relationship with God that we are friends with God, that we are not terrified of God any more, that God is not our enemy and our prosecutor but our Father and our friend, that we give God the trust and the obedience and the submission which naturally arise from this new relationship. And how does believing in Jesus tie up with that? The whole essence of Christianity is that we would never have known that God is like this had not Jesus come and lived and died to tell us so. It is only because Jesus came to tell us that God is our Father, that God loves us, that God cares, that God wants nothing more than to forgive, it is only because of that that the old strangeness and distance and enmity and suspicion of God are taken away and the new relationship is possible.

But that new relationship issues in a certain kind of life. Now we know what God is like, and our lives must answer to that which we know of God. Our answer will be in three directions, each of which corresponds to that which Jesus told us of God.

(i) God is love, and therefore in our lives there must be a love and a service of others which correspond to the love and the service of God; there must be a forgiveness of others which corresponds to the forgiveness of God.

(ii) God is holiness, and therefore in our lives there must be a purity which corresponds to the holiness of God. We must be holy because God is holy. It is only the pure in heart who may see God.

(iii) God is wisdom, and therefore in our lives there must be a complete and perfect submission and trust which correspond to the wisdom of God. If God is perfectly and completely wise then there is nothing left for us to do but completely to accept all His guidance and all that He sends.

It is Jesus' teaching that the whole essence of the Christian life is a new relationship to God, a relationship which was offered by God, a relationship which was alone made possible by the revelation which Jesus gave us of God, a relationship which issues in the service, the purity and the trust which are the reflection of God. To enter into such a relationship involves such a life, and that is the work which God wishes us and enables us to perform.

THE DEMAND FOR A SIGN

John 6: 30-34

> They said to Him: " What sign are you going to perform that we may see it and believe in you? What is your work? Our fathers ate the manna in the wilder-

ness. As it stands written: ' He gave them bread from heaven to eat.' " Jesus said to them: " This is the truth I tell you—Moses did not give you bread from heaven, but my Father gives you the real bread from heaven. The bread of God is He who comes down from heaven, and gives life to the world." They said to Him: " Sir, always give us that bread."

HERE the argument becomes specifically Jewish in its expression and its assumptions and allusions. Jesus had just made a great claim. The true work of God was to believe in Him. " Very well," said the Jews. " Prove it. This is in effect a claim to be the Messiah. Prove it." Now their thoughts were still on the feeding of the crowd and inevitably that turned their thoughts to the manna in the wilderness. They could hardly help connecting the two things. The manna had always been regarded as the bread of God (*Psalm* 78: 24; *Exodus* 16: 15). Now there was a strong Jewish rabbinic belief that when the Messiah came He would again give the manna. The giving of the manna was held to be the supreme work in the life of Moses and the Messiah was bound to equal and to surpass that work. " As was the first redeemer so was the final redeemer; as the first redeemer caused the manna to fall from heaven, even so shall the second redeemer cause the manna to fall." " Ye shall not find the manna in this age, but ye shall find it in the age that is to come." " For whom has the manna been prepared? For the righteous in the age that is coming. Everyone who believes is worthy and eateth of it." It was the belief that a pot of the manna had been hidden in the ark in the first temple, and that, when the temple was destroyed, Jeremiah had hidden it away and would produce it again when the Messiah came. In other words, the Jews were challenging Jesus to produce bread from God in order to substantiate His claims. They did not regard the bread which had fed the five thousand as bread from God; it had begun in earthly loaves and issued in earthly loaves. The manna, as they held, was a different thing and a real test.

Jesus' answer was twofold. First, He reminded them that it was not *Moses* who had given them the manna; it was *God*. Second, He told them that the manna was not really the bread of God; it was only the symbol of the bread of God. The bread of God is He who comes down from heaven and gives men, not simply satisfaction from physical hunger, but life. Jesus was claiming that the only real satisfaction was in Him.

THE BREAD OF LIFE

John 6: 35-40

Jesus said to them: " I am the bread of life. He who comes to me will never hunger, and he who believes in me will never thirst any more. But I tell you, though you have seen me, yet you do not believe in me. All that the Father gives me will come to me, because I came down from heaven, not to do my will, but to do the will of Him who sent me. This is the will of Him who sent me—that I should lose none of those He gave to me, but that I should raise them all up on the last day. This is the will of my Father, that everyone who believes on the Son, when he sees Him, should have everlasting life. And I will raise him up on the last day."

THIS is one of the great passages of the Fourth Gospel, and indeed of the New Testament. In it there are two great lines of thought that we must try to analyse.

First, what did Jesus mean when He said: " I am the bread of life "? It is not enough to regard this as simply a beautiful and lovely and poetical phrase. What does it mean? Let us analyse it step by step. We will number the steps so that the movement of the argument will be clear. (i) Bread sustains life. Bread is the staff of life. Bread is that without which life cannot go on. Bread is the essential for life. (ii) But what is life? Clearly this whole argument is moving above and beyond merely physical things. By life there is meant something far more than mere existence. What is this new spiritual meaning of life? (iii) Life is the new relationship with God. Real life is the new relationship with God, that relationship of trust and intimacy and obedience and love of which we have already thought. (iv) But that relationship is only made possible by Jesus Christ. Without Him and apart from Him no one can enter into that new relationship with God. (v) That is to say, Jesus gives life. Without Jesus life is impossible in the full sense of the term. Without Him life may be existence, but it is not life. (vi) Therefore, if Jesus gives life, if He is the essential of life, He can be described as the bread of life. To put this in a far less beautiful way, Jesus is the essential without which real life can neither begin nor go on. But, once we know Him and accept Him and receive Him, all the unsatisfied longings, all the insatiable desires of the heart and the soul are gone. The hunger and thirst of the human situation are ended when we know Christ, and when through Him we know God. The restless soul is at rest; the hungry heart is satisfied.

Second, this passage opens out to us the stages of the Christian life. In it Jesus speaks of those who come to Him, and whom God gives Him. Again we must number these steps so that we can follow this divine process. (i) We see Jesus. We are given the vision of Jesus. We see Him in the pages of the New Testament; we see Him in the teaching of the Church; we see Him sometimes even face to face. (ii) Having seen Him, we come to Him. We regard Him not as some distant hero and pattern, not as someone who is a figure in a book, but as someone to whom we come. (iii) We believe in Him. That is to say, we accept Him as the final authority on God, on man, on life. That means that our coming is not a matter of interest; it is not a meeting on equal terms; it is essentially and fundamentally a submission and a surrender. (iv) This whole process gives us life. That is to say, it puts us into the new and lovely relationship with God, wherein God becomes an intimate friend; we are now at home with the one whom we feared or never knew. (v) The possibility of this is free and it is universal. The invitation is to all men, and the invitation is to receive and to take. The bread of life is ours for the taking and the asking. (vi) The only way to that new relationship is through Jesus. Without Him it never would have been possible; and apart from Him it is still impossible. No searching of the human mind and no longing of the human heart can fully find God apart from Jesus. (vii) At the back of the whole process there is God. It is those whom God has given Him who come to Christ. God not only provides the goal; God moves in the human heart to awaken our desire for Him; and God works in the human heart to take away the rebellion and the pride which would hinder us from making the great submission. We could never even have sought Him unless He had already found us. (viii) But there remains that stubborn something which enables us to refuse the offer of God, to defy His moving in our hearts. In the last analysis, the one thing which defeats God is the defiance of the human heart. Life is there for the taking—and the refusing.

And when we take, what happens? Two things happen.

First, into life there enters the new satisfaction. The hunger and the thirst are gone. The human heart finds what it was searching for and life ceases to be mere existence and becomes a thing at once of thrill and of peace.

Second, even beyond life we are safe. Even on the last day when all things end we are still safe. As a great commentator said: " Christ brings us to the haven beyond which there is no danger."

The offer of Christ is life in time and life in eternity. It is that greatness and glory we cheat ourselves of when we refuse the invitation of Christ and the moving of God.

THE FAILURE OF THE JEWS

John 6: 41-50

> So the Jews kept murmuring about Him, because
> He said: "I am the bread which came down from
> heaven." They kept saying: "Is this not Jesus, the
> son of Joseph, whose father and mother we know?
> How can He now say: 'I have come down from
> heaven'?" Jesus answered: "Stop murmuring to
> each other. No one can come to me except the Father
> who sent me draws him; and I will raise him up on
> the last day. It stands written in the prophets: 'And
> all will be taught by God.' Everyone who has listened
> and learned from my Father comes to me. Not that
> anyone has seen the Father, except He who is from
> God—*He* has seen the Father. This is the truth I
> tell you—he who believes has eternal life. I am the
> bread of life. Your fathers ate the manna in the
> wilderness, and died. This is the bread of life which
> comes down from heaven that as many may eat of
> Him and not die. I am the bread of life which came
> down from heaven. If anyone eats of this bread he
> will live forever."

THE great interest of this passage is that it shows the
reasons why the Jews rejected Jesus, and in rejecting
Him, rejected eternal life.

(i) They judged things by human values and by external
standards. Their reaction in face of the claim of Jesus
was to produce the fact that He was a carpenter's son,
and that they had seen Him grow up in Nazareth. They
were unable to understand how one who was a carpenter
and a tradesman and who came from a poor home could
possibly be a special messenger from God. They rejected
Jesus because they tested Him by human assessments
and by social values and by worldly standards. T. E.
Lawrence was a close personal friend of Thomas Hardy,
the poet. In the days when Lawrence was serving as an
aircraftsman in the Royal Air Force he sometimes used
to visit Hardy and his wife in his aircraftsman's uniform.
It so happened that on one occasion his visit coincided

with a visit of the Mayoress of Dorchester. The Mayoress
was bitterly affronted that she had to submit to meeting
a common aircraftsman, for she had no idea who the
aircraftsman was. In French she said to Mrs. Hardy that
never in all her born days had she had to sit down to tea
with a private soldier. No one said anything; until T. E.
Lawrence said in perfect French: " I beg your pardon,
Madame, but can I be of any use as an interpreter? Mrs.
Hardy knows no French." A snobbish and discourteous
woman had made a shattering mistake because she judged
by externals and by worldly social standards. That is
what the Jews did. We must have a care that we never
neglect a message from God because we despise or do not
care for the messenger. A man would not refuse a cheque
for £1,000 because it happened to be enclosed in an envelope
which did not conform to the most aristocratic standards
of notepaper. God has many messengers. God's greatest
message came through a Galilaean carpenter, and that
was precisely why the Jews disregarded it.

(ii) The Jews complained and argued *with each other*.
They were so taken up with their private arguments that
it never struck them to refer the decision to God. They
were exceedingly eager to let everyone know what they
thought about the matter; they were not in the least
anxious to know what God thought. It might well be that
sometimes in some court or committee, when every man is
desirous of pushing his opinion down his neighbour's
throat, we would be better to stop and be quiet and pray
and ask God what He thinks and what He wants us to do.
After all it does not matter so very much what we think;
but what God thinks matters intensely; and we so seldom
take steps to find out what He thinks.

(iii) The Jews listened, *but they did not learn*. There
are different kinds of listening. There is the listening of
criticism; there is the listening of resentment. There is the
listening of superiority; there is the listening of indifference.
There is the listening of the man who only listens because

for the moment he cannot get the chance to speak. The only listening that is worth while is the listening which listens and learns. There is no other way to listen to God.

(iv) The Jews resisted *the drawing of God*. Only those accept Jesus whom God draws to Jesus. Now the word which John uses for *to draw* is interesting. It is the word which is used in the Greek translation of the Hebrew when Jeremiah hears God say: " With loving-kindness have I drawn thee " (*Jeremiah* 31: 3). But the interesting thing about the word (*helkuein*) is that it almost always implies some kind of resistance. It is the word for drawing a heavily laden net to the shore (*John* 21: 6, 11). It is the word which is used of Paul and Silas being dragged before the magistrates in Philippi (*Acts* 16: 19). It is the word for drawing a sword from the belt or from its scabbard (*John* 18: 10). Always there is this idea of resistance. God can and does draw men, but man's resistance can defeat the pull of God.

Now Jesus was the bread of life; we have seen that that means that Jesus is the essential for life; therefore to refuse the invitation and command of Jesus is to miss life and to die. The Rabbis had a saying: " The generation in the wilderness have no part in the life to come." In the old story in *Numbers* the people who cravenly refused to brave the dangers of the promised land after the report of the scouts who had been sent to spy out the land, were condemned to wander in the wilderness until they died. Because they would not accept the guidance of God they were for ever shut out from the promised land. But the Rabbis believed that the fathers who died in the wilderness not only missed the promised land, but that they also missed the life to come. To refuse the offer of Jesus is to refuse the essential of life; it is therefore to miss life in this world and in the world to come. Whereas to accept the offer of Jesus is to find life, a life which gives real life in this world, and glory in the world to come.

HIS BODY AND HIS BLOOD

John 6: 50-59

" The bread which I will give him is my flesh, which is given that the world may have life." So the Jews argued with each other. "How," they said, "can this man give us his flesh to eat?" Jesus said to them: "This is the truth I tell you—unless you eat the flesh of the Son of Man and drink His blood, you cannot possess eternal life within yourselves. He who eats my flesh and drinks my blood has eternal life, and I will raise him up on the last day. My flesh is the real food and my blood is the real drink. He who eats my flesh and drinks my blood remains in me and I in him. As the living Father has sent me, so I live through Him; and He who eats me will live through me. This is the bread which came down from heaven. It is not a case of eating, as your fathers ate and died. He who eats this bread lives for ever." He said these things when He was teaching in the Synagogue at Capernaum.

To most of us this is a very difficult passage. It speaks in language and moves in a world of ideas which is quite strange to us, and which may seem even fantastic and grotesque. But we must remember this—to the ancient world it was moving amidst familiar ideas, ideas which go back to the very childhood of the race.

The ideas in this section would be quite normal and usual to anyone who had been brought up in ancient sacrifice. In ancient sacrifice the animal was very seldom burned entire. Usually only a token part was burned on the altar, although the whole animal was offered to the god. Part of the flesh was given to the priests as their perquisite; and part of the flesh was given to the worshipper wherewith to make a feast for himself and his friends within the temple precincts. Now at that feast the god himself was held to be a guest. He was there sitting with his people and his worshippers. More, once the flesh had been offered to the god, it was held that the god had entered into the flesh;

and therefore when the worshipper ate it he was literally eating the god, taking the god into his very inmost being, nourishing himself with the very life and strength of the god. When people rose from such a feast they went out, as they believed, literally god-filled. We may think of it as heathen and idolatrous worship, we may think of it as a vast delusion; and yet the fact remains these people went out quite certain that in them there was now the dynamic vitality of their god. We may say and think what we like about this kind of worship. This vital experience happened. To people who were used to that kind of experience a section like this presented no difficulties at all.

Further, in that ancient world the one live form of religion was to be found in the Mystery Religions. Now the one thing these Mystery Religions offered was communion and even identity with some god. The way it was done was this. All the Mystery Religions were essentially passion plays. They were stories of some god who had lived and suffered terribly and who died and rose again. This story was turned into a moving play. Before the initiate could see it he had to undergo a long course of instruction in the inner meaning of the story. He had to undergo all kinds of ceremonial purifications. He had to pass through a long period of fasting and abstention from all sexual relationships. At the actual presentation of a passion play everything was arranged and designed to produce a highly emotional atmosphere. There was carefully calculated lighting; there was sensuous incense; there was exciting music; there was a wonderful liturgy; everything was designed to work up the initiate to a height and tensity of emotion and expectation that he had never experienced before. Call it hallucination if we like; call it a combination of hypnotism and self hypnotism—something happened. And that something was identity with the god. As the carefully prepared initiate watched he became one with the god. He shared the sorrows and the griefs; he shared the death; he shared the resurrection; he shared the life of the god; he and the god became for ever and for ever one; and there he was safe in life and in death.

Some of the sayings and prayers of the Mystery Religions are very beautiful. In the Mysteries of Mithra the initiate prayed: " Abide with my soul; leave me not, that I may be initiated and that the holy spirit may dwell within me." In the Hermetic Mysteries the initiate said: " I know thee Hermes, and thou knowest me; *I am thou and thou art I.*" In the same Mysteries a prayer runs: " Come to me, Lord Hermes, as babes to mothers' wombs." In the Mysteries of Isis the worshipper said: " As truly as Osiris lives, so shall his followers live. As truly as Osiris is not dead, his followers shall die no more."

We must remember that those ancient people knew all about the striving, the longing, the dreaming for identity with their god, for the bliss of taking the god into themselves and taking themselves into the god. They would not read phrases like eating Christ's body and drinking His blood with a crude and shocked literalism. They would know something of that ineffable experience of union, closer than any earthly union, of which these words speak. This is language that the ancient world could understand— and so can we.

It may be well that we should remember that here John is doing what he so often does. He is not giving, or trying to give, the actual words of Jesus. He has been thinking for seventy years of what Jesus said; and now, led and guided and inspired by the Holy Spirit, he is giving the *meaning*, the *inner significance* of the words of Jesus. It is not the words that he tells; that would merely have been a feat of memory. It is the essential meaning of the words; that is the guidance of the Holy Spirit.

HIS BODY AND HIS BLOOD

John 6: 50-59 (*continued*)

LET us see now if we can find out something of what Jesus meant, and of what John understood from words like this. There are two ways in which we can take this passage, and there are two ways in which we are meant to take it.

(i) We may take it in a quite general sense. Jesus spoke about eating His flesh and drinking His blood. Now the flesh of Jesus was His complete and full humanity. John in his First Letter lays it down almost passionately: " Every spirit that confesseth that Jesus Christ is come in the flesh is of God; and every spirit that confesseth not that Jesus Christ is come in the flesh is not of God." In fact, the spirit which denies that Jesus is come in the flesh is of antichrist (I *John* 4: 2, 3). John insisted that we must clutch and grasp and never let go the full humanity of Jesus, that Jesus was bone of our bone and flesh of our flesh. Now what does this mean? Jesus, as we have seen again and again, was the mind of God become a person. So this means that in Jesus we see God taking human life upon Him, facing our human situation, struggling with our human problems, battling with our human temptations, working out our human relationships. Therefore it is as if Jesus said: " Feed your heart, feed your mind, feed your soul on the thought of my manhood. When you are discouraged and in despair, when you are tired of life and beaten to your knees and disgusted with life and living— remember I took that life of yours and these struggles of yours on me." Suddenly life and the flesh are clad with glory for they are touched with God. It was and is the great belief of the Greek Orthodox Christology that Jesus deified our flesh by taking it on Himself. To eat Christ's body is to feed on the thought of His manhood until our manhood is strengthened and cleansed and purified and irradiated by His. Jesus said we must drink His blood. In Jewish thought *the blood stands for the life*. It is easy to understand why he thought that. As the blood flows from a wound life ebbs away. And to the Jew, *the blood belonged to God.* That is why to this day a true Jew will never eat any meat which has not been completely drained of blood. " But flesh with the life thereof, which is the blood thereof, shall ye not eat " (*Genesis* 9: 4). " Only be sure that thou eat not the blood, for the blood is the life " (*Deuteronomy* 16: 23). Now see what Jesus is saying— " You must drink my blood—you must take my life into the very centre of your being—and that life of mine is the life which belongs to God." When Jesus said we must drink His blood He meant that we must take His life into the very centre and core of our hearts. What does that mean? Think of it this way. Here in a bookcase is a book which a man has never read. It may be the glory and the wonder of the tragedies of Shakespeare. He may have bought that book, but so long as it remains unread upon his bookshelves it is external to him. It remains outside him. But then one day he takes it down and reads it. He is thrilled and fascinated and moved. The story sticks to him; the great lines remain in his memory; now when he wants to, he can take that wonder out from inside himself and remember it and think about it and feed his mind and his heart upon it. Once the book was external to him, on his shelf. Now it has got inside him and he can feed upon it. It is that way with any great possession and experience in life. It remains external until we take it within ourselves. It is so with Jesus. Here is Jesus, the life of God. So long as He remains a figure in a book He is external to us; but when He enters into our hearts He is within us, and we can feed upon the life and the strength and the dynamic vitality that Christ gives to us. Jesus said that we must drink His blood. He is saying: " You must take my life inside you; you must stop thinking of me as a figure in a book and a subject for theological debate; you must take me into you, and you must come into me; and then you will have life, real life." That is what Jesus meant when He spoke about us abiding in Him and He abiding in us. When Jesus told us to eat His flesh and drink His blood, He was telling us to feed our hearts and souls and minds on His humanity, and He was telling us to revitalize our lives with His life until we are drenched and permeated and saturated and filled with the life of God.

(ii) But John meant more than that, and in this second thing he was reading back how all the experience of Jesus Christ had brought him into the Galilaean days. Quite certainly John was thinking of the Lord's Supper, of the Sacrament. He is saying: " If you want life, you must come and sit at that table, where you eat that broken bread and drink that poured-out wine which somehow, in the grace of God, bring you into living contact with the love and the life of Jesus Christ." John was saying to men: " You cannot draw on the fullness of the Christian life and wonder unless you sit at that table of love." But—and here is the sheer wonder of John's point of view—we must note that *John has no account of the Last Supper.* He brings in his teaching about it, not in the narrative of the Upper Room, but in the story of a picnic meal on a hillside near Bethsaida Julias by the blue waters of the Sea of Galilee. There is no doubt what John is saying—he is saying that for the true Christian *every meal has become a sacrament.* It may well be that there were those who—if the phrase be allowed—were making too much of the Sacrament within the Church, who were making a fetish and a magic of the Sacrament, who were saying or implying that the Sacrament was the one place where we might find and meet and enjoy and rest in the nearer presence of the Risen Christ. It is true that the Sacrament is a special appointment with God; but John held with all his heart that every meal, in the humblest home, in the richest palace, beneath the canopy of the sky with only the grass for a carpet, is a sacrament. John refused to limit the presence of Christ to an ecclesiastical environment and a correctly liturgical service. He said: " At any meal you can find again that bread which speaks of the manhood of the Master, that wine that speaks of the blood which is life." It is the wondrous thought of John that the communion table, and the dinner table and the picnic on the seashore or the hillside are all alike in that at all of them we can taste and touch and handle the bread and the wine which bring us Christ. Christianity would be a poor thing if Christ were confined to Churches. It is John's belief that we can find Christ anywhere in a Christ-filled world. It is not that he belittles the Sacrament; it is that he expands the Sacrament, so that we find Christ at the table in the Church of Christ, and then go out to find Him everywhere where men and women meet together to enjoy the gifts of God.

THE ALL-IMPORTANT SPIRIT

John 6: 59-65

> When they had heard this discourse many of His disciples said: " This word is hard! Who is able to listen to it? " Jesus well knew within Himself that His disciples were murmuring about this; so He said to them: " Does this cause you to stumble? What then if you were to see the Son of Man ascending to where He formerly was? The life-giving power is the Spirit; the flesh is of no help. The words which I have spoken to you are spirit and life. But there are some who do not believe." For Jesus knew from the beginning who they were who did not believe, and who it was who was going to betray Him. So that was why He often said: " No man can come to me, except it has been given to him by the Father to do so."

IT is little wonder that the disciples had found the discourse of Jesus hard. The Greek word is *sklēros*; and *sklēros* does not mean *hard to understand*; it means *hard to accept, hard to tolerate*. The disciples knew quite well what Jesus had been saying. They knew that He had been claiming that He was the very life of God come down from heaven, and that no one could live this life or face eternity without accepting Him and submitting to Him. Here we come upon a truth that re-emerges in every age. Time and again it is not the intellectual difficulty of accepting Christ which keeps men from becoming Christians; it is the height of Christ's moral demand. When we begin to think honestly about the matter we are bound to see that at the heart of all religion there must be mystery, for the simple reason that at the heart of all religion there is God. It is in the nature of things that the finite can never comprehend the infinite, that the ways of God can never be grasped by the human mind, that man cannot ever fully understand God. Any honest thinker is bound to admit that. If we could fully grasp God, then God would cease to be God, and would simply be a kind of outsize man. Any honest thinker will accept the mystery. The real difficulty of Christianity is two-fold. It demands an act of surrender to Christ, an acceptance of Him as the final authority; and it demands a moral standard wherein only the pure in heart may see God. The disciples were well aware that Jesus had claimed to be the very life and mind of God come down to earth; their difficulty was to accept that that was true, with all the implications which are in it. And to this day many a man's refusal of Christ comes, not because Christ puzzles and baffles his intellect, but because Christ challenges and condemns his life.

So Jesus goes on, not to try to prove His claim, but to state that some day events will prove it. What He is saying is this: " You find it difficult to believe that I am the bread, the essential of life, which *came down* from heaven. Well then, you will have no difficulty in accepting that claim when some day you see me *ascending back* to heaven." In other words this is a forecast of the Ascension. Jesus is saying: " When the time comes for me to return to heaven and to my glory, then you will see that what I claim is true." That is important. It means that the Resurrection is the guarantee of all the claims of Jesus. He was not one who lived nobly and died gallantly for a lost cause; He was the one whose claims were vindicated by the fact that He died and rose again. He did not come to the end in defeat; He came to the end in triumph. The Resurrection is the proof of the indestructibility of the claims of Christ.

Jesus then goes on to say that the all-important thing is the life-giving power of the Spirit; that the flesh is of no help. We can put that very simply in a way which will give us at least something of its meaning—the most important thing is the spirit in which any action is done. Someone has put it this way: "All human things are trivial if they exist for nothing beyond themselves." The value of anything depends on its aim. If we eat food simply for the sake of eating food, we become gluttons, and it is likely to do us far more harm than good; if we eat food to sustain life, to do our work better, and to maintain the fitness of our body at its highest peak, then food has a real meaning and significance. If a man spends a great deal of time on sport simply for the sake of sport, he is at least to some extent wasting his time. But if he spends time on sport to keep his body fit and athletic, and thereby to do his work for God and men better, then sport ceases to be trivial and becomes intensely important. The things of the flesh all gain their value from the spirit in which they are done. So Jesus goes on: "My words are spirit and life." It is Christ who alone can tell us what life is, can put into us the spirit in which life must be lived, and who can give us the strength and the power so to live it. Life is like any other activity. It takes its value from its purpose and its goal. It is Christ who alone can give us the aim in life, the spirit of life, the purpose for life; and it is Christ alone who can give us the life, the strength, the power to work out that spirit and aim and purpose against the constant opposition that comes to us from without and from within. In His words are the spirit of life and the strength for life.

But Jesus was well aware that there were those who would not only reject His offer but who would reject it with hostility. Jesus had insight into human nature; He could read men's hearts; and the great responsibility of the human heart is that in it there is a core over which we and we alone have control. No man can accept Jesus unless he is moved by the Spirit of God to do so, but to the end of the day a man can resist that Spirit, and such a man is not shut out by God; he is shut out by himself.

ATTITUDES TO CHRIST

John 6: 66-71

> After this many of His disciples turned back and would not walk with Him any more. Jesus said to the Twelve: " Surely you too do not want to go away? " Simon Peter answered Him: " Lord, to whom are we to go? You have the words of eternal life; and we have believed and we have come to know that you are the Holy One of God." Jesus answered them: " Did I not choose you twelve, and one of you is a devil? " He meant Judas, the son of Simon Iscariot, for he was going to betray Him— and he was one of the Twelve.

HERE is a passage which is instinct with tragedy, for in it there is the beginning of the end. There was a time when it looked as if men would flock to Jesus. When He was in Jerusalem at the Passover many saw His miracles and believed in His name (2: 23). So many had come to be baptized by His disciples that the numbers were embarrassing (4: 1-3). In Samaria great things had happened (4: 1, 39, 45). In Galilee the crowds had flocked after Him just the day before (6: 2). But now the tone of things had changed; from now on there was a growing hatred which was going to culminate in the Cross. Already John launches us on the last act of the tragedy.

It is circumstances like these which truly reveal men's hearts and which show men in their true colours. And in these circumstances there were three different attitudes to Jesus.

(i) There was *defection*. There were those who turned back and who walked with Him no more. They had crowded to Him and now they were slipping away. They drifted away for various reasons. Some of them saw quite clearly where Jesus was heading. It was not possible to challenge the authorities and the powers like that and get away with it. He was heading for disaster and they got out in time. They were fair-weather followers. It has been said that the test of an army is how it fights when it is tired. Those who drifted away would have stuck by Jesus so long as His career was on the upward way, but at the first shadow of the Cross they left Him. There were those who drifted away because they shirked the challenge and the command of Jesus. Fundamentally their point of view was that they had come to Jesus to get something out of Him; when it came to suffering something for Him and to giving something to Him they quit. When following was romance and glamour they would follow Him; when it was a hard way and a tough job they left Him. They had really contemplated discipleship for purely selfish reasons. There is no one who can give us so much as Jesus, but, the fact remains, if we come to Him solely to get and never to give we will certainly turn back. The man who would follow Jesus must remember that in following Jesus there is always a Cross.

(ii) There was *deterioration*. It is in Judas above all that we see this deterioration. Jesus must have seen in him a man whom He could use for His purposes. But Judas, who might have become the hero, became the villain; and he who might have become the saint became the name of shame. There is a terrible story about the experience of an artist who was painting the picture of the Last Supper. It was a great picture and it took him many years to paint it. He went out to find a model for the face of Christ, and he found a young man with a face of such transcendent loveliness and purity that he painted him as Jesus. Bit by bit the picture was filled in and one after another of the disciples was painted. There came the day when he needed a model for Judas whose face he had left to the last. He went out and searched in the lowest haunts of the city and in the dens of vice. At last he found a man with a face so depraved and vicious that he took him as a model for the face of Judas. When the sittings were at an end the man said to the artist: " You painted me before." " Surely not," said the artist. " O yes," said the man, " and the last time you painted me, you painted me as Christ." The years had brought the terrible deterioration. There is always a terrible danger in life. The years can be cruel. They can take away our ideals and our enthusiasms and our dreams and our loyalties. They can leave us with a life that has grown smaller and not bigger. They can leave us with a heart that is shrivelled and not expanded in the love of Christ. There can be a lost loveliness in life—God save us from that!

(iii) There was *determination*. This is John's version of Peter's great confession at Caesarea Philippi in the other gospels (*Mark* 8: 27; *Matthew* 16: 13; *Luke* 9: 18). It was just such a situation as this that called out the loyalty of Peter's heart. To Peter the simple fact was that there was just no one else to go to. For him Jesus alone had the words of life. Now we must note one thing. Peter's loyalty was based on a personal relationship to Jesus Christ. There were many things that Peter did not understand; he was just as bewildered and puzzled as anyone else. But there was something about Jesus for which he would willingly die. In the last analysis Christianity is not a philosophy which we accept; it is not a theory to which we give allegiance; it is not something which is thought out; it is not something which is intellectually arrived at. It is a personal response to Jesus

Christ. It is the answer of the heart to the magnet of Christ.
It is an allegiance and a love which a man gives because
his heart will not allow him to do anything else.

NOT MAN'S TIME BUT GOD'S

John 7: 1-9

> After these things Jesus moved about in Galilee,
> for He did not wish to move about in Judaea, because
> the Jews were out to kill Him. The Festival of the
> Jews which is called the Festival of Tabernacles
> was near. So His brothers said to Him: " Leave
> here and go down to Jerusalem so that your disciples
> will get the chance to see the works that you do.
> For no one goes on doing things in secret, when he
> wishes to draw public attention to himself. Since
> you can do these things, show yourself to the world."
> For even His brothers did not believe in Him. So
> Jesus said to them: " The time of opportunity that
> I am looking for has not yet come; but your time is
> always ready. The world cannot hate you, but it
> hates me, because I bear witness about it that its
> deeds are evil. Go up to the Festival yourselves. I
> am not yet going up to the Festival, because my time
> has not yet come." When He had said these things
> to them He remained in Galilee.

THE Festival of Tabernacles fell at the end of September
and the beginning of October. It was one of the obligatory
festivals of the Jews and every adult male Jew who lived
within twenty miles of Jerusalem was legally bound to
attend it. But devout Jews from far outside the twenty
mile radius delighted to go to it. It lasted altogether for
eight days. Later in this chapter we shall have occasion
to deal more fully with it. When the time of it came round,
Jesus' brothers urged Him to go to Jerusalem for it;
but Jesus rejected their arguments and went in His own
good time.

There is one unique thing in this passage which we must
note. According to the Authorised Version (verse 7)

Jesus says: " My time is not yet come." Now Jesus
frequently spoke about His *time*, or His *hour*. But in
this passage He uses a quite different word, and He uses
it for the only time. In the other passages (*John* 2: 4;
7: 30; 8: 20; 12: 27) the word that Jesus or John uses
is *hōra*, which means the *destined hour of God*. Such a time
or hour was not movable; it was not avoidable; it had
to be accepted without argument and without alteration
because it was the hour at which the plan of God had
decided that something must happen. But in this passage
the word is not *hōra*; the word is *kairos*, which characteristically means an *opportunity*; it means the best time, the
most suitable opportunity to do something; it means the
moment when the circumstances are most suitable; it
means what we often call *the psychological moment*; it
means that moment when an opportunity must be grasped
lest it never return. What Jesus is saying here is not
that the destined hour of God has not come; He is saying
something much simpler; He is saying that that moment was
not the moment which would give Him the chance for which
He was waiting. That explains why Jesus later actually
did go to Jerusalem. Many people have been troubled
about the fact that Jesus first told His brothers that He
would not go and then in fact actually went. Schopenhauer,
the German philosopher, actually said: " Jesus Christ
did of set purpose utter a falsehood." Other people have
argued that it means that Jesus said that He was not
going up to the Festival *publicly* but that did not preclude
Him from going *privately*. But if we look at the Greek,
what Jesus is saying is simply this: " If I go up with
you just now I will not get the opportunity that I am
looking for. The time is not opportune." So He delayed
His going until the middle of the Festival, for to arrive
with the crowds all assembled and expectant gave Him
a far better opportunity than to go at the very beginning.
This simply shows us Jesus choosing His time with careful
prudence in order to get the most effective results.

From this passage we learn two things.

(i) We learn that we cannot force Jesus' hand. Jesus' brothers tried to force Him into going to Jerusalem. It was in effect what we should call a dare and a challenge. In a way they were quite right from the human point of view. Jesus' great miracles had been wrought in Galilee. Galilee is the scene of the changing of the water into wine (*John* 2: Iff); of the healing of the nobleman's son (*John* 4: 46); of the feeding of the five thousand (*John* 6: Iff). The only miracle that He had wrought in Jerusalem was the curing of the impotent man at the pool (*John* 5: Iff). It was a not unnatural thing to tell Jesus to go to Jerusalem and to let His supporters there see what He could do. The story makes it clear that the healing of the impotent man had been regarded far more as an act of Sabbath breaking than as a miracle. Further, if Jesus was ever to succeed in winning men, He could not hope to do so by hiding in a corner; He must act in such a way that everyone could see what He did. Still further, Jerusalem was in actual fact the keypoint. The Galilaeans were notoriously hot-blooded and hot-headed. Anyone who wanted a following would have no difficulty in raising one in the excitable atmosphere of Galilee; but Jerusalem was a very different proposition. Galilee was no real test; Jerusalem was the acid test. Jesus' brothers could have put up a good case for their insistence; but Jesus' hand is not to be forced. Jesus does things, not in man's time, but in God's time. The impatience of man must learn to wait on the wisdom of God. The world goes to God's time-table, not to ours.

(ii) We learn that it is impossible to treat Jesus with indifference. It made no difference when Jesus' brothers went to Jerusalem. Any day would do for them, for no one would notice that they were there. Nothing whatever depended on their going to Jerusalem; they could go in their own time, and it made no difference. But if Jesus went it was a very different thing. Why? Because Jesus' brothers were part of the world; their sympathies were with the world; they were in tune with the world; they did not make the world uncomfortable and the world had no quarrel with them. But Jesus enters with a disturbing dynamic power. His very presence is a condemnation of our way of life. His very coming is a challenge to our selfishness and our lethargy. Jesus had to choose His moment, for when He arrives something happens.

REACTIONS TO JESUS

John 7: 10-13

> When His brothers had gone up to the Festival, then He too went up, not openly, but, as it were, in secret. So the Jews searched for Him at the Festival, and kept saying: "Where is He?" And there was many a heated argument about Him among the crowds. Some said: "He is a good man." But others said: "No; far from it; He is leading the people astray." But no one spoke about Him openly because of their fear of the Jews.

So in the end Jesus chose His own moment and went to Jerusalem. Here we have the reactions of the people when they were confronted with Jesus. Now one of the supreme interests of this chapter is the number of reactions of which it tells us; and we will here collect the different reactions to Jesus, not only in this passage, but from the whole chapter.

(i) There was the reaction of His brothers (verses 1-5). It was really a reaction of half-amused and teasing contemptuous amusement. When they urged Him to go to Jerusalem, they were offering Him a dare. They did not really believe in Him; they were really egging Him on, as they thought, as you might egg on a precocious boy. We still meet that attitude of tolerant contempt to religion. George Bernaños in *The Diary of a Country Priest* tells how the country priest used sometimes to be invited to dinner at the big aristocratic house of his parish. The aristocratic owner would encourage him to speak and argue before his guests, but he did it with that half-amused, half-contemptuous tolerance with which he might encourage a child to show off or a dog to display his tricks. There are still people who tolerate religion and who forget that religion is a matter of life and death.

(ii) There was open hatred. There was the sheer hatred of the Pharisees and of the chief priests (verses 7, 19). They did not hate Him for the same reason, because in point of fact they hated each other. The Pharisees hated Him because Jesus drove through their petty rules and regulations. If He was right, they were wrong; and they loved their own little system more than they loved God. No matter what God said to them, they would cling to their rules and their regulations. The Sadducees were a political party. They did not observe the Pharisaic rules and regulations. Nearly all the priests were Sadducees. They were characteristically the collaborationist party. They collaborated with their Roman masters, and they had a very comfortable and even luxurious time. The Sadducees did not want a Messiah; a Messiah was in fact the last thing they wanted; for when the Messiah came their political set up would disintegrate in fragments and their wealthy comfort would be gone. They hated Jesus because Jesus interfered with the vested interests which were dearer to them than God. It is still possible for a man to love his own little system more than he loves God, and to place his own vested interests above the challenge of the adventurous and the sacrificial way.

(iii) Both these reactions issued in the consuming desire to eliminate Jesus (verses 30, 32). When a man's ideals clash with the ideals of Christ, either the man must submit and surrender, or he must fight Christ and seek to destroy Him. Hitler would have no Christians about him, for the Christian owed a higher loyalty than loyalty to the state. A man is faced with a simple alternative if he allows Christ into his orbit at all. He can either do what he likes, or he can do what Christ likes; and if he wishes to go on doing as he likes, there is nothing left for him to do but to seek to eliminate Christ.

(iv) There was arrogant contempt (verses 15, 47-49). What right had this man, quite untrained in the theological schools, to come and lay down the law? Jesus had no cultural background; He had no training in the rabbinic schools and colleges. How had He ever learned to read? Surely no intelligent person was ever going to listen to Him? Here is the reaction of academic snobbery. And yet the fact remains that many of the greatest poets and writers and evangelists have had no technical qualifications at all. That is not for one moment to say that technical qualifications and study and culture and education are to be despised and abandoned; but it is to say that we must have a care that we never wave a man away and usher him out and consign him to the company who do not matter because he lacks the technical equipment of the schools.

(v) There was the reaction of the crowd. The crowd reaction was twofold. First, there was the reaction of sheer *interest* (verse 11). The one thing that is impossible when Jesus really invades life is indifference. So long as Jesus remains an historical figure in a book, indifference is possible; but when Jesus comes alive then indifference is no longer possible. Apart from anything else, Jesus is the most interesting figure in the world. Second, there was the reaction of *discussion* (verses 12, 43). They talked about Jesus. They argued their opinions about Jesus; they put forward their views about Jesus; they debated about Jesus. There is value and there is danger there. The value is that nothing helps us to clarify our own opinions like pitting them against someone else's. The mind sharpens the mind as iron sharpens iron. The danger is that religion can so very easily come to be regarded as a matter for argument and debate and discussion, a series of fascinating questions, about which a man may talk for a life-time—and do nothing. There is all the difference in the world between being an argumentative amateur theologian, willing to talk until the stars go out, and a truly religious person, whose religion has passed from talking about Christ to knowing Christ, and from discussing Christ to living Christianity.

VERDICTS ON JESUS

John 7: 10-13 (*continued*)

IN this chapter there is a whole series of verdicts on Jesus.

(i) There is the verdict that He was a *good man* (verse 12). That verdict remains, and it is true, but it is not the whole truth. It was Napoleon who made the famous remark: " I know men, and Jesus Christ is more than a man." Jesus was indeed truly man; but in Him there was the mind of God. When He speaks it is not one man speaking to another. If that were so we might argue about and discuss His commands; when He speaks it is God speaking to men; and Christianity means not arguing about His commands, but accepting them.

(ii) There is the verdict that He was a *prophet* (verse 40). That too is true. The prophet is the forth-teller of the will of God, the man who lived so close to God that he knows the mind and the purposes of God. That is true of Jesus; but there is this difference. The prophet says: " Thus saith the Lord." His authority is a borrowed and a delegated authority. His message is given to him and is not his own. Jesus says: " I say unto you." He has the right to speak, not with a delegated authority, but because He is who He is.

(iii) There is the verdict that He was a *deluded madman* (verse 20). Now it is true that either Jesus is the only completely sane person in the world, or that He was mad. He chose a Cross when He might have had power. He was the Suffering Servant when He might have been the conquering king. He washed His disciples' feet when He might have had men kneeling at His feet. He came to serve when He could have subjected the world to servitude. It is not common sense that the words of Jesus give us, but uncommon sense. Jesus turned the world's standards upside down, because into a mad world He brings the supreme sanity of God.

(iv) There is the verdict that He was a *seducer*. The Jewish authorities saw in Him one who was leading men away from true religion. The fact that Jesus was accused of every crime in the calendar against religion. He was accused of being a Sabbath-breaker, of being a dunkard and a glutton, of having the most disreputable friends, of destroying orthodox religion. It is quite clear that, if we prefer our idea of religion to His, He will certainly appear a seducer —and it is one of the hardest things in the world for any man to do to admit that he is wrong.

(v) There is the verdict that He was a *man of courage* (verse 26). The one thing that no one ever doubted about Jesus was His sheer courage. He had the moral courage to defy convention and to be different. He had the physical courage that could bear the most terrible and searing pain. He had the courage to go on when His family abandoned Him, and His friends forsook Him, and one of His own Circle betrayed Him. Here we see Him courageously entering Jerusalem when to enter it was to enter the lions' den. Jesus " feared God so much that He never feared the face of any man."

(vi) There is the verdict that He had a *most dynamic personality* (verse 46). The verdict of the officers who were sent to arrest Him and who came back empty-handed was that never had any man spoken like this. Julian Duguid tells how he once voyaged on the same Atlantic liner as Sir Wilfred Grenfell, and he tells us that when Sir Wilfred Grenfell came into a room you could tell it even if you had your back to him and could not see him, for a kind of wave of vitality emanated from him. When we think of how this Galilaean carpenter faced the highest in the land and dominated them, until it was they who were on trial and not He, we are bound to admit that He was at least one of the supreme personalities in history. The picture of a gentle, anæmic Christ will not do. From Christ there flowed a power that sent those despatched to arrest Him back in empty-handed bewilderment.

(vii) There is the verdict that He was the *Christ*, the Anointed One of God. Nothing less will do. It is the plain fact that Jesus Christ does not fit into any of the available human categories. To describe Him and His effect on men human categories break down; and only the category of the divine will do.

Before we leave this general study of this chapter there are three other reactions to Christ in it that we must note.

(i) There was the crowd's reaction of *fear* (verse 13). They talked about Him but they were afraid to talk too loud. The word that John uses for their talking is an onomatopoetic word—that is, a word which imitates the sound of that for which it stands. It is the word *goggusmos* (two *g*'s in Greek are pronounced *ng*). The Authorised Version translates it *murmuring*. It indicates a kind of growling, muttering, discontented undertone. It is the regular word used for the grumbling of the children of Israel in the wilderness when they complained against Moses. They muttered the complaints that they were afraid to utter. Fear can keep a man from making a clarion call of his faith and can turn it into an indistinct, semi-audible mutter. The Christian is never afraid to tell the world in ringing tones that he believes in Christ.

(ii) The reaction of a certain number of the crowd was *belief* (verse 31). Now these were the men and women who could not deny or disbelieve the evidence of their own eyes. They heard what Jesus said; they saw what Jesus did; they were confronted with that dynamic person; and they believed. If a man rids himself of prejudice and fear, he is bound in the end to finish in belief.

(iii) There was the reaction of Nicodemus. His reaction was to *defend* Jesus (verse 50). In that council of the Jewish authorities he was the one lone man to raise his voice in the defence of Jesus Christ. There lies the duty of every one of us. Ian Maclaren used to tell students when they preached: " Speak a good word for Jesus Christ." We live to-day in a strange world. We live in a world which is hostile to Christianity in many ways and in many places, but the strange thing is that never was the world more ready to talk about Christ and to discuss religion. We live in a generation when every one of us can earn the royal title, " Defender of the Faith." It is the privilege that God has given us that we can all be advocates and defenders of Jesus Christ in face of the criticism—and sometimes the mockery—of men.

THE ULTIMATE AUTHORITY

John 7: 14-18

> The Jews were amazed. " How," they said, " can this fellow read when He is quite uneducated? " " My teaching," said Jesus, " is not mine, but it belongs to Him who sent me. If anyone is willing to do His will, he will understand whether my teaching derives from God, or whether I am speaking from no source beyond myself. The man who speaks from no other source beyond himself is out for his own glory. He who seeks the glory of Him who sent him is true, and there is no wickedness in him."

WE have already had occasion to see that it is very likely that some parts of John's Gospel have become misplaced. Maybe he never had time to put it fully in order; maybe the leaves on which it was written were finally assembled in the wrong order. This section, and the section which follows, form one of the clearest cases of misplacement. As these two passages come in here they hardly make sense; they have no connection at all with their context. It is almost certain that they should not come in here,

but that they should come after 5: 47. Chapter 5 tells
of the healing of the impotent man at the healing pool.
That miracle was done on the Sabbath and was regarded
by the Jewish authorities as a breach of the Sabbath.
In His own defence Jesus has cited the writings of Moses,
and has said that if they really knew what these writings
mean, and if they really believed in them, they would
also believe in Him. The chapter finishes: " If you had
believed in Moses, you would have believed in me, for he
wrote about me. If you do not believe in his writings,
how will you believe in my words? " (*John* 5: 47). If
we go straight from there and read *John* 7: 15-24 the
connection is clear. Jesus has just referred to the writing
of Moses, and immediately the astonished Jewish leaders
break in: " How can this fellow read when He is quite
uneducated? " We will understand the sense and the
relevance and the connection of *John* 7: 15-24 far better
if we assume that in its present position that passage is
misplaced, and originally came after *John* 5: 47. With
that connection in our minds let us now turn to the passage
itself.

The criticism of the leaders of the Jews was that Jesus
was quite uneducated. It is exactly the same accusation
that was made against Peter and John when they stood
before the Sanhedrin (*Acts* 4: 13). Jesus had been to no
rabbinic school. It was the practice that only the disciple
of an accredited teacher, only one who had studied under
one of the great Rabbis, was entitled to expound scripture,
and to talk about the law. No Rabbi ever made a statement
on his own authority. He always began: " There is a
teaching that. . . . " And he then went on to cite quotations
and authorities for every statement which he made. And
here was this Galilaean carpenter, this man with no training
whatever, daring to quote and to expound Moses to them.
Now Jesus could very well have walked straight into a
trap here. He might well have said: " I need no teacher;
I am self-taught; I got my teaching and my wisdom and

my doctrine from no one but myself." But that is not what He said. In effect He said: "You ask who was my teacher? You ask what authority I produce for the things I say and for my exposition of scripture? *My teaching and my authority is God.*" Jesus never claimed to be self-taught; He did claim to be God-taught. It is in fact a claim which He makes again and again. "I have not spoken of myself; but the Father which sent me, He gave me a commandment, what I should say, and what I should speak" (*John* 12: 49). "The words that I speak unto you, I speak not of myself" (*John* 14: 10).

Frank Salisbury tells of a letter he received after he had painted his great picture of the burial of the unknown warrior in Westminster Abbey. A fellow artist wrote to him saying: "I want to congratulate you on the great picture that you have painted—or rather the picture that God has helped you to paint." All great productions of the human mind and spirit are given by God. No great man would claim to have discovered the truth; he would only humbly and thankfully say that God had revealed His truth to him. If we glory in being self-taught, if we claim that any discovery we have made is our own unaided discovery, we are, in the last analysis, only glorifying our own reputation and our own selves. The great man thinks not of the power of his own mind or hand; he thinks always of the God who told him what he knows and taught him what he can do.

But further, Jesus goes on to lay down a universal truth of life. He says that it is only the man who does God's will who can truly understand God's teaching. Now that is not a theological truth; it is a universal truth. *We learn by doing.* A doctor might learn the technique of surgery from text-books. He might know in theory how to carry out every possible operation. But that would not make him a surgeon; he has to learn surgery by actually operating; he has to learn by doing. A man might learn the way in which an automobile engine works; in theory he might be able to carry out every possible repair and adjustment; but that would not make him an engineer; he has to learn by doing. It is the same with the Christian life. If we wait until we have understood everything, we will never start at all. But if we begin by doing God's will as we know it, God's truth will become clearer and clearer to us. We learn by doing. If a man says: " I cannot be a Christian because there is so much of Christian doctrine that I do not understand, and I must wait until I understand it all," the answer is: " You never will understand it all; but if you start here and now trying to live the Christian life, you certainly will understand more and more of it as the days go on." In Christianity, as in all other things, the way to learn is to do.

Now, let us remember that this passage really ought to come after the story of the healing of the impotent man. Jesus has been accused of wickedness in that He healed the man on the Sabbath day. Now He goes on to demonstrate that He was utterly sincere in seeking only the glory of God and that there is no wickedness whatsoever in the action which He did.

A WISE ARGUMENT

John 7: 19-24

" Did not Moses give you the law—and not one of you really keeps it? Why do you try to kill me? " The crowd answered: " You are mad! Who is trying to kill you? " Jesus answered them: " I have done only one deed and you are all astonished by it. Moses gave you the rite of circumcision (not that it had its origin in Moses—it came down from your fathers) and you circumcise a man on the Sabbath. If a man can be circumcised on the Sabbath, without breaking the law of Moses, are you angry at me for making the entire body of a man whole on the Sabbath? Stop judging by appearances, and make your judgment just."

BEFORE we begin to look at this passage in detail, we must note one point here. We must picture this scene as a debate between Jesus and the leaders of the Jews with the crowd standing all around. The crowd is listening as the debate goes on. Jesus is aiming to justify His own action in healing the impotent man on the Sabbath day, and thereby technically breaking the Sabbath law. He begins by saying that Moses gave them the Sabbath law, and yet none of them keeps it absolutely and literally. What He meant by that we shall very shortly see. If He then breaks the law to heal a man, why do they, who themselves break the Sabbath law, seek to kill Him? At this point it is the *crowd* who break in with the exclamation: " You are mad! " and the question: " Who is trying to kill you? " The crowd have never yet realised the malignant hatred of their leaders; they are not yet aware of the plots and the plans to eliminate Him. Remember this passage is really part of chapter 5 and not of chapter 7. They think that Jesus has a persecution mania, that His imagination is disordered and His mind upset; and they think that because they do not know the facts. In point of fact Jesus did not answer the question of the crowd. It was not really a question; it was a kind of bystanders' interjection; He goes on with His argument.

The argument of Jesus is this. It was the law that a child should be circumcised on the eighth day after his birth. " And in the eighth day the flesh of his foreskin shall be circumcised " (*Leviticus* 12: 3). Obviously the eighth day would often fall on a Sabbath. And the law was quite clear that " everything necessary for circumcision may be done on the Sabbath day." That is actually laid down in so many words in the *Mishnah*, which is the codification of the scribal law. So Jesus' argument runs like this. " You say that you fully observe the law which came to you through Moses. You say that you observe the law which lays it down that there must be no work done on the Sabbath day, and under work you have included every kind of medical attention which is not necessary actually to save life. And yet you yourselves have quite definitely allowed circumcision to be carried out on the Sabbath day. Now circumcision is two things. It is medical attention to one part of a man's body; and the body has actually two hundred and forty-eight parts. (That was the Jewish reckoning.) Further, circumcision is a kind of mutilation; it is actually taking something from the body. How can you in reason blame me for curing the whole of a man's body; and how can you blame me for making a man's body whole and entire when you allow yourselves to mutilate it on the Sabbath day?" That is an extremely carefully wrought and an extremely clever argument. If it is lawful to carry out an operation on the Sabbath day which mutilates, it cannot be unlawful to carry out an operation which makes the body whole.

So Jesus finishes by telling them to try to see below the surface of things, to try to judge fairly; and if they do, they will not be able any longer to accuse Him of breaking the law. It may be that a passage like this sounds remote to us; but the fact remains that, when we read a passage like this, we can see the keen, acute, clear, logical mind of Jesus in operation, and we can see Him meeting the wisest and cleverest and most subtle men of his day with their own weapons and on their own terms; and we can see Him, in that contest, defeating them.

THE CLAIM OF CHRIST

John 7: 14, 25-30

When the Festival was now half way through Jesus went up to the Temple precincts and began to teach. So some of the people of Jerusalem said: " Is not this the man whom they are trying to kill? And look! He is speaking publicly, and they say nothing to Him! Can it be that the authorities have really discovered that this is the Anointed One of God?

But He cannot be because we know where He comes from. When the Anointed One of God comes no one knows where He comes from." So Jesus, as He taught in the Temple, cried: " So you know me? And you know where I come from? But it is not on my own authority that I have come; but He who sent me is real—and you do not know Him. *But I know Him,* because I have come from Him, and it was He who sent me." So they would like to have found a way to arrest Him; but no one laid a hand upon Him, because His hour had not yet come.

WE have already seen that the likelihood is that verses 15-24 should come after 5: 47; the introduction to this passage is really in verse 14; so, to get the connection, we begin at verse 14 and then go on to verse 24.

The crowd were surprised to find Jesus preaching in the Temple precincts. Along the sides of the Court of the Gentiles there ran two great pillared colonades or porticoes —the Royal Porch and Solomon's Porch. These were places where people walked and where Rabbis talked and it would be there that Jesus was teaching. The people well knew the hostility of the authorities to Jesus; and they were astonished to see the courage of Jesus in thus defying the authorities; and they were still more astonished to see that He was allowed to teach unchecked and unmolested. A thought suddenly struck them: " Can it be that after all this man is the Messiah, the Anointed One of God, and that the authorities know it? " But no sooner had the thought struck them than it was dismissed. Their objection was that they knew where Jesus had come from. They knew that His home was in Nazareth; they knew who His parents and who His brothers and sisters were; there was no mystery about His antecedents. Now that was the very opposite of popular belief, for it was the common belief that the Messiah would *appear*. The idea was that He was waiting concealed and that some day He would burst suddenly upon the world and no one would know where He had come from. They believed that they did know that the Messiah would be born in Bethlehem, for that was David's town, but they also believed that nothing else would be known about Him. There was a rabbinic saying: " Three things come wholly unexpectedly, the Messiah, a godsend, and a scorpion." The Messiah would *appear* as suddenly and unexpectedly as a man stumbles on a godsend or steps on a hidden scorpion. In later years when Justin Martyr was talking and arguing with a Jew about his beliefs, the Jew says of the Messiah: "Although the Messiah be already born and exists somewhere, yet he is unknown and is himself ignorant of his Messiahship, nor has he any power until Elijah comes to anoint him and to make him known." All popular Jewish belief believed in the sudden *appearance* of the Messiah. He would burst upon the world mysteriously, no man knew from where. As for Jesus, He did not measure up to that kind of standard at all. To the Jews there was no mystery about where He came from.

This belief was characteristic of a certain attitude of mind which prevailed among the Jews and which is by no means dead yet—the attitude of mind which seeks for God in the abnormal and the unusual. They could never be persuaded to see God in the ordinary common things. A thing had to be extraordinary before God could be in it. The teaching of Christianity is just the reverse of that. If God is only to enter the world in the abnormal, and the unusual, and the extraordinary, it means that God will very seldom be in the world; whereas if we can look for and find God in the common things, it means that God is always present. Christianity does not look on this world as a world which God very occasionally invades; it looks on it as a God-filled world from which God is never absent.

In answer to these complaints and objections of the people Jesus made two statements, both of which shocked the people and the authorities. He said that it was quite true that they knew who He was and where He came from; but it was also true that ultimately He had come direct from God. Quite true, He came from Nazareth; but still truer, He came from God. Second, He said that they did not know God, but He did. It was a bitter insult to tell the chosen people that they did not know God. What greater insult could there be than to tell God's people that they did not know God? It was an incredible claim to make that He alone knew God, that He stood in such a unique relationship to God, that He in such a way had come from God and was returning to God, that He knew God as no one else did.

Now here is one of the great turning-points, one of the crucial moments in Jesus' life. Up to this point the authorities had looked on Jesus as a rebellious and revolutionary Sabbath breaker, which was in truth a serious enough charge; but from now on He is guilty, not of Sabbath-breaking; He is guilty of the ultimate sin, *the sin of blasphemy*. As they saw it, He was talking of Israel and talking of God as no human being has any right to speak.

In point of fact this is precisely the choice which is still before us. Either, what Jesus said about Himself is false, in which case He is guilty of such blasphemy as no man ever dared to utter; or, what He said about Himself is true, in which case He is what He claimed to be and can be described in no other terms than the Son of God. Jesus leaves us with the definite choice—we must accept Him fully or reject Him absolutely. That is precisely why every man has to decide for or against Jesus Christ.

SEARCHING—IN TIME

John 7: 31-36

> Many of the crowd believed in Him. " When the Anointed One of God comes," they said, " surely He cannot do greater signs than this man has done? " The Pharisees heard the crowds carrying on these discussions about Him; and the chief priests and Pharisees despatched officers to arrest Him. So Jesus

said: " For a little while I am to be with You, and
then I go back to Him who sent me. You will search
for me and you will not find me. You cannot come
where I am." So the Jews said to each other: " Where
is this fellow going to go that we will not be able to
find Him? Surely He is not going to go to the Jews who
are dispersed among the Greeks and teach the Greeks?
What can this word of His mean—' You will search
for me and you will not find me ' and ' You cannot
come where I am '? "

THERE were certain of the crowd who could not help
believing that Jesus was the Anointed One of God. They
believed that no one could possibly do greater things than
He was doing. That was in fact the argument which Jesus
Himself used when John the Baptist was in doubt about
whether He was the one who was to come, or if they had
to look for another. When John sent his messengers, Jesus'
answer was: " Go back and tell John the things you
have seen me do. That will convince him " (*Matthew*
11: 1-6). The very fact that there were those who were
trembling on the brink of acceptance moved the authorities
to action. They sent their officers—most likely, the Temple
police—to arrest Him. Jesus' answer was that He was only
with them for a little time; and the day would come
when they would search for Him, not to arrest Him, but to
obtain what only He could give, but it would be too late.
He would be gone where they could never follow.

Jesus meant that He would return to His Father, from
whom they by their disobedience and rebelliousness had
shut themselves out. But they did not understand.
Throughout the centuries the Jews had been scattered
throughout the world. Sometimes they had been forcibly
removed as exiles; sometimes in the time of their country's
misfortune they had emigrated to other lands. There
was one comprehensive term for these Jews who lived
outside Palestine. They were called *The Diaspora*, the
dispersion. Scholars still speak of the *Jews of the Diaspora*,
when they wish to use a short term to describe the Jews

who live outside Palestine. That is the phrase that the people used here. " Is this Jesus," they said, " going to leave Palestine? Is He going away to the *Diaspora*? Will He even go the length of going away and preaching to the Greeks and so become lost in the masses of the Gentile world? Is He going to run away so far that He will be completely out of reach? " It is an amazing thing how a taunt became a prophecy. The Jews meant it for a jest, and as the years went on it became blessedly true that it was to the Gentiles that the Risen Christ went out. These scoffing Jews were speaking truer than they knew.

This passage brings us face to face with *the promise and the threat of Jesus*. Jesus had said: " Seek and ye shall find " (*Matthew* 7: 7). Now He says: " You will search for me and you will not find me " (verse 34). Long ago the ancient prophet had put the two things together in a very wonderful way: " Seek ye the Lord *while He may be found* " (*Isaiah* 55: 6). It is characteristic of this life that time is limited; it is the grim truth of life that there comes a time when the opportunity to do something, and even the possibility of doing it, are gone. Physical strength decays, and there are things a man can do at thirty that he cannot do at sixty. Mental vigour weakens and there are mental tasks to which a man can address himself in his youth and in his prime which are beyond him in his age. Moral fibre grows less muscular; and if a man allows some habit to dominate him there may come the day when he cannot break himself of it, although at the beginning he could, even easily, have ejected it from his life. It is so with us and Jesus Christ. What Jesus was saying to these people was: " You can awaken to a sense of need too late." A man may so long refuse Christ, he may so long take the wrong way, that in the end he does not even see the beauty of Christ, and evil becomes his good, and repentance becomes impossible. So long as there is life, and so long as sin still hurts us, and so long as the unattainable good still beckons us and haunts us, the chance to seek and find is still there. But a man must have a care lest he grow so used to sin that he does not know that he is sinning, lest he grow so indifferent to Christ that he sees in Christ no loveliness, lest he neglect God so long that he forgets that there is a God, for then the sense of need dies, and if there is no sense of need, we cannot seek, and if we cannot seek, we will never find. The one thing that a man must never lose is his sense of sin.

THE FOUNTAIN OF LIVING WATER

John 7: 37-44

On the last, the great day of the Festival, Jesus stood and cried: " If anyone thirsts, let him come to me and drink. As the scripture says: ' He who believes in me—rivers of living water shall flow from his belly.' " It was about the Spirit, whom those who believed in Him were to receive, that He said this. For as yet there was no Spirit because Jesus was not yet glorified. When they heard these words some of the crowd said: " This is really the promised Prophet." Others said: " This is the Anointed One of God." But some said: " Surely the Anointed One of God does not come from Galilee? Does the scripture not say that the Anointed One of God is a descendant of David, and that he is to come from Bethlehem, the village where David used to live? " So there was a division of opinion in the crowd because of Him. Some of them would have liked to arrest Him, but none laid hands on Him.

ALL the events of this chapter took place during the Festival of Tabernacles; and now in order properly to understand this passage we must know the significance, and at least some of the ritual of that Festival.

The Festival of Tabernacles or Booths was the third of the trio of great Jewish Festivals, attendance at which was compulsory for all adult male Jews who lived within twenty miles of Jerusalem. The three were The Passover,

The Festival of Pentecost, and the Festival of Tabernacles. It fell on the fifteenth day of the seventh month, that is, about 15th October. Like all the great Jewish Festivals it had a double significance.

First, it had an *historical* significance. It received its name from the fact that all through it people left their houses and lived in little booths. During the Festival the booths sprang up everywhere, on the flat roofs of the houses, in the streets, in the city squares, in the gardens, and even in the very courts of the Temple. The law laid it down that the booths must not be permanent structures, but that they must be built specially for the occasion. The walls of the booths were made of branches and fronds, and must be such that they would give protection from the weather but not shut out the sun. The roof had to be thatched, but the thatching had to be wide enough for the stars to be seen through the roof at night. The historical significance of all this was to remind the people in such a way that they would never forget it that once upon a time they had been homeless wanderers in the desert without a roof over their heads (*Leviticus* 23: 40-43). The purpose was " that your generations may know that I made the children of Israel to dwell in booths, when I brought them out of the land of Egypt." Originally it lasted seven days, but by the time of Jesus an eighth day had been added. So then the historical significance of the Festival of Booths was to be a reminder that the children of Israel had been wanderers in the desert before they reached the settled life of the Promised Land.

Second, it had an *agricultural* significance. It was supremely a harvest-thanksgiving Festival. It is sometimes called *The Festival of the Ingathering* (*Exodus* 23: 16; 34: 22). To the Jews it was the most popular Festival of all. For that reason it was sometimes called simply *The Feast* (I *Kings* 8: 2), and sometimes *The Festival of the Lord* (*Leviticus* 23: 39). It stood out above all other Festivals. The people called it " the season of our gladness." Coming as it did in the late autumn, it was the gladdest of all times, for it marked the ingathering of all the harvests, for by this time the barley-, the wheat-, and the grape-harvest were all safely gathered in. As the law had it, it was to be celebrated " at the end of the year when thou gatherest in thy labour out of thy field " (*Exodus* 23: 16); it was to be kept " after that thou hast gathered in from thy threshing-floor and thy wine-press " (*Deuteronomy* 16: 13, 16). It was not only the thanksgiving for one harvest; it was the glad thanksgiving for all the bounty of nature which made life possible and which made living happy. In Zechariah's dream of the new world it was this Festival which was to be celebrated all over the world (*Zechariah* 14: 16-18). Josephus called it " the holiest and the greatest festival among the Jews " (*Antiquities of the Jews*, 3: 10: 4). It was not only a time for the rich and for the wealthy and for those who normally had plenty. It was laid down that the servant, the stranger, the widow and the poor were all to share in the universal joy.

There was one particular ceremony connected with it. The worshippers were told to take " the fruit of goodly trees, branches of palm trees, the boughs of thick trees, and the willows of the brook " (*Leviticus* 23: 40). The Sadducees said that that was a description of the material out of which the booths had to be built; the Pharisees said that it was a description of the things the worshippers had to bring with them when they came to the Temple. Very naturally, the people accepted the interpretation of the Pharisees, for it gave them a vivid ceremony in which to participate.

This special ceremony is very closely connected with this passage and with the words of Jesus. Quite certainly He spoke His words with it in His mind, and very possibly, even with it as an immediate background. Each day of the Festival the people came with their palms and their willows to the Temple; with them they formed a kind of screen or roof and marched round the great altar. At the same time a priest took a golden pitcher which held three *logs*—that is, about two pints—and went down to the Pool of Siloam and filled it with water. It was carried back through the Water Gate while the people recited Isaiah 12: 3: " With joy shall ye draw water out of the wells of salvation." The water was carried up to the Temple and to the altar and poured out on it as an offering to God. While this was being done *The Hallel*—that is, Psalms 113-118—was sung to the accompaniment of flutes by the Levite choir. When they came to the words, " O give thanks to the Lord " (*Psalm* 118: 1), and again to the words, " O work now then salvation " (*Psalm* 118: 25), and finally to the closing words, " O give thanks unto the Lord " (*Psalm* 118: 29), the worshippers shouted and waved their palms towards the altar. The whole dramatic ceremony was a vivid thanksgiving for God's good gift of water, and an acted prayer for rain, and a memory of the water which sprang from the rock when they travelled through the wilderness. On the last day the ceremony was doubly impressive for they marched seven times round the altar in memory of the sevenfold circuit around the walls of Jericho, whereby the walls fell down and the city was taken.

It was against that background, maybe it was at that very moment, that Jesus' voice rang out: " If any man thirst, let him come to *me* and drink." It is as if Jesus said: " You are thanking and glorifying God for the water which quenches the thirst of your bodies. Come to Me if you want water which will quench the thirst of your soul." Jesus was using that dramatic moment to turn men's thoughts to the thirst of men for God and for the eternal things.

THE FOUNTAIN OF LIVING WATER

John 7: 37-44

Now that we have seen the vivid background of this passage we must turn to look at it in more detail.

The promise of Jesus presents us with something of a problem. Jesus said: " He who believes in me—rivers of water shall flow from his belly." And He introduces that statement by saying, " as scripture says." Now no one has ever been able to identify that quotation satisfactorily, and the question is, just what does it mean? There are two distinct possibilities.

(i) It may refer to the man who comes to Jesus Christ and who accepts Him. That man will have within him a river of refreshing water. It would be another way of saying what Jesus said to the woman of Samaria: " The water that I shall give him shall be in him a well of living water springing up into everlasting life " (*John* 4: 14). It would be another way of putting Isaiah's beautiful saying: " And the Lord shall guide thee continually and shall satisfy thy soul in drought, and make fat thy bones; and thou shalt be like a watered garden, and like a spring of water, whose waters fail not " (*Isaiah* 58: 11). The meaning would be that Jesus can give a man the refreshment of the Holy Spirit. The Jews placed all the feelings and the thoughts and the emotions in certain parts of the body. The *heart* was the seat of the thought and the intellect; the *kidneys* and the *belly* were the seat of the inmost emotions and feelings. As the writer of the *Proverbs* had it: " The spirit of man is the candle of the Lord, searching all the inward parts of the belly " (*Proverbs* 20: 27). This would mean that Jesus was promising us that cleansing, refreshing, life-giving stream of the Holy Spirit so that our thoughts and feelings and emotions and inmost desires would be purified and revitalised and filled with new life. It is as if Jesus said: " Come to me; accept me; trust me; and I will put into you

263

through my Spirit a new life which will give you purity
and satisfaction, and which will take away all your frus-
trations and unsatisfied hungers and give you the kind
of life you have always longed for and never had." Whichever interpretation we take, it is quite certain that that
interpretation is true.

(ii) The other interpretation is that this sentence may
refer to Jesus Himself. " Rivers of living water shall
flow from His belly " may refer to Jesus. It may be a
description of the Messiah which Jesus is taking from
somewhere which we cannot identify, and applying to
Himself. The Christians always identified Jesus with
the rock which gave the Israelites water in the wilderness
(*Exodus* 17: 6). Paul took that image of the rock and
applied it to Christ (I *Corinthians* 10: 4). It is John who
tells how there came forth at the thrust of the soldier's
spear *water* and *blood* from the side of Jesus (*John* 19: 34).
The water stands for the purification which comes in
baptism and the blood for the atoning death of the Cross.
This symbol of the life-giving water which comes from God
is often in the Old Testament (*Psalm* 105: 41; *Ezekiel*
47: 1, 12). Joel has the great picture: " And a fountain
shall come forth out of the house of the Lord " (*Joel* 3: 18).
It may well be that John is thinking of Jesus as the fountain
from which the cleansing stream flows. Water is that
without which man cannot live; and Christ is the one
without whom man cannot live and dare not die. From
Him there comes the gift of the Spirit which cleanses
and strengthens life. Again, whichever interpretation we
choose, that too is deeply true.

Whether we take this picture as referring to Christ or to
the man who accepts Christ, it means that from Christ
there flows the strength and power and cleansing which
alone give us life in the real sense of the term.

In this passage there is one startling thing. In verse 39
the Authorised Version tones it down, but in the best
Greek manuscript there is the strange statement: " For

as yet there was no Spirit." What is the meaning of that? Think of it this way. A great power can exist for years and even centuries without men being able to tap it. The power is there even when men do not know that it is there. To take a very relevant example—there has always been atomic power in this world. Men did not invent atomic power; it has always been there. But only in our own time have men tapped and used what has always been there. The Holy Spirit has always existed; but men never really enjoyed the full power of that Spirit until after Pentecost. They had had glimpses of Him, foretastes of Him, but it was only after Pentecost that the floodgates were opened and the tide of the Spirit flowed out on to men. And, as it has been finely said, " There could be no Pentecost without Calvary." It was only when men had known Jesus that they really knew the Spirit. Before that the Spirit had been a power, but now the Spirit is a person, for the Spirit to us has become nothing other than the presence and the power of the Risen Christ always with us. In this apparently startling sentence John is not saying that the Spirit did not *exist*; but He is saying that it took the life and the death of Jesus Christ to lead up to Pentecost, and to open the floodgates for the Spirit to become real and powerful to all men.

But we must notice how this passage finishes. Some people thought that Jesus was the Prophet whom Moses had promised (*Deuteronomy* 18: 15). Some thought that He was the Anointed One of God; and there followed a wrangle about whether or not the Anointed One of God must come from Bethlehem. Here is tragedy. A great religious experience had ended in the aridity of a theological wrangle. That is what above all we must avoid. Jesus Christ is not someone about whom to argue; He is someone to know, and love and enjoy. If we have one view of Him and someone else has another, it does not matter so long as both of us find Him Saviour and accept Him as Lord. Even if we do explain our religious experience in different ways, that should never divide us, for it is always the experience that is important, and not any man's explanation of it.

UNWILLING ADMIRATION AND TIMID DEFENCE

John 7: 45-52

> So the officers came to the chief priests and the Pharisees. They said to them: " Why did you not bring Him here? " The attendants answered: " Never did a man speak as He speaks." So the Pharisees answered: " Surely you too have not been led astray? Has anyone from the authorities believed in Him? Or anyone from the Pharisees? *They* have not; but the mob which is ignorant of the law and which is accursed believes in Him! " Nicodemus (the man who came to Him before) said to them, for he was one of them: " Surely our law does not condemn a man unless it first hears a statement of the case from him, and has first-hand information about what he is doing? " They answered him: " Surely you too are not from Galilee? Search and see that no prophet arises from Galilee."

HERE we have certain vivid reactions to Jesus.

(i) The reaction of the officers was bewildered amazement. They had gone out to arrest Jesus, and they had come back without Him, because never in their lives had they heard anyone speak like that. Really to listen to Jesus is a new and an unparalleled experience for any man.

(ii) The reaction of the chief priests and Pharisees was contempt. The Pharisees had a phrase by which they described the ordinary, simple people who did not observe the thousands of regulations of the ceremonial law. They called them contemptuously *The People of the Land*. To them they were beneath contempt. To marry a daughter to one of them was like exposing her bound and helpless to a beast. " The masses who do not know the law are accursed." The rabbinic law said: " Six things are laid down about the People of the Land: entrust no testimony to them, take no testimony from then, trust them with no secret, do not appoint them guardians of an orphan, do not make them custodians of charitable funds, do not accompany them on a journey." It was forbidden to be a guest of one of the People of the Land, or to entertain such a person as a guest. It was even laid down that, wherever it was possible, nothing should be bought or sold from one of the People of the Land. In their proud aristocracy and in their intellectual snobbery and spiritual pride the Pharisees looked down from their vast height of contempt on the ordinary man. Their plea was: " Nobody who is spiritually and academically of any account has believed on this Jesus. Only ignorant fools accept him." It is indeed a terrible thing when a man thinks himself either too clever or too good to need Jesus Christ—and it can happen yet.

(iii) There was the reaction of Nicodemus. It was a timid reaction. For Nicodemus did not defend Jesus directly. He only dared to quote certain legal maxims which were relevant. The law laid it down that every man must receive justice (*Exodus* 23: 1; *Deuteronomy* 1: 16); and part of justice was and is that he must have a right to state his case, and he cannot be condemned on second-hand information. The Pharisees proposed to break that law. It is clear that Nicodemus did not carry his protest any further. His heart told him to defend Jesus but his head told him not to take the risk. The Pharisees flung catchwords at him; they told him that obviously no prophet could come out of Galilee and taunted him with having a connection with the Galilaean rabble, and he said no more.

Often a man finds himself in a situation in which he would like to defend Jesus and in which he knows he ought to show his colours. Often he makes a kind of half-hearted defence, and is then reduced to an uncomfortable and an ashamed silence. In the defence of Jesus Christ it is better to be reckless with our hearts than prudent with our heads. To defend Jesus Christ may bring us laughter and unpopularity in time; it may even mean difficulty and sacrifice. But the fact remains that Jesus said that He would confess before His Father the man who confessed Him on earth, and He would deny before His Father the man who denied Him on earth. Loyalty to Christ may produce a cross on earth, but it brings a crown in eternity.